THE BIG FOUR BRITISH BANKS

The
Big Four
British Banks

Organization, Strategy and the Future

David Rogers

St. Martin's Press
New York

THE BIG FOUR BRITISH BANKS

Copyright © 1999 by David Rogers

St. Martin's Press, Scholarly and Reference Division, 175 Fifth Avenue, New York, N.Y. 10010

First published in the United States of America in 1999

This book is printed on paper suitable for recycling and made from fully managed and sustained forest sources.

Printed in Great Britain

ISBN 0–312–22869–4

Library of Congress Cataloging-in-Publication Data
Rogers, David, 1930–
The big four British banks / David Rogers.
p.   cm.
Includes bibliographical references and index.
ISBN 0–312–22869–4 (cloth)
1. Banks and banking—Great Britain.   2. Banks and banking, British.   I. Title.
HG2988.R64   1999
332.1'0941—dc21   99–40680
                                                             CIP

For Ben, Sam, Gabe and Hannah

Contents

Acknowledgements

I HAD assumed that, as an outsider from the US, writing a book about British banking would be difficult. Not only was I unfamiliar with the banks and their cultures, but I came from a country whose banks were generally more advanced in management, technology and performance than their British counterparts. Might not British bankers be defensive and consequently reluctant to talk about their achievements and travails?

Contrary to those expectations, I received a most hospitable welcome from bankers and knowledgeable observers of the industry. In many cases, their welcome was more generous than that of American bankers I interviewed in my previous study. It had taken months and in some cases more than a year to get access to American senior bankers. I knew I would not have that kind of time in Britain. Fortunately, I did not need it.

The overwhelming majority of British bankers and informed observers I interviewed were extraordinarily generous and forthright in discussing the problems of leading their institutions through such turbulent times. I thank them all for that, fully aware that I could not have written this book without their co-operation.

Since I promised anonymity to all informants, I will not list them here. Suffice it to say that many senior managers and staff at the banks often went out of their way to honour my requests for information and re-interviews. The same generosity was extended by many outsiders: bank reporters, analysts, consultants, regulators, and academics who spent hours of their time, for some over several meetings, sharing with me their insights into the industry's evolution and how individual banks worked.

One person I must acknowledge, however, is Christopher Fildes, banking analyst for the *Daily Telegraph* and *The Spectator* who helped me in this project in ways too numerous to mention. A man of great wisdom, wit and warmth, he shared with me his knowledge and counsel way beyond what I had any right to expect.

Another of my biggest debts in writing this book is to the London Business School and its Department of Organizational Behaviour. I was a Visiting Professor there in the summer and autumn of 1995 while doing much of the research for the book and could not have asked for a more supportive institutional environment. LBS's excellent library, office space and computer facilities made it possible for me to pursue this study in productive ways for the limited time I was there. I thank in particular Nigel Nicholson and Rob Goffee, and several colleagues as well, including Tim Morris, Costas Markides and John Hunt. I also thank Angie Quest, administrator of the Organizational Behaviour Department, and Jane Murphy for their many kindnesses.

Several colleagues in my home institution, the Stern School of Business, NYU, have been of help. Two I continue to rely on in so many ways are Ingo Walter and Roy Smith. Walter has supported my work for more than a decade, while Smith read several chapters in early draft. Both have provided much intellectual stimulation. They are among the world's leading scholars in the field of global banking, and I find that the more I get to know about the subject, the smarter they appear.

I also acknowledge the grant awarded to me by the Bank and Financial Analysts Association, through the Salomon Center at Stern. It supported research on the book during my residence in London in 1995.

In addition, I thank colleagues Peter Grinyer and George Smith. Grinyer, a Visiting Professor of strategy at Stern from the University of St Andrews and a former Londoner, read several chapters and provided helpful substantive and editorial suggestions. Smith, a business and financial historian, read a couple of chapters and introduced me to some of the recent literature on British culture and economic development. Also, I am indebted to Karen Angelillo, Administrator of the Management Department at Stern, and Alice Wong for their cheerful assistance in response to my many requests for their help. Bill Guth graciously covered for me as Department Chair on my semester's sabbatical in London. Finally, I thank Randy Schuler for his initiative in helping arrange my visit to the London Business School.

Jonathan Ferguson, Juliet Sotnick, Ashish Raythatha, and Gabrielle Upton, MBA students at Stern, helped in the research. I appreciate their conscientious work and suggestions in pulling together needed data.

Bernard Barber, long-time friend and colleague, read an early book outline and précis and gave helpful comments.

I finally want to thank my family for their extraordinary support. My wife, Terry, also a sociologist, read and edited every chapter. Her critical eye, combined with her love and support, contributed more than I can easily describe. Also, each of my sons, Ed, Alex, and Paul, was a sensitive sounding board in conversations about the book.

Special thanks are due to my editor, Stephen Rutt, who showed much patience and administrative skills in managing this project, in addition to providing valuable substantive suggestions. It is not easy to manage on a long-distance basis the production of such a book, notwithstanding modern communications technology. Stephen showed how well that can be done. I also thank the copy editor, Derek Atkins, for his excellent work.

It was clear from my field experiences that the British bankers and people in London who are involved in their industry constitute a close-knit community, with strong social ties that go back many years. I feel grateful to those people who went out of their way to introduce me to that community and encourage many of its members to share their experiences with me. I hope that the insights developed in the book merit their courtesy.

Foreword

WRITING A BOOK in the late 1990s about commercial banking in Britain, or, for that matter, in any industrial nation, is a lot like trying to track a series of accelerating changes whose future is unknown. Academics writing about corporate strategy refer to this industry as one in a situation of hypercompetition and hyperturbulence. The changes that commercial banking is facing, both in the external marketplace and internal to its firms, have accelerated to such a degree since the 1970s that writing about them, even in Britain, where four major banks have dominated the industry, is a formidable challenge – second only to that of managing them. It involves dealing with a fast-moving target, where the only seeming constant is the increasing pace of change itself. Volatility is the hallmark.

This book, I hope, will add to an understanding of factors contributing to that volatility through an institutional analysis of what happened in the recent evolution of British banking. The book is based on over two hundred interviews, conducted between June 1994 and March 1999, with board members, senior bankers, headquarters staff and branch managers in the four clearers, as well as with informed outsiders. The latter include regulators, bank analysts, consultants, journalists and academics who have studied or worked with banks. In addition, the book draws on such archival materials as past studies, company histories, annual reports, coverage in the financial press, and internal documents.

On the surface, the driving forces behind the industry's change, in Britain and elsewhere, are well known: increasing globalization, technological changes, deregulation, and a disintermediation of the industry. Stated more simply, a long-term decline in traditional credit businesses of deposits and loans is taking place, accompanied by a rise of worldwide capital markets and of new securities products, by a blurring of boundaries separating all segments of financial services from one another, and by a consequent massive consolidation within and across these segments.

Indeed, a so-called 'feeding frenzy' of enormous scale has been taking place worldwide, involving acquisitions within and among commercial and investment banking, insurance, and asset management, and crossing national boundaries.

Consider the following recent developments as indications of how fast the major changes are taking place in Britain: Since late 1997, both NatWest and Barclays have abandoned much of their decade-long effort to develop world-class wholesale and investment banks, giving up on their universal banking strategy. Martin Taylor, previously hailed as a glittering star of British banking, suddenly resigned in late 1998 as Barclays' CEO. Midland, one of Britain's most venerable banks, having been taken over by Hongkong & Shanghai Banking Corporation (HSBC) in 1992, lost even more of its past identity in 1998 by taking on the HSBC brand name for all its products.

The exits from investment banking by NatWest and Barclays raised larger questions about their strategic direction, about breakdowns in their risk-management controls, and about inadequacies in their governance, all contributing to the losses that drove them to withdraw. These exits also raised serious questions about Britain's capacity for global leadership in a world where its major merchant banks had been acquired since the early 1990s by competitors from abroad and where its last two major global investment banks, NatWest Markets (NWM) and Barclays de Zoete Wedd (BZW), were being dismembered and sold off.

Lloyds' exit from investment banking, as those by NatWest and Barclays, have led in the short term to the concentration of British banks on domestic retail banking, a financial services sector in which they traditionally had much core competence and that was generating most of their revenues. Even that seemingly secure market niche has become increasingly threatened, however, by the entry of new competitors – both banks and non-banks, both domestic and foreign. It is now not at all clear what the British clearing banks' future is in that once seemingly impregnable niche. We do know, however, that there are no more safe havens in the banking industry.

It was in this context that I did the research for the book. Having done one on how the US banks fared in the 1970s and 1980s, I wanted to see what the US experience might teach us about developments in Britain and, conversely, what might be learned for the US and other nations from the British experience. I particularly wanted to analyse what lessons can be taken from the British banking experience of the past few decades, when the pace of change began accelerating so much. There is every indication that all the driving forces listed above will be with us for the indefinite future, and that the actions and non-actions that senior managers of these banks take will have significant effects on their respective institutions' performance.

The result of these considerations is the organizational case studies that constitute the core of the book (Chapters 4–9). The first three chapters set the stage for the case studies by analysing what has happened to commercial banking worldwide, comparing developments in recent decades in the US and Britain, and highlighting the industry's increasing competition and pace of change in Britain. Chapter 10 synthesizes the case studies by benchmarking how universal banking has fared in Britain and raising the larger question as to its viability as a strategy in other nations.

Given what we know at this point in history about the more sophisticated technologies and management practices in US commercial and investment banks relative to their British counterparts, it would have been easy to focus on how far behind and limited the British banking industry has been. The facts are more complex. US banks continue to go through their own problems, as witness their difficulties in the 1990s in managing the post-merger integration issues of their consolidations.

Also, as difficult as it has been to manage British banks in this period of turmoil, most big universal banks in Europe have not fared that well either. Constraints of state controls and rigid labour practices, along with bureaucratic rigidities of many of these banks, may suggest that British banks, for all their problems, are farther along in modernizing their management than their European competitors.

It was my judgement that an institutional analysis, based on interviews and archival data, would cast light on what is happening to British banking and what are its future prospects. My training is as a sociologist and student of management, and the analysis to follow reflects the perspective that those fields bring to bear on their subject. The data that I gathered and the analysis of those data, driven by the concepts of my field, hopefully generate new insights that complement what traditional scholars and observers of the industry provide.

Many others will do studies of this industry in the future. The institutional analysis provided here, carried out with a cross-national perspective and while many changes were taking place, should provide some benchmarks of the industry's prospects on which future studies may build.

On a final note, I intend this book to provide a balance between empathy and criticism in analysing how British banking has fared in recent decades. British bankers should have undertaken many more thoughtful actions in the past and should be able to do so in the future. Much of the book deals with those actions. It is much easier, however, given the situation that the banks face, to detail what the actions should be than to be in the firing line. Trying to move these old, established institutions into agile, high-performing competitors in an industry as volatile as this one is a challenging task.

The reader will note that although there is much presentation of statistical data on the banks' financial performance throughout the case study chapters, there are no tables to crystallize and support the argument. Such tables are presented, however, in an appendix that summarizes the comparative performance of the banks in the 1990s.

1 *Introduction*

THIS IS a book about the evolution of the British commercial banking industry, as reflected primarily in the experiences of its four clearing banks – Barclays, Lloyds, Midland, and NatWest. The book concentrates mainly on the period since the 1960s, when the cosy, cartel position of the UK banks began to erode in the face of increasing competition. Though acknowledging the importance of history in shaping more recent developments, I limited myself to the past few decades for at least two reasons. First, banking scholars had already produced many detailed studies of the industry's long history.[1] Second, the changes taking place since the 1960s have been so momentous that they merit intensive study in their own right. Moreover, having reviewed several studies on how the industry had evolved before then, I could take that context into consideration in analyzing what was happening now.

This book thus constitutes a case study of an industry in very rapid change, aiming to give some understanding of how its main players are adapting and what its future prospects are likely to be. Contrary to previous researchers on this subject, I am a student of management and organizational behaviour and apply concepts of my field in seeking new insights into what is happening to the UK banking industry. Those concepts relate to how institutions adapt to change, particularly to the strategies and organizational infrastructures they develop to do so.

Looking at the larger context, the prospects for this industry are increasingly affected by developments in related financial services. In that sense, what is happening in such related industries as investment banking, insurance, home mortgages, and asset management will also be discussed, because such influences cast light on trends in commercial banking, since the boundaries have become increasingly blurred in recent decades.

The main question is: what will this industry be like a decade from now? What strategies, cultures, and organizational forms will distinguish the survivors from the non-survivors, the winners from the losers? Will the dominant form be the highly diversified, global, financial supermarket known nowadays as the 'universal' bank, will it be the more focused niche player, or will it be both – or some other type altogether? In brief, what will it take to become a world-class and/or top domestic player in UK banking?

While such forecasting is perilous at best, given the volatility and indeterminacy of markets and institutions worldwide, it is still important for key players in this industry – bankers, regulators, and other public policy makers – to deal with competitive challenges more proactively than they have in the past. They have little choice, given the fact that the global competitiveness of the nations in which banks are located will be vitally affected by how well they adapt.

An industry in secular decline

The context for the study is that commercial banking worldwide is an industry in secular decline.[2] Major indicators of this decline include commercial banks' share of total financial assets and their shares of deposits and loans. In both the US and the UK, all those shares have decreased over the past several decades as other products and competitors have moved to a stronger market position. In the US, for example, the commercial banks' share of financial assets of selected domestic financial institutions dropped from 57.3 per cent in 1946 to 31.2 per cent in 1990.[3] They were being displaced by private, state, and local pension funds, mutual funds, money-market mutual funds, and finance companies. The decline in the UK was even more dramatic, with the clearing banks' share of total UK bank deposits falling from just under 70 per cent in the early 1950s to 18.2 per cent in 1979.[4]

One of the main new competitors has been the building societies, and by the mid-1980s they accounted for about 44 per cent of resident sterling deposits compared with the clearers' share of 33 per cent. As Sir Timothy Bevan, chair of Barclays in the mid-1980s, said at that time: 'It is now the building societies, not the clearers, which dominate the retail deposits markets.'[5]

This decline has resulted from a familiar litany of forces: globalization, deregulation, disintermediation and the rise of capital markets, and, most importantly of all, new electronic communications and information technology, all of which have lowered entry barriers for many new players, particularly non-banks.

In many respects, commercial banking worldwide is facing the same problems that manufacturing industries faced in the 1970s and 80s, namely how to restructure for survival in the face of increasing competition. Banking faces, in this regard, commoditization and shrinking margins in its traditional products, and the need to cut back drastically on inflated costs built up from its protected, cartelized market from the past. More generally, banking must develop new strategies, cultures, organizational forms, and expertise in order to survive in a vastly different competitive environment. This book is meant to help bankers do that, by providing a deeper understanding of forces contributing to the industry's evolution.

Given commercial banking's record profits of recent years in the UK, the US and many other industrial nations, it may seem quite anomalous to argue that it is an industry in secular decline. In fact, banking is very much a boom-and-bust industry, whose fortunes are tied closely to business-cycle conditions in the economies in which it is embedded. Notwithstanding such record profits and the industry's cyclical performance, data such as those just cited – indicating the banks' shrinking portion of total financial assets and of deposits and loans – are consistent and unambiguous. And the consensus among many banking scholars is that, given the industry's increasing competitive pressures, only those banks that restructure radically will survive and be dominant players in the next century.

Another factor contributing to the industry's decline, and resulting from its cyclicality, may well be bankers' recurring misjudgements in boom years about long-term growth prospects. A common pattern in both the US and UK has been for bankers to pile up loans in boom years that later turn sour, based on a misplaced euphoria about how much longer such bull markets would continue (a 'feel good' factor) and then get caught holding large batches of those loans in subsequent recessions.

If such misjudgements happened in isolated instances, they might not have negative, industry-wide impacts; but they have been recurrent events in recent decades. Loans to developing countries (LDC) and commercial real-estate loans are cases in point. Bankers did not learn from losses in both these markets in earlier times and, acting as a herd, were doomed to repeat mistakes of the past. A policy research group in London, the Centre for The Study of Financial Innovation, has referred to this as the industry's tendency to keep 'slipping on banana peels'.

A comparative perspective

In order to understand better this industry's future prospects in the UK, I have couched the book in a broad comparative perspective. Indeed, a significant quantity of literature has developed in recent years, analyzing the forms that commercial banking takes in different industrial nations.[6]

This book has three characteristics that distinguish it from most studies of banking. First, it relates variations in the banking industry's evolution in different nations to variations in those nations' cultures, markets, and institutions.

Second, it looks inside the banks to ascertain how they are managed and, in particular, how their cultures, strategies, organizational structures, and CEOs shape performance.[7] Regarding this second point, one can often learn much about the future prospects of an industry by analyzing in depth the functioning of its prototypical firms. I had done that in a previous study of the US banking industry and have applied a similar approach in this book.[8]

Finally, the book uses concepts from the fields of strategic management and organizational studies so as to help interpret the dynamics of individual banks and the future of the industry. These fields are concerned with how firms position themselves in their industry and how they implement the strategies (relating to mix of products, customers, and geographic markets) that they choose.

In sum, finance scholars and economists writing about banking have adopted an industry-wide approach in looking at its evolution and performance, with little attention given to individual banks. Industries rise and fall, however, as a result of how individual managers and firms adapt, notwithstanding the influence of more macro-market and other endogenous forces.

In brief, the actions of managers count. It makes a lot of sense, then, to try to understand in some depth the dynamics of that adaptation – namely, how and why these managers and firms behave in the way they do.[9]

Students of the industry have concluded that, although the structure of banking is different in various countries (for example, whether it is banking-driven or capital-markets-driven), as well as the extent of concentration, the role of regulators, how far regulation has gone, and the strategies banks have followed, there are significant transnational similarities in the competitive threats that the industry faces and how bankers have responded. One obvious reason for this is that the industry has become more global, with developments in any single country increasingly shaped by worldwide forces.

Adaptation strategies since the 1970s

Commercial banking worldwide has thus been challenged to re-invent itself in the face of increasing competition or else to experience possible extinction in its traditional form. The forces mentioned above that have contributed to this challenge – globalization, the rise of capital markets, deregulation, new technology, and the emergence of new competitors – are obviously not that recent, having had an accelerating impact since the 1970s. And it is likely that the industry will take many years, perhaps decades, to change in fundamental ways in response to the pressures. That response has already been ongoing in various industrialized nations, chiefly in the form of consolidation through bank mergers,[10] diversification, branch closure, downsizing and other forms of cost cutting, experimenting with new delivery systems that bypass the traditional branch (for example, phone banking, pc banking, and ATMs in shopping malls, supermarkets, train stations, and other public places). Overcapacity and inflated cost structures (particularly in relation to administrative, personnel and physical facilities) are regarded worldwide as problems that must be managed.

Academics, consultants, regulators and bankers themselves have proposed many different strategies to adapt to the increasing competitive threats that the industry faces. One is to become more like the classic European 'universal banks' by diversifying into such new fields as investment banking, insurance, asset management, and home mortgage banking. There are various versions of universal banking in different nations, but all involve banks in multiple product areas of both retail and wholesale businesses.[11]

A main difference between the UK and classic European (German, Swiss and French) versions is that the latter involve commercial banks as big shareholders of non-financial firms, existing as financial– industrial conglomerates. Those ownership patterns do not exist in the UK.

Another adaptation strategy is to move in the opposite direction, focusing instead on core competencies and competing as specialized niche players.[12] This may also involve diversification – but only within a segment of financial services – as a predominantly retail or wholesale bank. Lloyds in the UK is an example of this, being highly diversified beyond its traditional loan and deposit business into home mortgages, life assurance, and asset management, but still a predominantly UK retail bank, unlike its three universal bank competitors.

More recently, partly in line with new management paradigms gaining increasing popularity among both academics and consultants, there has been discussion of the importance of banks externalizing many of their businesses, instead managing networks of strategic alliances and joint ventures as the best way of competing. Notions of the bank of the future as a 'virtual organization' whose main skills are managing such networks as they develop to meet customers' needs for a variety of financial services have gained recent support.[13]

Each of these strategies has its advocates. Each has potential costs and benefits. And it is not at all clear which may lead to the best performance. It may well be that all have their place, depending on how well they are implemented. As Smith and Walter suggest, 'strategy isn't everything. Implementation is at least as important.' [14] This book will provide data relevant to arguments regarding the strengths and weaknesses of various adaptation strategies, particularly universal banking and its opposite, the more focused niche strategy.

Why the UK banking industry

I have selected the UK as my site in light of my previous book on the US commercial banking industry.[15] US banking, I concluded, although obviously shaped in idiosyncratic ways by its societal setting, illustrated several findings worthy of comparative investigation:

(1) Strategic focus, concentrating on areas of core competence, beats diversification;

(2) implementation intensity (paying close attention to its dynamics and making early corrective changes where required) is essential for success; and

(3) the effective managing of internal integration issues, particularly around getting more collaboration and synergies across product groups, is a key component of implementation intensity.

The US experience of the 1970s and 1980s seemed to suggest that an intensive growth and diversification strategy, such as Citicorp pursued, was no longer viable in an industry characterized by increasing competition and turbulence: there were too many strong niche players in several of the markets into which Citicorp and others (pursuing their strategy) had diversified – for instance, securities brokerage, mergers and acquisitions (M&A), and information services. And the fact that Citicorp's dramatic turnaround in the nineties coincided with its increasing willingness to sell off losing businesses in these product markets and focus itself more reinforces that conclusion.

Moreover, becoming a high performer requires more than concentrating on areas of core competence. It is also necessary to develop a strong infrastructure, or what students of strategic management call a strategic architecture: a culture, an organizational structure, control systems, technological capability, human resources practices and change-management skills that together match the implementation requirements of the strategy.

Finally, a big part of that infrastructure must be geared to generating much collaboration across product groups. Many observers of the industry have noted that success in serving both retail (individual and small business) and wholesale (large corporate and governmental) customers involves providing them with innovative, customized packages of products and services. This strategy is referred to in the industry as 'cross selling' at the retail level and 'structuring deals' (through the equivalent of project teams) at the wholesale level.[16] It involves achieving synergies across product groups and divisions that multiproduct firms in other industries have been notoriously deficient at doing.[17]

UK bankers, along with their counterparts in other nations, give considerable lip service to the notion of achieving synergies through cross-product collaboration. Except in isolated cases where the corporate culture strongly supports it (for instance at TSB, JP Morgan and Goldman Sachs), getting such synergies through collaboration is extremely difficult, making universal banking a highly problematic strategy. Given the difficulties, reflecting the different cultures, compensation systems and social backgrounds of investment bankers and those in traditional corporate and retail banking, as well as their political interests (for example, in gaining access to the capital pool at headquarters), it is no wonder that managing a multiproduct financial services firm is a daunting task. One might assume that commercial banks would shy away from universal banking as these problems become more obvious throughout the industry.

But it hasn't turned out that way. Despite the many problems that US money centres, including Citicorp, and the big UK clearing banks have had in pursuing this diversification strategy, the banking industry worldwide – and certainly in the US and UK – has been moving toward universal banking as a model.[18] The many arguments in its favour – that it spreads risk and smoothes income streams, provides for economies of scale and scope, provides opportunities for synergies, and limits customers' transaction costs by providing packages of services from a single source (known as 'one-stop shopping') – seem to be prevailing, even if they are not demonstrated empirically, or at least not on a consistent basis.

The UK experience is of particular interest in this regard in that, unlike the US, it has been engaged in universal banking at least since 'Big Bang' and the deregulation of UK capital markets in 1986. An analysis of its experiences should thus have some relevance for US banks that are at an earlier stage in this development, because of more restrictive legislation there. Moreover, since both nations have been characterized as sites of capital-market rather than banking-oriented financial systems, the comparison has particular relevance.

The two main issues of the book

Taking the US banking industry as a point of comparison, the book deals with two related issues.

The first involves an analysis of the changing *strategies* of the four clearers, particularly since the early 1970s. For example, since the early 1990s, marking the end of the UK's deep recession, the banks have tempered their relentless pursuit of bigness (asset size) and market share with an increased emphasis on focus, core competence and shareholder value.

The second looks at the *strategic architecture* (in other words, strategy–structure relations) that these clearing banks have developed to implement their strategies. More specifically, it analyzes how the banks have managed the complexities of integrating their various businesses, so as to achieve lateral linkages and synergies across separate divisions and product groups.

Few studies exist on how universal banking actually gets carried out, in particular on how inevitable conflicts (both cultural and political) across product groups and divisions, and between them and headquarters, are actually managed. Universal banking may lead to economies of scale and scope and to synergies, or it may not, depending on how the conflicts are managed. Where it does not so lead, the addition of new businesses to add value is likely to inflate costs without any compensating benefits.

Each of the two issues is explored for its relevance in suggesting what works and what does not. Who are the high and low performers, and what do they do that makes them that? Are they more or less diversified, and do they have particular configurations of internal characteristics (infrastructures) to implement their strategies?

Design and method

To summarize the argument so far, given the fact that commercial banking as traditionally conceived – taking deposits and providing loans – has been increasingly disintermediated, with new capital markets products replacing old banking ones, there is a need for the industry to re-invent itself. This is happening worldwide, with the particulars varying in different national contexts.

The strategies the banks should follow in re-inventing themselves are not at all clear, however, as competing visions exist. The two most pronounced are the conglomerate strategy of universal banking, where the banks' future survival is seen to lie in diversifying into many other financial services, and the niche-market strategy of banks specializing on what they do best. And there are various types within each.

In an industry driven by fad and fashion, UK banking has both strategies, with Lloyds pursuing the latter and the other three the former. Of additional significance in the UK case is the fact that the country's three clearing banks implementing universal banking have been doing so since Big Bang in 1986, in contrast to the US, which has been much more constrained domestically by Glass Steagall and the power of the insurance lobby.

There may be lessons in that respect for US banks from the UK experience in attempting to manage such multiproduct firms. Assumed economies of scale and scope, for example, may or may not take place. The only way to understand this process is to get inside the banks undergoing such diversification and analyze how it unfolds.

My field strategy for this book has been based on that approach and calls for the use of both archival materials and interviews. The former included company histories, articles in the financial press, annual reports, bank analyst reports, internal company documents, and industry studies. While these sources provided useful preliminary data on the industry and on the banks' histories and present characteristics, I found it necessary to probe more deeply to ascertain the cultures, strategies and management practices that drove these banks' and their industry's evolution. I did so through conducting qualitative, informant interviews both inside and outside the banks.

I began by searching out a pool of knowledgeable outsiders, including bank analysts, management consultants, journalists, academics providing training programmes or consulting services for the banks, regulators, trade association staff, and retired bankers. In most instances, this outsider panel included senior people who had dealt with top management at the banks. My interviews with these outsiders covered both industry and bank-level issues. The former related to the main driving forces affecting the industry's evolution – in particular, its increasing competition and how this was impacting on the individual banks.

Those portions of the interviews dealing with the banks themselves focused largely on comparisons of their characteristics and performance. Needless to say, they generated many insights that made me that much more informed and therefore credible when I later talked to the bankers themselves. In addition, proceeding with a so-called 'snowball' approach, I was often successful in gaining an entry to later informants from earlier ones. I am most grateful for the generous help several early outside informants provided in that regard, opening many doors to people who might otherwise not have been so readily available.

These interviews with outsiders were begun in Spring 1995 and continued throughout the study, but in August of that year I began a series of intensive interviews with senior managers and board members of the four clearing banks. I ended up doing some 100 interviews with outsiders and another 100 with bankers. The latter included CEOs, board chairs, HQ staff heading up strategic planning and human resource management departments, divisional and product heads, and some middle- and lower-level staff. Barclays and NatWest were the banks where I spent most of my time, followed by Lloyds and then Midland.[19]

The chapters that follow contain the many insights I was able to glean about the future of British banking from an analysis of data from these two sources. Wherever possible, I make comparisons with US banking and will be focusing on what can be learned through such comparisons about the characteristics that British banks will need in order to be major players in the future, both in their own country and globally.

'Universal banking' and the decline of conglomerates

Before analyzing British banking and the four clearers' experiences, a brief literature review is relevant on the performance of conglomerates in other industries, because this bears on the viability of the equivalent in financial services, namely the universal bank. The short answer to the viability of the conglomerate strategy is that it has not worked well in many manufacturing industries and has been increasingly abandoned there. As Robert Grant has concluded from an exhaustive review: 'During the 1980s and 1990s, there has been a clear reversal of the diversification trend.'[20] He notes a strong 'back to basics' movement in both North America and Western Europe, meaning by that the divestment of unrelated businesses and a restructuring around fewer, more closely related ones. A main reason for the trend seems to have been that high levels of diversification give rise to problems of managing complexity. The assumed synergies from exploiting the linkages across businesses within diversified companies must be managed, and that has been very difficult given cultural and political conflicts across multiple businesses in the conglomerate firm. It may well be that managers don't have the experience or skills to deal effectively with these conflicts.

Markides has written extensively in that regard about inefficiencies resulting from disproportionate increases in the costs of co-ordination and control in highly diversified firms, suggesting that there are theoretical limits to diversification. He also attributes the marginal costs of diversification to a more volatile and uncertain economic environment, in which maintaining profitability in many different businesses is extremely difficult. His conclusion is that there is a curvilinear relationship between diversification and profitability. Diversification increases profitability up to a point, beyond which, for the reasons specified above, proftability goes down.[21]

These are all theoretical arguments. What is the evidence to support them? Markides provides the following:

(1) There has been a significant shedding of businesses and refocusing activity displayed by conglomerates in the UK and Western Europe in the 1980s and 1990s.

(2) The firms that refocused were highly diversified and had poor performance relative to their industry counterparts before making this change, implying that firms refocus in response to

a performance crisis, possibly brought about by 'excessive' diversification.

(3) Refocusing announcements were accompanied by positive abnormal stockmarket returns.[22]

A still larger implication is that the era of conglomerates may be over and that companies will *have* to refocus.

Closer to our subject, Grant has done a study comparing the performance of focused and conglomerate firms among US financial services corporations between 1977 and 1986. His sample of conglomerate firms identified the six most active diversifiers during this period and included two commercial banks, namely BankAmerica and Citicorp. Comparing the performance of the conglomerates with that of specialist companies, Grant found that the return on equity (ROE) and the return on assets (ROA) by the conglomerate companies were, overall, below that earned by the specialists. He also found that diversification failed to improve performance over time.[23]

Grant concluded that the appeal of one-stop shopping to individual and corporate customers proved to be limited and he included the following observation from Henry Kaufman, prominent economist and financial adviser: 'Managing financial conglomeration will be an exceptional challenge and poses great risk. I am not convinced that financial institutions today have the management skills at the most senior level to perceive and understand the developments in five or six or seven different areas of their business.'[24]

In brief, as other industries are increasingly abandoning diversification and the conglomerate strategy, commercial banking seems to be moving the other way. To be sure, the diversification that universal banking entails is not quite the same as that in industrial conglomerates. In the latter case, their diversification had been to unrelated fields, while most if not all of the banks' diversification is in financial-services-related businesses. Nevertheless, many of the same economic, political, and managerial problems mentioned for industrial conglomerates exist in financial services. We address these issues as we analyze the recent evolution of the Big Four UK clearing banks.

Notes and references

1. See, for example, Michael Collins, *Money and Banking in the UK: A History*, Croom Helm, London, 1988.
2. David T. Llewellyn, 'A Strategic Perspective on the Global Banking Industry', in *Revue de La Banque*, 6, 1995, pp. 302–12; and his 'Universal Banking and the Public Interest: A British Perspective', Ch. 5, pp. 161–204, in Anthony Saunders and Ingo Walter (eds), *Universal Banking*, Chicago, Irwin, 1996. Llewellyn, an economist and banking scholar, has written insightfully on this trend, particularly as exemplified in the UK. See also Jordi Canals, *Universal Banking*, Clarendon Press, Oxford, 1997, Ch. l.
3. Board of Governors of the Federal Reserve System, *Flow of Funds Accounts*, various editions.
4. Collins, *op. cit.*, p. 405.
5. *Ibid.*, p. 411–12.
6. Two recent examples are Itzhak Swary and Barry Topf, *Global Financial Deregulation*, Blackwell, Cambridge, 1992; and Anthony Saunders and Ingo Walter (eds), *Universal Banking*, Irwin, Chicago, 1996.
7. One exception is Canals, *op. cit.*
8. David Rogers, *The Future of American Banking*, McGraw Hill, New York, 1993.
9. Interestingly, Channon had provided some prescient comments on precisely this point in 1977. As he noted: '... the literature to date has not treated these firms as the individual and unique business organizations that they are, but rather has considered them collectively – as clearly defined, yet somehow characterless, groups of like enterprises. The research evidence, however clearly revealed that, while, for instance, the different clearing banks had features in common, there were also notable differences in the policies they were pursuing and the structures used to implement these policies.' Derek Channon, *British Banking Strategy*, Macmillan, London, 1977, Preface, xi. Despite Channon's admonitions, banking industry researchers have not looked at the strategy and structure of individual banks to any degree, with the exception of the author's previous banking study and Canals' recent work.
10. See Roy C. Smith and Ingo Walter, 'Global Patterns of Mergers and Acquisition Activity in the Financial Services Industry', a paper presented at the Conference on Mergers of Financial Institutions, New York University Salomon Center, Leonard N. Stern School of Business, 11 October 1996.
11. For a discussion of different types of universal banks, see Anthony Saunders and Ingo Walter, *Universal Banking in the United States*, Oxford University Press, New York, Oxford, 1994, Ch. 4.
12. This is the thesis of Roy Smith in his book, *Comeback*, Harvard Business School Press, Boston, 1993.
13. I am indebted to Professor David Llewellyn of Loughborough University for insights on this issue.
14. Smith and Walter, *op.cit.*, p. 22.
15. Rogers, *op. cit.*
16. Robert Eccles and Dwight Crane, *Doing Deals*, Harvard Business School Press, Boston, 1988.

17. Andrew Campbell and Kathleen Sommers Luchs (eds), *Strategic Synergy*, Butterworth-Heinemann, Oxford, 1992.
18. Saunders and Walter, *op. cit.*
19. Originally, given their size and complexity, I was intending to do case studies of Barclays and NatWest alone. After gaining significant entry into the two other clearing banks, contrary to my expectations, I decided to include Lloyds and Midland also.
20. Robert M. Grant, *Contemporary Strategy Analysis*, Blackwell, Cambridge MA, 1995, p. 369.
21. Constantine C. Markides, *Diversification, Refocusing, and Economic Performance*, MIT Press, Cambridge MA, 1995.
22. *Ibid.*, p. 164.
23. Robert Grant, 'Diversification in The Financial Services Industry', in Campbell and Luchs, *op. cit.*, pp. 201–42.
24. *Ibid.*, p. 231, quoted from Henry Kaufman, 'Financial Institutions and the Fragile, Volatile Financial Markets', in Arnold W. Sametz (ed.), *The Emerging Financial Industry*, Lexington Books, DC Heath, Lexington MA, 1985, pp. 26–7.

2 UK *and US Banking: Similarities and Differences*

I ARGUED in Chapter 1 that the banking industry worldwide has evolved since the 1960s from a protected, cartel-like state to one subject to continued competitive threat. This parallels the evolution of financial services more broadly, from a condition of segmentation in which sharp market boundaries separated investment banking, commercial banking, insurance, home mortgages and asset management to one in which each was diversifying onto the others' territory.[1] The driving forces behind these changes – globalization, the rise of capital markets, new technology, lowered entry barriers, and a consequent disintermediation of banks – have proceeded on a transnational basis, forcing banks in all countries of the world to adapt.

Historical and transnational comparisons

Notwithstanding transnational similarities indicated in Chapter 1, this evolutionary process will proceed differently in different nations. The more comparative a perspective we can get on the process, looking at the varied adaptation efforts of banks both within and across nations, the more insight we should gain about what drives the changes and how they can best be managed.

My approach in this regard was to choose the US as my site for comparison. I had already studied US banking; and its recent experience suggests that some propositions relate to conglomerate and specialist banking which I wanted to explore in Britain. Since Britain is farther along in trying out its own version of conglomerate banking, it could in that respect be a benchmark case for the US when it too undertakes conglomerate or universal banking.

Conversely, there may also be lessons that British bankers may learn from their counterparts in the US. For example, US banking has moved faster than some British clearers to incorporate advanced electronic communications technology, sales and marketing techniques, and strategic analysis.

This comparative approach is particularly important in increasing our understanding of why some banks fail and others succeed as the industry is becoming increasingly competitive. More comparisons of individual banks, both within and across nations, may provide insights into how the industry is adapting to change.[2]

Key similarities between UK and US banking

In comparing the US and UK banking industries there are several similarities and differences, with the latter a function of the different cultures, institutions, markets and regulatory structures of each nation.

In relation to similarities, both nations have economies whose financial systems are capital-markets-driven – in contrast, for example, to Germany and Japan, which are more banking-driven and which have weak capital markets. A banking-driven financial system is one where banks actually own companies that they monitor and where the stock and bond markets are relatively underdeveloped.[3] The German *hausbank* system and the Japanese *keiretsus* are examples, with the former involving large corporations relying on a single or main bank for external financing. The German system also involves banks participating actively in strategic decisions through heavy stock ownership and control, including bankers sitting on company boards.

In the US and Britain, by contrast, banks for the most part do not own non-financial corporations, and there are strong restrictions prohibiting stock ownership, informal in Britain and legislative in the US.

The other main similarities are historical experiences that the US and British banking industries have in common with those of many other industrial nations. Both have experienced the worldwide trend from segmentation and specialization in financial services, to increasing permeability where each segment is diversifying onto the others' domain.[4] Both have thus evolved from a protected, cartel-like past to a condition of increasing competition, including from non-banks, foreign banks and other domestic financial service institutions, as entry barriers erode. And both have been particularly impacted by new technology and are in the process of reconfiguring traditional branches, closing many and experimenting with new, electronically driven alternative delivery systems – ATMs, pc banking, home banking, point-of-sale banking, and new sites for deposits and withdrawals.

At the same time, in adapting to increased competition in wholesale and retail banking, banks in both nations have become increasingly global, have diversified in their products and customer base, and are undergoing continued consolidation. The global expansion had been underway since World War I, with Citicorp, Barclays, and Lloyds having branches abroad dating back to the 1910s; but banks expanded globally on a big scale in the 1960s and 1970s, with the US leading the way. This coincided with the growth of multinational corporations, international money markets, and (particularly) the Euromoney markets.

In addition, British and US banks began diversifying into such new product markets as credit cards, asset management, investment banking, and insurance in these years. Banks in both countries were responding to the same competitive conditions.

Most importantly, banking in both nations has continued to consolidate during these years, as the US and Britain both experienced a condition of overcapacity. Being 'overbanked', both have been in a process of shake-out that is likely to continue for many years.

Key differences

Notwithstanding the similarities outline above, the differences between US and UK banking are significant. Indeed, I judge them as so significant they may well outweigh the similarities in explaining British banking's recent history and its future prospects. The differences fall under seven main headings: economic concentration, regulation, universal banking, recruitment policy, marketing methods, bank failure, and investment banking. These are each described in more detail below.

Economic concentration

British banking is much more concentrated than in the US. In fact, the banks represent extreme cases on this dimension. Britain did much of its consolidation in the nineteenth century, and by 1918 there was a 'Big Five' – Barclays, Lloyds, National Provincial, Westminster and Midland – that held 80 per cent of the nation's deposits. Those five banks operated as a cartel, limiting competition on interest rates.[5] There is now a Big Four, with National Provincial and Westminster having merged into NatWest in 1970.

By contrast, the US had 25 000 banks in the 1920s, 18 000 in 1986, and still had 9528 at the end of 1996.[6] The big numbers reflect the US's dual banking system, which includes both state and federally chartered banks. One of the main reasons for this was the strong populist tradition in the US, reflecting an historic distrust of bigness and centralized economic power. The US as a nation was founded in revolt against what the colonies regarded as the arbitrary, coercive power of a monarchy, and the US's banking system reflects that. Two centralized 'Banks of the United States', one founded by Alexander Hamilton in 1791 and the other started in 1816, were both closed down, in each case as a reflection of this tradition. The Second Bank, for example, was closed in the Jacksonian populist era in 1836.[7]

Even in 1997, with bank consolidation and mergers proceeding at a rapid pace, there remain up to 8000 small community banks in the US. Moreover, until the McCarran Act of 1927 was repealed in 1996, there remained strong legal constraints against interstate banking that continued to protect many community banks, even though some were charging monopolistic prices and were insufficiently modernized in terms of technology and range of products. The US may well be down to 7500 banks by the year 2000, but although that represents considerable consolidation over the past couple of decades, it is still sharply different from the UK banking system as well as that of every other industrial nation.

In many respects, the US is now undergoing the amalgamation that took place in the UK in the nineteenth century, though for the reasons stated above it will not reach anywhere near the same degree of economic concentration. Since restrictions on interstate banking are now being lifted, it is nonetheless likely that the US will soon have a small number of national banks – for instance, BancOne, NationsBank, Bank of America, First Union, Fleet, Key Corp – having branches throughout that country. In the UK, although each of the Big Four has tended to be concentrated in a particular region, national branch networks have existed since the 1880s and were certainly well developed by 1918, when a Big Five emerged.[8]

In summary, the US has had thousands of banks and limited branching, while Britain has had a small number of them, each with many branches.[9] As one observer of UK banking noted: 'You go to towns throughout the UK and you find a bank on every corner. And so it is in London as well.' As at the end of 1994, for example, and excluding the UK's Girobank that operates through post offices, the UK still had over 11 000 branches.[10] Both nations are overbanked, although with different structures and in different ways.

Regulation

A second major difference between US and British banking is in regulation. Britain has historically been very lightly regulated in comparison with the US, which has one of the most restrictive regulatory systems in the world. In Britain, there had been no branching limits, no interest-rate caps, no deposit insurance, no minimum capital requirements, no legal demands for banks to provide financial services to poor minority populations, few limits on banks getting into insurance, and no Glass–Steagall equivalent to prevent diversification into investment banking. US banking, in sharp contrast, by having to live with all these constraints, has thus been micro-managed to an extreme degree. Attempts since the early 1980s to repeal Glass–Steagall, for example, have always been defeated.

Observers of UK banking note a different pattern of regulator controls from those in the US. The Bank of England had regulated much more informally than US regulators, using 'raised eyebrows' or 'a wink and a nod'. As Swary and Topf note: 'The system was notable for its considerable reliance upon self-regulation by the institutions concerned. There was very little in the way of formal regulation, mandatory rules, or prescribed codes.'[11]

Instead, moral or gentlemanly persuasion was the prevailing regulatory style. For example, some high-ranked Bank of England officials had serious reservations about Barclays pursuing its aggressive global expansion strategy throughout much of this century, as Britain's premier 'empire' bank. The regulators' classic behaviour, however, as many knowledgeable observers have noted, was to do little to curb it, except indirectly by making reportedly negative comments about it to Barclays' senior managers. As one banking writer explained: 'Many Bank of England officials were not happy about Barclays' global expansion, but they wouldn't say so directly or do anything about it. It took the form of comments like "How's your madcap foreign banking going?" said with raised eyebrows. The joke was that the banks' and regulators' relation was much like grandmother and grandchild. The latter would take a few footsteps and soon was expecting to be grabbed or hugged by the former.'

At the same time, the Bank of England did not play a completely *laissez-faire* regulatory role. When its top officials saw a serious threat to the future stability of the banking system, they intervened aggressively. This happened in the early 1970s, when it got the Big Four to bail out the industry's so-called 'secondary banks', lest the latter's poor performance destabilize the entire industry.[12]

Later, in 1986, when Midland was in danger of collapsing after having lost an estimated £1 billion in the acquisition and later sale of Crocker Bank of San Francisco, the Bank of England prevailed on one of its most senior officials, Sir Kit McMahon, to be Midland's CEO. And again, in 1991, after McMahon had been unable to turn Midland around, it urged Barclays to allow its Chief Financial Officer, Sir Brian Pearse, to succeed McMahon as CEO. In this respect, senior officials from the Bank of England, along with the most senior managers of the Big Four clearers, functioned as an informal 'club' to maintain the banking system's stability.

Historian Michael Collins suggests that the Bank of England even tolerated cartel pricing practices of the Big Four, precisely because of the stability they brought to the banking system and the wider UK economy.

As the pace of change in financial services accelerated in the 1970s and thereafter, however, the Bank of England issued more formal regulations and, by 1979, there was at last significant legislation controlling the banks' activities. But even then, the regulatory constraints on British banking were still much more limited than the micro-management by US banking regulators.

Universal banking

It is in that limited regulatory context that a significant third difference emerges between the US and UK banking industries. This is that universal banking has been much more in evidence in the UK, with Barclays, NatWest, and Midland all having an active presence in global investment banking since at least 1986, the time of Big Bang and the deregulation both of fixed commissions for brokers and of the UK securities markets. Even before then, all of the Big Four had their own merchant banks.

The UK clearing banks were also increasingly active in insurance, unlike in the US where a combination of legislative constraints and a powerful insurance lobby in Washington and the states prevented the banks from entering that industry.

Recruitment policy

On a number of characteristics, then, the UK banking system differs significantly from that in the US. One might argue that the UK's limited regulatory constraints should have made possible greater experimentation than in the US. Offsetting their freedom to experiment, however, has been the limiting and homogenizing effect of the UK's class structure on the cultures and consequent actions of the banks. Until very recently, commercial banking in the UK has been largely the preserve of a non-university-educated, lower-middle-class, drawn from its 'grammar school' graduate population. Until the 1990s, managers at all levels in British banks came disproportionately from this non-university class. The typical career of a CEO or other senior manager was to enter a bank branch as a clerk at age 16 or 17, fresh out of secondary school, usually in the locale where he or she lived, and gradually move up the ranks by dint of expertise in traditional banking and bureaucratic survival.

Contrast this with US banks, which have been recruiting MBAs and people with other graduate degrees, let alone college graduates, since at least the late 1950s. Huertas and Cleveland describe, for example, how George Moore, then CEO of Citicorp, aggressively recruited people from business schools and other graduate programmes in the 1950s and 1960s to build an élite corps of global bankers, supporting its expanding multinational banking strategy.[13] Even the small community bankers in the US generally sent their children to college, with many of their sons later taking over the bank.

That development took place much later in Britain and may account in part for the fact that its banks were later to incorporate modern technology and management systems than the US. If university education does, indeed, broaden one's horizons, increase analytical skills, and sharpen thinking, it would follow that employing a greater proportion of graduates is likely to increase the number of bankers with the ability to handle new technology and modern approaches to management.

The differences between Britain and the US in this regard are narrowing, as British commercial banks have recruited new university graduates in greater numbers since the late 1970s. The process has been gradual, however, since the arrival of these graduates was often resisted by an 'old guard', who sometimes contemptuously referred to the newcomers as the 'officer class'. There was clearly little respect initially among the veteran bankers in some of the clearing banks for such people. A senior human resource manager in one of the clearers reported, for example, that the turnover among these university-educated newcomers was as high as 90 per cent until recently.

Thus, the UK banks' 'clubbiness' and their lateness relative to the US in the use of technology, strategic management and planning, sales and marketing expertise, and more broadly what might be called change-management concepts and techniques has held back development. This is certainly not to glorify US bankers as uniformly sophisticated change managers, a goal that many US management consultants have prodded them to pursue more actively;[14] but banking in the US clearly modernized earlier in its management practices than it did in the UK.

Academics writing about UK banking, for example, commonly portray the UK banks as playing catch-up relative to the US. Professor Derek Channon referred to how UK banks were always later than the US in adopting many products and management practices that they in fact borrowed from it:[15] in credit finance, factoring, leasing, the use of term loans, using aggressive marketing techniques and cold calling, and developing an increased understanding of industrial corporations to become competitive in providing both advisory services and packages of investment-banking products. He concluded that UK banks were well behind those in the US in management and marketing skills associated with running large, multiproduct organizations. One of his most telling observations in this regard was in essence that US banks expanded more internationally in the 1960s than the UK banks had in more than a century.[16]

Lord Alexander, board chairman at NatWest from 1989 to 1997, put it well when he said on numerous occasions that he saw the UK banks as beginning to be run much more like businesses than institutions. Basically, what he was saying was that UK banks, traditionally functioning like social clubs, were not advanced in using rational business-management techniques to adapt to the rapid changes that their industry was experiencing. There was an exclusivity in who the banks recruited, leading to much homogeneity in social backgrounds and perpetuated by the bankers' resistance to accepting a new, more educated generation.

Here, the difference with the US is more a matter of degree. Certainly, the big US banks were traditionally bastions of their own homogeneous, male-dominated, Protestant élite. That was the case, for example, with Chase, Bankers Trust, and even JP Morgan, as well as some of the big regional banks. But that homogeneity broke down earlier in the US than in Britain. By the late sixties and seventies, senior Chase managers, for example, were making reference to the bank's large number of Irish Catholics in top positions. Then, when Bankers Trust converted in the late 1970s to investment banking, it brought in an entirely new population of traders, referred to as 'scrappy ethnics', very different in social backgrounds from the old-line loan officers.

A larger implication of this discussion of different social backgrounds of bankers in the US and Britain is that banking in all industrial nations has had to modernize as it has lost its old cartel status since the 1960s and now faces escalating competition. In Britain, because of the traditional, national, class structure, that modernization had proceeded more slowly than in the US. New, university-educated managers were not accepted as readily as in the US.

In addition, as part of their particular genre of clubbiness, the British banks had a strong, if informal, 'no-poaching' rule, at least among the Big Four, that has only gradually broken down in recent years. The loyalty that UK bankers had for their institutions was so great that it was considered bad form to voluntarily leave one clearer to work for another. And this practice most likely reinforced both the homogeneity of the banks and their adherence to traditional ways, further slowing down the pace of strategic and organizational change. As an example, a senior Barclays manager in the early nineties who had originally worked in Martins Bank (which Barclays acquired in 1968) continued to identify himself as a Martins man.

Also, British banks had a 'jobs for life' culture until the 1990s, supported by narrowly specialized banking qualifications, obtained by part-time study. This further reinforced the banks' homogeneity of personnel and their exclusivity.

Marketing methods

Still another difference between the British and US banking industries, reflecting the wider society and its culture, relates to the particularly negative UK bankers' attitudes about using aggressive sales practices in the branches. Many branch employees regarded aggressive salesmanship as undignified and inappropriate for gentlemanly UK bankers. Such phrases as 'we're tellers, not sellers' captured this sentiment. To the extent that it was widespread and strongly held, it slowed down the modernization of the branches and their improved capacity to compete.

Bank failure

One other difference is that the UK has not experienced the same widespread bank failure that the US has. Though the US has traditionally followed a 'too big to fail' policy for its large banks, with the understanding that the regulators would prop them up in the event of a possible failure, that has not at all been the case for smaller and medium-sized banks. Contrast this with the Secondary Banking Crisis in 1973, when the Bank of England prevailed on the Big Four to bail out smaller banks, a large number of which would otherwise have failed – a development that Bank of England officials and students of the industry foresaw as having potentially catastrophic consequences.

On the other side, the prospects of competitive threat from foreign banks had traditionally been much greater in the UK than in the US, mainly due to the restrictive legislation in the latter. That has had a significant negative impact on UK banks as, for example, in the 1970s when global US wholesale banks gained 25 per cent of the market share of the UK large corporate loan business within a year or two of their entry, because of their superior products and lower prices. Japanese banks made similar inroads.

Investment banking

London being a major financial centre dating back several centuries is, willingly or otherwise, integrally related to the wider European Union. It is in that sense subject to EU legislation on capital markets and insurance. As a capital of the Euromarkets, it attracts much of its financial business. At the same time, its capital markets are much less well developed than those in the US. Thus, the main so-called 'bulge bracket' firms in investment banking had never been the British merchant banks, but rather the global US investment banks such as Goldman Sachs, Merrill Lynch, Salomon, and Morgan Stanley.

The traditional British investment banks were increasingly unable to compete in the late 1980s and early 1990s without a massive infusion of capital. This weakness became so pronounced that four of the most prestigious were acquired by large, continental European commercial banks: Morgan Grenfell by Deutsche Bank, Kleinwort Benson by Dredsner, SG Warburg by Swiss Bank Corporation (SBC), and Barings by ING. Only Schroder has survived as an independent firm from among the large British merchant banks.

This is not to say that the newly merged European global investment banks will now be able to match the US bulge-bracket firms in performance. A recent article in *The Economist* suggests that these European global investment banks are 'out of their league' and will have to 'dream on'. Now that these European global aspirants are owned by commercial banks, 'whose conservative traditions clash with the fast-paced, deal-making culture of successful investment banking', it will be difficult for the investment bankers in their newly-formed conglomerate to move fast enough to compete effectively. In addition, the biggest investment banking market worldwide is in the US, and American firms are reluctant to 'concede their fertile home turf, and [are] well positioned to hold it'.[17]

Britain's global investment banks face the same kinds of problems as their European counterparts. They must compete with the American bulge-bracket investment banks that already have well over 50 per cent of market share in such mainstream product markets as investment bond and equity underwriting and placement, M&A advice, and lead management of syndicated loans and medium-term notes. In addition, having investment banking has yielded uneven returns, huge costs (particularly on compensation), and many complex management problems. On the last of these, the investment bankers' huge compensation demands, the difficulty of engendering loyalty to the firm and a team sense, developing strong infrastructure controls, and the many culture and class conflicts between the investment and commercial bankers have together been overwhelming. It is little wonder, then, that the returns on equity of all of the universal banks – and certainly of their investment banks – in Britain and Europe have been so modest relative to those of the US bulge-bracket banks.

Since the US capital markets are much more developed than those in Britain, it should not be surprising that securitization is much farther along in the US, where banks have moved more aggressively to get loans off their balance sheets. Also, traditional banking with business in the form of loans to small and middle-market businesses remains much stronger in Britain.

In summary, the British banking industry is a critical case through which to explore the viability of universal v. more specialist banking, as well as the larger issue of what strategies and organizational forms are likely to distinguish the winners from the losers. By placing the British experience in a larger, transnational context, comparisons with US and secondarily with European universal banks should enhance our understanding of the dynamics of the British industry's evolution. With these perspectives in mind, we discuss the evolution of British banking since the 1960s.

Notes and references

1. Itzhak Swary and Barry Topf, *Global Financial Regulation*, Blackwell, Cambridge, 1992, p. 4.
2. Banking scholars Steven Pilloff and Anthony Santomero argue that we need more field-based, managerial-process, case studies that are more longitudinal and with more organizational detail in order to understand better why some banks fail and others succeed. See their paper, 'The Value Effects of Bank Mergers and Acquisitions', presented at the Conference on Mergers of Financial Institutions, New York University Salomon Center, Stern School of Business, in association with New York University Law School, Center for The Study of Central Banks.
3. Lawrence Ritter, William Silber and Gregory Udell, *Principles of Money, Banking and Financial Markets*, (9th edn), Addison Wesley, Reading MA, 1997, Ch. 14.
4. Swary and Topf, *op. cit.*, p. 4.
5. Collins, *Money and Banking in the UK: a History*, Croom Helm, London, 1988, p. 19ff.
6. *American Banker*, 7 July, 1997 p. 9.
7. Sidney Ratner, James H. Soltow, and Richard Sylla, *The Evolution of the American Economy* (2nd edn), Macmillan, New York, 1993, p. 171.
8. Collins, *op. cit.*, pp. 78ff.
9. Michael D. Bardo and Richard Sylla (eds), *Anglo-American Financial Systems*, Irwin, New York, 1995.
10. *Annual Abstract of Banking Statistics*, British Bankers Association, Vol. 14, 1997, pp. 66–7.
11. Swary and Topf, *op. cit.*, p. 125.
12. Collins, *op. cit.*, pp. 382–3.
13. Harold van B. Cleveland and Thomas F. Huertas, *Citibank*, Harvard University Press, Cambridge MA, 1985, p. 285.
14. See Lowell Bryan's books: *Breaking Up the Bank: Rethinking an Industry Under Siege*, Dow Jones-Irwin, Homewood IL, 1988; and *Bankrupt*, Harper Business, New York, 1991.
15. Derek Channon, *British Banking Strategy*, Macmillan, London and Basingstoke, 1977, p. 161ff.
16. *Ibid.*, p. 153.
17. *The Economist*, 21 June 1997, p. 72.

3 Recent History and Strategic Adaptations

A SERIES of critical events since the 1960s moved British banking away from its previously protected, cartel-like state to increasing competition. Many reflected the blurring of boundaries across financial services sectors. This chapter highlights those events in encapsulating the industry's main trends in recent decades.

Forces contributing to increasing competition

The Bank of England

By 1970, as banking worldwide had become more competitive, the Bank of England concluded that maintaining Britain's traditional, cartelized system was too costly. It undertook a series of initiatives to encourage more competitive practices among the clearers.[1] The first initiative in that direction was a Bank of England requirement in 1970 that banks publish reports on their true costs and profits. Before then, the banks had used a variety of 'creative' accounting procedures to mask their performance. As one bank reporter explained: 'Before 1970, they could fudge their profits through accounting procedures so that neither the banks nor any outsiders knew how they were doing. Soon the banks were in shock, because Midland, for example, felt it was doing well when in fact it was not.'

The introduction of a new policy in 1971, referred to as Competition and Credit Control, was a landmark event in this regard. It removed regulatory constraints on bank lending. Most importantly, it eliminated the clearing banks' right to collude on interest rates, thus ending the price-fixing cartels that the Bank of England had implicitly supported before. The clearing banks were urged to compete much more with one another and with other rival financial services organizations.[2]

This was followed in 1974 by the secondary banking crisis.[3] Smaller quasi-banks and fringe banks had engaged in reckless property lending that threatened to destabilize the entire industry and, potentially, the wider UK economy as well. 'It was quite a severe crisis,' reported a bank analyst, 'and it ended up with some fifty smaller, fringe banks having to be rescued.' This strengthened the big banks' position, because the Bank of England had urged that they be the main 'lifeboat' players in the bail out. Equally importantly, it forced more formal controls from the Bank of England over bank practices, replacing the former approach of informal co-operation and consultation between it and the banks.

A final landmark legislative event was the 1979 Banking Act that formalized the status of banks and the Bank of England's supervisory role. The 1979 Act established criteria relating to liquidity and capital adequacy, managerial integrity, and the judicious conduct of the overall business. The criteria were to be applied at the time a bank applied for a licence and through periodic monitoring.[4]

In the past, the Bank of England had been intent on ensuring stability rather than competitiveness in the banking industry. Its officials realized increasingly in the 1970s, however, that they needed a regulatory system flexible enough not to stifle innovation in the face of increasing competition. In essence, they wanted a balance between stability and adaptability.

Globalization as another driver

Throughout the 1970s, London increasingly became an offshore centre for the newly emerging Eurodollar market, which grew tremendously during those years and involved foreign banks entering the UK wholesale banking markets. Many US banks had opened offices in London, partly because of regulatory restrictions at home, and these banks quickly captured a big share in the corporate loan market. While foreign banks did not penetrate the UK retail market, by 1989 they accounted for over 60 per cent of loans to UK industry, primarily to the large public companies.[5]

During this time, UK banking went from being predominantly domestic to becoming much more global.[6] Barclays, the first to do so, had formed its DCO (dominion and countries outside) division in the 1920s, following the flag of the British empire to various colonies around the world. Lloyds, later to reduce its international businesses, bought a big bank in Latin America in 1971, one in New Zealand in 1974, and opened branches in the US and Europe in the 1970s. NatWest, having inherited virtually no business in international banking, set itself up in money centres in major industrial nations. And Midland, also late to globalize, first had correspondent banking and later a consortium approach.

Deregulation and the building societies

Another significant development that increased competition in UK banking was the deregulation of the building societies (the UK equivalent to the US savings and loans companies). Having originated as mutually owned mortgage banks, obtaining funds from depositors and financing home purchases, the building societies nowadays increasingly compete with the banks in commercial banking services and mortgage lending.[7] The 1986 Building Societies Act deregulated them to the extent that up to 25 per cent of their total commercial business was permitted to be in non-traditional (home mortgage) services that included insurance, credit cards, money transaction accounts and personal banking.

Building societies are a formidable competitor to the banks. They have significantly lower costs than the clearing banks. They are well placed geographically. And they were early in using ATMs and other new electronic communications technology. One informant stated that the Bank of Scotland, recognizing the competitive strengths of the building societies, used them to gain access to the English consumer banking market.

Meanwhile, the building societies themselves had undergone massive consolidation in the eighties and nineties, with the larger ones 'hoovering up', in the words of one analyst, the smaller ones. This was accompanied by a demutualization of several of the larger building societies, which converted legally to commercial banks. The latter trend was so pronounced that banking industry analysts nowadays sometimes refer to a 'Big Eight' rather than a Big Four, the additional four being Abbey National, Halifax, Woolwich, and Alliance & Leicester.[8]

The largest of the societies, Abbey National, was the first to go public and obtain a banking licence in 1989. Others have followed suit in the late 1990s, including the three just mentioned.[9] They have become formidable competitors to the banks because of their substantially lower costs, allowing them to underprice the banks on many retail banking products. Moreover, even those societies that have not formally demutualized and become banks compete increasingly in the wholesale money markets. Thus, the wholesale borrowing of this group as a percentage of its other liabilities or fund-raising increased from 1.5 per cent in 1980 to 18.2 per cent at the end of 1989. It has done so through issuing bonds, floating rate notes, and CDs (Certificates of Deposit) – all in competition with banks. As a result, boundaries between retail banks and building societies have been progressively eroded since the 1980s.

Deregulation and investment banking

A further significant trend towards increasing competition was the deregulation of the Stock Exchange and investment banking in 1986, resulting from Big Bang. It blurred yet another market boundary in financial services, namely that between investment and commercial banking. In this instance, it led to commercial banks diversifying into other financial services rather than the other way round. Nevertheless, it did make global wholesale banking much more competitive than before. Big Bang enabled commercial banks to enter investment banking on a considerable scale, even though the Big Four had already been doing so on a more limited basis through their own merchant banks. Furthermore, under Big Bang, various investment banking businesses previously separated by law – brokerage, trading, merchant banking, and asset management – could merge in one financial services corporation. The clearers could thus become involved into all these securities-related businesses.

After Big Bang, all four clearing banks in fact made the change, through acquisitions and expanding subsidiaries. County NatWest, BZW, Midland Montagu, and Lloyds Merchant Bank all got formed and/or expanded at this time in such fields as securities underwriting and trading, asset management, and mergers and acquisitions. The rationale was that they were following their large corporate customers to the capital markets, providing them with a wider array of securities-related products and services, and thereby being able to compete effectively against European-based universal banks as well as investment banks.

The main point again is the pronounced trend in financial services toward reduced segmentation and specialization. All financial services institutions were diversifying onto one another's turfs, heightening the competition for each. The rise of capital markets products, providing substitutes for deposits and loans, was contributing to the disintermediation of commercial banks and to the vastly increased competition that they were facing.

Technology and competition

The accelerating impact of technology throughout this period also increased competition. By the 1990s, banks no longer had a monopoly on risk-management-related information on currencies, interest rates, creditworthiness of clients, etc. As a result, many new non-banks gained entry – Marks & Spencer, British Telecom, GE Capital, Tesco, for example. All were offering bank-like services.[10]

Technology changed the entire nature of retail and wholesale banking. On the retail side, new, more low-cost delivery systems became possible – phone banking, pc banking, ATMs, banking in supermarkets, airports, railway stations and shopping malls. Those new distribution options, in conjunction with the entry of lower-cost building societies into retail banking, increased competitive threats. And, on the wholesale side, the decline of the corporate loan business, with the advent of new capital markets products and players, also created increased competition.

In brief, the industry moved from a protected cartel to one in which competition had become very intense. Having existed in the past in protected markets in stable and simple environments with few competitive threats, banks could afford the static-style, vertical, command-and-control bureaucracies they had then. Now they would need entirely new, more competitive strategies and more flexible organizations, cultures, HR practices, information-and-control systems, as well as change managers to support the new strategies.[11]

One challenge for British banks was how fast they could adapt to these new competitive opportunities and threats. Related to that challenge was what they might learn from the adaptations of firms in manufacturing industries that had faced many of the same competitive forces at an earlier time. In addition, what could 'first mover' banks, which had aggressively embarked on a series of such changes (Lloyds in UK banking, Barclays in investment banking, Midland in its electronic and telephone retail banking arm called First Direct) provide as positive and/or negative role models for others that had been more cautious initially? While there are no definitive guidelines for managing change under increasingly competitive conditions, a description and analysis of how Britain's commercial banks adapted should provide some useful benchmarks of how to proceed, by suggesting what is successful and unsuccessful practice.

Changing strategies in UK banking

Since the early 1970s, when competition increased substantially, the UK banks have gone through several dominant strategies. Over time, they have gradually differentiated themselves from one another, but it is possible to discern different stages that all went through.

Stage One: size, growth, and market share at any cost – 'Big is Beautiful'

Through the 1970s and 1980s, the British clearing banks mindlessly pursued growth through mergers and geographic and product diversification. In doing so, they were simply following a strategy that had become all too common amongst commercial bankers worldwide. One of the leaders in this strategy was Walter Wriston, CEO of Citicorp from 1968 until 1982, who changed the paradigm of the industry from banks functioning as public utilities to their functioning as growth stocks. His explicit goal was for Citicorp to increase its gross income at 15 per cent a year; and his broader goal was for it to become a highly diversified, global and conglomerate bank.[12]

The UK banks pursued a similar strategy, increasing their diversification (both geographic and product), internationalizing, consolidating, trying to increase their market share in as many products as possible, and increasing their size as measured by total assets. These goals were pursued often without regard to loan quality, profitability or shareholder value. In fact, little or no attention was given to the latter concerns, and many observers of the industry in the UK concluded that the banks had no coherent and thought-out strategy other than to become bigger and more diversified.

One way that the banks pursued this growth strategy was to have big rights issues to raise capital. A rights issue involved selling new shares of stock at lower prices than existing ones. NatWest, Barclays and Midland continued to pursue this practice through the 1980s so as to remain competitive.

This growth strategy was expressed in its most extreme form in the race for first place in asset size between NatWest and Barclays, a rivalry that had taken place since the 1970s. Barclays had temporarily pursued a more risk-averse strategy in the mid-1980s, under Timothy Bevan as CEO and Chair, allowing NatWest to catch up. When NatWest passed it in size in 1988, Barclays' new CEO, Sir John Quinton, reportedly took this as a serious challenge. His slogan was 'Number One in '91', accompanied in 1989 by a £900 million rights issue, thereby depressing existing shareholder value. A London banking reporter later added: 'In the loo by '92' as a more likely outcome, after Barclays incurred big losses in using its new capital for commercial real-estate loans in the UK and bank acquisitions in France and Germany.

The obsession with size, however, extended beyond Barclays. Earlier, the senior managers at Midland, the largest bank in the world in the 1920s and 1930s, were reportedly very distraught when they found out in the 1970s that it was not at all the biggest, even in the UK. This only became evident to them after the Bank of England required the banks to report true assets and profits, without accounting gimmicks.

Even Lloyds, which abandoned this growth and diversification strategy much earlier than the other three, had concerns about being seen as the smallest of the four clearers. One senior Lloyds manager explained: 'Sir Brian Pitman, our CEO, is very sensitive to backhanded compliments in the press relating to our size. One such compliment is that "Lloyds showed once again that it is top among the clearers in financial performance, but once again, that smallest is the best." That really gets to him and his ego; and he may end up being the biggest and the best, because it bothers him so much. He hates being called a small bank.'

This growth strategy had devastating impacts on the UK banks in the late 1980s and early 1990s, just as it had with Citicorp and its many US money-centre imitators. To illustrate: Midland, in a desperate attempt to catch up in market share internationally after a very slow start, bought Crocker Bank of San Francisco in 1980, without taking into account Crocker's weaknesses and without developing controls over its operations.[13] Crocker, widely known as one of the low-performing banks in the US, with an abundance of poorly performing loans, proceeded to squander Midland's capital in more bad loans. Six years later, Midland sold Crocker at a $1 billion loss, from which it never recovered and which contributed to its decline and later acquisition by Hongkong and Shanghai Banking Corporation (HSBC).

NatWest, anxious to gain market share on Barclays' BZW and other competitors in investment banking after a slow start, over-reached itself in 1988 on a big underwriting of the Blue Arrow

Manpower Training Agency share issue. This soon turned into a highly publicized scandal, referred to as Blue Arrow, in which NatWest was charged with misrepresenting the size of the sale and with purchasing more securities itself than regulations allowed. An unprecedented court case soon followed, and the episode eventually cost the jobs of NatWest's chairman and several senior managers in its investment banking division, County NatWest, and speeded up the retirement of its CEO. The episode cast such a cloud over the division that it changed its name to NatWest Markets and started from scratch in 1992.[14]

Then Barclays, loaded with capital from its 1989 rights issue, booked many bad loans in commercial real-estate projects and made several questionable acquisitions of retail banks in Europe – particularly in France and Germany. This led, in turn, to a shareholder revolt, followed by the exit of the Barclays CEO, as well as a continuing barrage of strong criticism of his second-in-command and later successor, Andrew Buxton, the last senior manager from the old Barclays families. Buxton was then pressed to give up his CEO position, followed by the board's unprecedented move of recruiting as CEO a complete outsider, Martin Taylor, who had never been either a commercial banker or an investment banker.[15]

Also, along the way, a distinguished Bank of England official, Sir Kit McMahon, was brought in as CEO in 1986 to try to turn around Midland. He then left in 1991 when it was clear to him and his board that Midland was not recovering sufficiently.[16]

What had been going on? An old growth strategy that the clearing banks had followed unthinkingly had led them not just to a few bad decisions but to major débâcles big enough to unseat their CEOs, chairmen and many other senior managers. For boards and/or shareholder groups to exert that much power was an unusual event in the UK at this time, as it was in the US.

Seen in larger perspective, commercial banking, like investment banking, is mostly an industry of boom and bust, following the business cycle. Yet bankers throughout this century – in the UK and elsewhere – have kept making the same mistakes, falling into the same 'black holes', because they failed to see the implications of that fact. They consistently loaded themselves with questionable loans as they acquired more capital in the latter stages of boom periods; they booked substantial loans in those periods, and then got caught holding them in the immediate downturn, when the loans turned bad. It was as though the bankers had no institutional memory and instead had a kind of repetition compulsion, as they kept making the same mistakes again and again. Suffering perhaps from an unwarranted optimism or 'feel good' psychology, the banks seemed in boom times to lose their credit culture. In some cases, such as the Latin American loans, their behaviour was understandable, since similar losses had last taken place a full 50 years before. But for commercial real estate, the memory of previous losses in the recession and the Real Estate Investment Trust (REIT) failures of the early 1970s had to have been fresher; and yet the same pattern repeated itself, little more than a decade later. A London-based policy analysis group, the Centre for the Study of Financial Innovation, issued two papers on this subject in 1994 and 1995, referring to the phenomenon as bankers 'slipping on banana peels'. Martin Taylor, Barclays' CEO, urged his banking colleagues to expand and contract their operations more proactively in congruence with economic cycles, as a way of avoiding the problem in the future.[17]

A significant part of this growth strategy for the British banks was for them to become global wholesale banks, and it had the same mixed results for British banks as it did for those in the US. Some, like Lloyds, have since then scaled down considerably their international operations; the others have withdrawn selectively, with the US in particular seen as a graveyard for UK banks, except in investment banking.[18] First Lloyds in the mid-1980s, then Barclays in the early 1990s, and finally Natwest in 1995, sold off their US branches on the rationale that they couldn't reach the scale and diversity to compete there with indigenous US banks. All of them converted their international business to global investment banking. And when NatWest and Barclays experienced big losses in their investment bank in the middle and late 1990s, they scaled down considerably most of those businesses as well.

Stage Two: a new strategic focus and shareholder-value paradigm

A new strategic focus and shareholder-value paradigm has gradually been adopted in the 1990s, as the UK banks and their competitors around the world have realized that big is not always beautiful and that they had to begin to focus more on their core competencies. Sir Brian Pitman, CEO of Lloyds, led the way in this change in the late 1980s by scaling down his bank's commitments to wholesale investment banking and international operations. As a newly focused UK retail bank, Lloyds soon far outperformed the other three. Later, Barclays, under its new CEO Martin Taylor, also began to emphasize gaining more focus and shareholder value, although without scaling down investment banking until the late 1990s. Even NatWest, slower-moving than Barclays or Lloyds, began in the early nineties under its new CEO, Derek Wanless, to evaluate its performance in various businesses as a prelude to deciding which ones it would grow, which it would continue at the same level, and which ones it would scale down or sell.

What had happened to precipitate this change of strategy? As students of organizations continually remind us, institutions only change in response to crises, and the continued pursuit of the growth-and-size paradigm during a period of deep recession (1988–1992) certainly created such a crisis in UK banking in the early 1990s. This resulted in Barclays, NatWest and Midland all bringing in new CEOs. Barclays and NatWest skipped generations and chose CEOs in their early 40s – an unprecedented move in the UK and indicating the necessity for a paradigm shift.

The new paradigm emphasized profitability over profits, loan quality over market share, and shareholder value over asset size, attained through portfolio analysis. Driven both by such management consultants as McKinsey, BCG, Arthur Andersen and Gemini, and by a new generation of senior managers, this portfolio analysis is now involving the banks in a searching scrutiny of every business. For each, the growth potential of its markets and the likelihood that the bank can gain a significant market share without depleting its capital from other high-performing businesses are primary considerations. Forced by the pressures of lower entry barriers and increasing competition, the banks are making decisions informed by more sophisticated analysis and yet taking faster action on which businesses to grow, which to hold on to but not grow, which to downsize, and which to sell immediately. The pressure has never been greater, and it is likely to increase still further over time.

This means that the banks most likely to survive will have such competitive competences as: first, a strong enough strategic analysis capability to assess and forecast trends in various financial services markets; and, second, an implementation capability to follow through quickly in focusing on the markets where the bank is likely to be a strong player. In brief, the successful banks will have to read the trends well and quickly, and be agile enough to act equally quickly on the basis of such an analysis.

Key aspects of this new paradigm are to get more focus by divesting the banks of loss-making businesses and make a big commitment to technology to drive down costs, develop new products and improve delivery. A big part of that focus has been for the British banks to concentrate more than before on domestic retail and related businesses. Within retail banking, this has involved closing branches, reconfiguring remaining ones, and moving on to alternative delivery systems in phone banking, pc banking at home and in the workplace, point-of-sale banking, postal banking, etc. And on the wholesale banking side, technology is being used to develop innovative products and to improve service delivery through rapid global communications across product and functional groups regarding interest rates and currency changes.

It is not clear that banks have the skills to develop, let alone implement, these new strategies. But they are hiring increasing numbers of technically trained non-bankers for senior management positions to help them – as CFOs, IT directors and marketing directors. As mentioned earlier, Barclays even brought in a non-banker, Martin Taylor, as its new CEO in 1994.

Moreover, all the big clearing banks are now recruiting MBAs and university graduates in increasing numbers, to help them develop new non-banking (generic) competences in marketing and sales, information technology, finance, strategic planning, and matrix management. The competitive threats are of such a magnitude, however, and the high cost structures, inertia and other excess baggage residual from the banks' cartel past are so great, that it is not clear how much time the banks will have and how many mistakes they can tolerate as they move into new activities where mistakes are inevitable.

Stage Three: the 'virtual bank'?

Meanwhile, there is increasing discussion in the late nineties – although it is only discussion so far – on how the banks could provide diverse financial services products, particularly to wholesale customers, without necessarily having to incorporate them all within each organization itself. A new emphasis on strategic alliances and joint ventures, externalizing many banking services, is seen as a way of having product diversity, thereby meeting customers' many financial services needs without being vulnerable to the complex internal conflicts involved in managing them. The new concept of the 'virtual organization', commonly used in academic and management circles to justify such an outsourcing or externalizing strategy, has been raised as possibly applicable to banking.[19]

As the UK clearing banks diversified into investment banking, for example, since Big Bang in 1986, they have had to deal with many cultural and political conflicts between their investment and commercial bankers. The investment bankers' high levels of remuneration and benefits not only impose high costs on firms but lead to considerable jealousy from the commercial bankers, particularly in years when investment banking contributes so little to the banks' overall revenues.

Part of this conflict in the UK relates as well to sharp social class and educational differences between the two groups. Quite consistently, the investment bankers are university-trained and regard themselves as several cuts above the commercial bankers, the vast majority of whom are not. The head of NatWest Markets reported in late 1995, for example, that over 90 per cent of his staff were university-trained. By contrast, the proportions in the retail bank were the reverse, with roughly only 10 per cent university-trained.

Each side has strong negative stereotypes of the other. Investment bankers in securities trading and corporate-finance-related businesses regard commercial bankers as risk-averse, rigid and bureaucratic in their work habits, uncultured, and ignorant of the new world of capital-market products in banking. Commercial bankers see investment bankers, in turn, as undisciplined 'loose cannons', making outrageous, obscene bonus and salary demands, holding their bank hostage if it doesn't meet those demands, and having little or no loyalty to the bank.

Differences in careers, labour markets, and organizational loyalty also contribute to conflict. The vast majority of commercial bankers in middle and senior management entered the bank in an era when there was an implicit psychological contract for lifetime employment, and when a non-poaching rule prevailed; they were employed at one bank all their working lives and could be characterized as extreme 'locals' in career orientation. Investment bankers, by contrast, exist in different labour markets and with different career orientations. Their primary reference group of colleagues are not so much others within the bank of their present employment, but rather their peers elsewhere in the investment banking industry. They are in that sense 'cosmopolitans' in career orientation.

In addition to these cultural differences, there are recurring political conflicts between investment and commercial bankers over which group will get what shares in the central capital pool of the bank. Such conflicts always exist across divisions and departments in large organizations, but that between these groups has a particular intensity because of their different cultures.

One may well argue, then, that commercial banks pursuing this diversification strategy into investment banking have created a kind of internal 'pollution' that is very difficult to manage. The costs of managing the ensuing conflicts may be greater than the benefits of having all these financial services under one corporate umbrella. And it is partly in the context of this issue that some senior banking managers and industry observers have begun talking about new organizational forms that would potentially give banks the best of both worlds by having contractual rather than internal administrative relations across these product groups.

One issue relates to how much control the banks lose by externalizing such services. A related issue has to do with whether the banks have the skills to manage the contracts involved in such strategic alliances and joint ventures. We will discuss these issues below in Chapter 10 on how the banks approach managing across product and service boundaries.

Finally, there is serious question about the banks' capability to develop appropriate infrastructures – for risk management, auditing and other organizational controls – to manage efficiently the new investment banking businesses they take on. Senior managers in commercial banks do not have the technical training or experience in investment banking necessarily to manage it well. They must then rely on people who do, while still being held accountable for the investment bank's performance.

These issues of the UK clearing banks' capacity to manage such diversity periodically come to a head, raising larger questions about how well or poorly the banks are managed. One of the more recent episodes has involved the discovery in NatWest Markets in June 1997 that its traders had engaged in the mispricing of options for several years. This resulted in a loss to NatWest of £77 million, declines in its share price, and increasing fury among its large shareholders about how it was being managed.[20] The event was then followed by the resignations of the head of NatWest Markets and six senior managers.

More importantly, a series of larger questions about the competence of British bank management then got raised as a result of this incident:

(1) Was investment banking really a viable strategy for these banks, since it had been such a serious drain on the banks' capital since the clearers got into it? It was also noted that the banks bore huge costs to establish a presence in investment banking, particularly in staff remuneration and benefits, and that

managing investment bankers was very hard, given their high turnover, limited loyalty to the firm, huge compensation demands, and little collegial commitment.

In addition, how could the limited controls at NatWest Markets have existed to allow this kind of trader behaviour, which most likely took place with some help from colleagues? While the NatWest incident wasn't quite in the category of some of the extreme cases of rogue trader behaviour, as in Barings, Daiwa, Kidder and Salomon, it was creating serious reputational problems for NatWest and its senior management – and the same could happen to the other clearing banks.

(2) Didn't the incident highlight once again the weak senior and middle management below the very top levels, both at NatWest and perhaps at the other clearing banks? And didn't it say something as well about the limitations of clearing bank CEOs, who weren't knowledgeable enough about investment banking to have detected and stopped such behaviour much earlier – and thus at much less cost?

(3) And what did the incident imply about the ultimate viability of universal banking? While the event happened at NatWest, a close look at Barclays indicated that it, too, was having trouble with its investment bank. Indeed, Martin Taylor was reported to have given Bill Harrison, the new head of Barclays' investment bank, two years to show measurable progress toward a 20 per cent return on equity or have his resources drastically cut back.

In short, perhaps diversifying into investment banking was a flawed strategy for the UK clearers, and perhaps they should phase it down. Or, at a minimum, perhaps they should do much more of their investment banking through strategic alliances and joint ventures.

The implication of this recent NatWest incident and its aftermath, as well as the larger discussion of the UK banks' evolution, is that they have to improve their management tremendously in order to survive as strong players both in the UK and internationally. And it is to this issue of how the banks have managed the many changes that they have faced since the early 1970s that we now turn.

Notes and references

1. Forrest Capie, Ch. 2, in Michael Bordo and Richard Sylla (eds), *Anglo-American Financial Systems*, Irwin, Burr Ridge IL, 1995, p. 43.
2. Michael Collins, *Money and Banking in the UK: a History*, Croom Helm, London, 1988, p. 416.
3. *Ibid.*, p. 381–3.
4. *Ibid.*, p. 384.
5. Itzhak Swary and Barry Topf, *Global Financial Deregulation*, Blackwell, Cambridge, 1992, p. 148.
6. A good summary of these developments is in Derek Channon, *British Banking Strategy*, Macmillan, London and Basingstoke, 1977, Ch. 7.
7. Swary and Topf, *op. cit.*, p. 144.
8. These eight banks are among the twelve that are part of the Lehman Brothers annual reviews of UK clearing banks.
9. *The Economist*, 7 June 1997, p. 78.
10. Swary and Topf, *op. cit.*, p. 148.
11. For an analysis of how these organizational changes took place in US banks, see David Rogers, *The Future of American Banking*, McGraw Hill, New York, 1993, Chs 1 and 9.
12. *Ibid.*, Chs 3–5.
13. Russell Taylor, *Going for Broke*, Simon & Schuster, New York, 1992, pp. 223–35.
14. Roy Smith, *Comeback*, Harvard Business School Press, Boston, 1993, pp. 212–14.
15. See Chapter 6 below.
16. Taylor, *op. cit.*, pp. 271–3.
17. *Banking Banana Skins*, June 1994; and *Banking Banana Skins II*, November 1994, Centre for the Study of Financial Innovation.
18. *Financial Times*, 23 December 1995.
19. B.J. Hodge, William P. Anthony and Lawrence Gales, *Organization Theory*, Prentice Hall, Upper Saddle River NJ, 1996, pp. 202–3 and 225 for an explication of this new organizational form.
20. *Financial Times*, 16 July 1997.

CHAPTER

4 Lloyds: a Deviant Case, Rejecting Universal Banking

When the UK banks were in a risk-free environment, they had a volume culture. And they applied the same mentality to investment banking. Pitman [the Lloyds CEO] was an exception to this culture. He pursued a different strategy and a blindingly obvious one. Instead of volume and size, he looked at return on capital and shareholder value and got out of the losing businesses. He closed down his small investment bank and many international businesses. Instead, he chose personal banking, where the higher profits were, and now he has added to that many other retail businesses through a series of mergers. All this was blindingly obvious, but none of the others did it. It merely involves concentrating on what you do well.

Banking journalist

Pitman talked about ROE and his formula was simple: if it makes money, we'll do it, and if not, we won't. This was an extraordinary concept for British banking at that time. It was out of line with how our banks were managed.

Bank analyst

Lloyds' numbers are indeed impressive. Pitman is the master of the simplified agenda, but I am not sure that it has a true strategic view. He did get rid of some nasty eggs in the portfolio and he is a master of managing it all. And he doesn't have the other baggage (investment banking) of the clearers. Beyond that, he has bought well. He is a test of the big baron theory. He is very charismatic in representing his agenda and carrying it home. But ego sometimes gets in the way of big barons on capital allocation decisions, and he may make some bad ones in the future. So the big baron stuff is a worrier.

Management consultant

AN ANALYSIS of institutions that do not fit existing paradigms often reveals more significant insights about the industries of which they are a part than does a similar analysis of those that fit the mould. Lloyds is such a case in the recent history of its industry, and an analysis of its leadership and strategic choices since the early 1970s can tell us a lot about the recent evolution of British banking and about what configurations of strategy and organization are likely to distinguish the high from the low performers in the future.

Historically, Lloyds had been by far the smallest of the Big Four clearers. Even as late as 1988, for example, its total assets were £51.8 billion, compared with £55.7 billion for Midland, £98.6 billion for NatWest, and £104.6 billion for Barclays.[1] By the end of 1997, however, after several mergers in retail financial services, Lloyds had overtaken Midland and moved into a strong third position, though it has remained behind NatWest and Barclays. The latter had total assets of £185.4 billion and £234.6 billion respectively at the end of 1997, compared with Lloyds' £158.1 billion.

At present, Lloyds has five main businesses: retail banking, mortgages, insurance, wholesale markets, and international banking. The latter two, while important, have assumed a distinctly secondary role in the bank's overall portfolio, as it has pursued a strategy of becoming a UK-based retail financial services firm. Broadening its consumer-related business was in large part a way to reduce Lloyds' vulnerability to volatile economic swings in wholesale and international banking. Thus, in 1997, retail financial services (reckoned as the first three businesses listed) accounted for 70 per cent of Lloyds' profits, well beyond the equivalent proportion for Barclays and NatWest.[2]

Lloyds is significant in UK banking as both a pace setter and a deviant case. After Big Bang, while the other three clearing banks adopted a universal banking strategy of supplementing their traditional UK retail banking business with a heavy involvement in global investment and wholesale banking, Lloyds, under the leadership of Sir Brian Pitman, its CEO from 1983 to 1996, and board Chair since then, moved in a radically different direction. Out of both necessity and foresight, Lloyds became highly focused as a UK retail bank in the eighties and nineties. This took place while the industry was becoming increasingly globalized, and it turned a small, mediocre performer into one of the world's leading banks. As at 13 January 1998, for example, Lloyds had a market capitalization of $68.7 billion, the highest in the world. None of the other British clearing banks was in the top eight in the league.[3]

This performance represented a dramatic turnaround. In the late seventies and early eighties, Lloyds had suffered from huge losses in Latin American and commercial real-estate loans. Many informed observers during those years regarded Lloyds as the industry's 'basket case'. In recovering from its losses, Lloyds' 70%:30% ratio of retail to wholesale proportions of its total revenue in the late 1990s represented a complete reversal from the 1970s, when the percentages were 70%:30% the other way. The results have been equally dramatic, as Lloyds' ROE of 41 per cent in 1997 was more than double that of NatWest, Barclays and Midland.[4]

A focus on UK retail banking constituted a radical departure, both from the directions taken by the other clearers as well as from the earlier strategies of Lloyds itself. Lloyds, along with Barclays, was one of the first UK banks to go international. It developed branches in France in 1911, in South America in 1918, and made a major commitment to global expansion in the 1970s. This included its acquisition in 1971 of Bank of London South America (BOLSA) in 1971, merging it with Lloyds Bank Europe acquired in the 1950s; gaining full control of National Bank of New Zealand in the 1970s; and opening branches during the same time period in New York City, Chicago, Los Angeles and elsewhere in the US.[5] In 1978, Lloyds even made a brief foray into investment banking through the formation of Lloyds Merchant Bank. 'We had a big investment in a global network and many of our people felt that the way ahead for Lloyds was as a global bank,' explained a senior manager. 'We were building up the international side.'

At the same time, there was no coherent strategy in Lloyds' international banking efforts, other than to be global. 'In all these international acquisitions,' reported a Lloyds wholesale banker, 'we had no big strategic view. Our view was that we'll grow our international business where we can.'

Particularly since 1983, when Pitman became CEO and began working with his board chairman, Sir Jeremy Morse, the history of Lloyds is one of radical discontinuity with its past. It illustrates in dramatic fashion a central theme of this book, namely that management counts heavily in shaping an institution's strategic choices. Notwithstanding the importance of market forces in shaping and constraining these choices for Lloyds, the leadership provided by these two men, particularly Pitman, moved the bank to become a paradigm breaker in its industry. Moreover, Pitman soon became known as a leader in commercial banking worldwide, along with such

American banking CEOs as Wriston of Citicorp, and Brittain and Sanford of Bankers Trust.[6] John Aitken, a leading British bank analyst, is quoted as characterizing Pitman as 'the best British banker since the Second World War'.[7]

Recent history and leadership

Lloyds, a full service bank bent on global expansion and product diversification in the seventies and early eighties, experienced the same problems of income volatility and non-performing loans that so many other US and UK banks did at that time. For example, its portfolio of non-performing loans to Latin American nations was one of the biggest among the UK banks.[8] Yet, as the smallest of the Big Four in asset size, it had less capital to use to write down the loans than any of its UK competitors.

Lloyds had been deeply involved in providing financial services to Latin America through BOLSA, and it used that business as a springboard to spread its commitments there. It also accumulated a large portfolio of non-performing commercial real-estate loans during these years. Before Pitman's becoming CEO, then, Lloyds was not that different in strategy or performance from the other clearing banks. In fact, if anything, it was one of the low performers in the industry, notwithstanding a distinguished history dating back to 1765.[9] Moreover, it had severe capital problems, associated in part with its small size relative to its peers. It therefore had little organizational slack to draw on in hard times. That undoubtedly contributed to Lloyds making a radical departure from its past, global, expansionist strategy. It wasn't inevitable that this new focus on UK retail banking take place, however. Lloyds could have continued some modified version of its past strategy, as the other clearing banks did.

One of the things that turned Lloyds around in the 1980s was the leadership role that Pitman and Morse played. When Pitman became CEO in 1983, Lloyds' board engaged in a searching analysis of its strategy. It concluded that, contrary to the diffuse strategy it had before, where it was pursuing several different businesses – wholesale and retail, domestic and global – it would now focus on creating increased shareholder value. Other British clearing banks continued to equate size with strength in the 1980s and only came to embrace shareholder value as a goal after Britain's severe recession of the late eighties and early nineties. Even then, they were slow in adopting it.

By 1994, several European banks had followed Lloyds in this respect. As a board member of that time recalled:

> We had multiple, woolly objectives in 1983, and some of us felt they were *too* woolly. We had a big philosophical debate over two board meetings and switched from having multiple objectives to a single objective. Not everybody on the board agreed, but that was where we ended. Our single objective was creating increased shareholder value. We looked at the best performers in the world as models and found two in particular that stood out: GE [General Electric] and Coca-Cola. We then set a goal of doubling our shareholder value every three years, and we have done that every three years since then. That became our benchmark.

The strategy of enhancing shareholder value was achieved by growing the businesses that were performing well and phasing down and selling off those that were doing poorly. Lloyds closed down its investment bank in 1987 and many branches in the US, Europe, and the Far East. Moreover, it did so earlier than its clearing bank competitors. Lloyds even took the unprecedented step in late 1987 of withdrawing its application for a licence to trade securities in Tokyo, following from an earlier decision to withdraw from market making in British government bonds and Eurobonds.[10]

Lloyds had closed down its branches in the late 1980s, several years ahead of Barclays. Meanwhile, NatWest only sold off its large US business, US Bancorp, in 1995. A former Lloyds executive, Fred Crawley, recalled in referring to Pitman: 'He was the first to realize that planting flags around the world was not always the best way to make money.'[11] 'We at Lloyds were losing more money than we were making in our branches in many countries,' explained a senior wholesale banker, 'and we backed away from that. We were making money in the UK and then pouring it down a big black hole in other countries. It made no sense. We spent too much time sorting out brush fires around the world, and we decided to stop. Also, we just decided that diversification into investment banking and global expansion was yesterday's game.'

To Pitman and Lloyds, retail banking was by contrast *not* yesterday's game. That was where Lloyds decided to focus its resources, starting in the mid-1980s, and it has deepened that commitment ever since. The strategy was to become a multiproduct, multiregional and multi-customer retail financial services firm within the UK, rather than a universal bank or just a traditional bank. 'We became financial services retail stores, selling products,' explained a Lloyds senior banker, 'and we were very retail-oriented.'

This strategy was implemented under Pitman's leadership through a series of acquisitions, all of which UK bankers, bank analysts, consultants and knowledgeable academics generally regarded as well conceived. The three most prominent were Abbey Life in 1988, expanding Lloyds' growing insurance businesses; Cheltenham & Gloucester in 1995, adding to its home mortgage businesses; and Trustee Savings Bank (TSB) in 1996, expanding its customer base and providing a portfolio of other insurance and savings products as well. Eventually, Pitman was referred to as 'the high priest of banking consolidation'.

The financial services model that Lloyds followed was that of classic European 'bancassurance', perhaps most typified by TSB, which was the most advanced among UK banks in integrating insurance with traditional deposits and loan products.[12]

The acquisitions were so central to Lloyds strategy that its CEO became known in the financial press as 'Pitman the hit man'. *The Economist* referred to 'a frenetic pace of acquisitions' that Pitman was pursuing in the mid-1990s.[13] A central point in this new strategy was Pitman's awareness that while investment and global wholesale banking had thin, volatile margins, UK retail banking by contrast generated huge, steady profits. 'Pitman realized his bank could make more money by feeding the core franchise in the UK, which he increasingly saw as a money machine and much more profitable than international wholesale and investment banking,' reported a Lloyds manager. 'So, we began feeding the UK business. He wanted sustainable earnings; and he viewed wholesale and corporate business as having razor-thin pricing margins for limited returns, in contrast to the UK business that he saw as a cash machine.'

Lloyds became in this sense more strategic and more rationally managed than its clearing bank competitors. It did so by building up businesses and markets that generated profits and phasing down those that did not. The issues for Pitman in evaluating businesses were always the same: Does it make money? If so, how much? Does it fit the Lloyds strategy and organization? And what are its risks and rewards? Based on the answers to those questions, Lloyds sold off and rejected many businesses, particularly international ones, and Pitman become known as a CEO who not only pursued key acquisitions but who also divested his bank of many losing businesses. Sceptics sometimes referred to Pitman's strategy as 'growing by retreating', but it was in fact much more sophisticated than that.

While such an approach hardly seems innovative for any well managed business organization, it actually *was* innovative for British bankers at that time. They were oriented mainly toward bigness – for example, growth, asset size, diversification, global coverage, market share, and so on – without particular concern for profit margins, shareholder value, or whether the bank had significant core competencies in its various businesses. In brief, they confused size with strength. Most did not even know what their profits were before 1970, when a new Bank of England policy required that the clearers ascertain their profits on a sound accounting basis and declare them.

This shareholder-value approach was one that both Pitman and Morse found attractive, and since 1983 Lloyds has increasingly followed the strategy. Not surprisingly, Lloyds was not completely consistent in this direction. It did acquire an investment bank in 1978, Lloyds Merchant Bank, but it sold that bank in 1987. Furthermore, it made an aggressive bid in 1986 to acquire Standard Chartered, the UK's most global bank, with strong holdings in the Far East. That would have diverted Lloyds quite considerably from its domestic, UK retail strategy. Fortunately for Lloyds it did not acquire Standard Chartered, and therefore it was not forced to integrate that bank into its own operations a fit that seemed most unlikely.[14]

Pitman: the paradigm breaker of UK banking

A critical question is why Pitman, a non-university graduate who joined the bank on leaving school like the vast majority of his contemporaries in UK banking at the time, should have become such an iconoclast and paradigm breaker within his industry. While the other banks continued pursuing the goals of global expansion and product diversification, he was winding down Lloyds' merchant bank and foreign branches, 'like a turtle that pulled in its legs and was shrinking to survive' in the words of one competitor.

There are several explanations, some relating to Lloyds' dismal performance in the 1970s and many relating to Pitman's own experiences and character. First were Lloyds' big losses and the industry's progressively thinning margins in global wholesale banking up through the early eighties. 'Wholesale profits were gone by then,' explained a Lloyds senior banker. 'We had overlent, with all the others.' In addition, the competition had increased, making it that much more difficult to be successful in these markets. 'Other foreign banks and indigenous banks kept getting stronger,' this senior banker went on.

A turning point for Lloyds, though not for its clearing bank competitors, was Mexico's announcement in 1982 that it could not repay its debts. 'In 1981, we still had very good results in international banking,' reported a board member who had wanted to continue that business. 'We put a lot of effort into making sure we didn't overfocus on one area or market.' That commitment ended with Mexico's announcement. 'Our international strategy came to a grinding halt in 1982, with the Mexican announcement of its default. From then on, it was seen as a crazy strategy, and this is when we changed,' explained a senior manager.

UK domestic politics was another consideration contributing to the change. The diversification away from the UK in the 1970s coincided with the perception among some senior Lloyds bankers that the UK's more socialist government of that time was hostile to banks. Likewise, these bankers interpreted Lloyds' move back to UK banking as coinciding with the more supportive political atmosphere after 1979:

> In the 1970s, when we were building up the international side, we felt we could diversify away from the UK, particularly since it was seen as going Socialist and becoming anti-banks. Then, when the Conservative Party returned to power in 1979, there was a friendlier political atmosphere that also contributed to our wanting to be a UK bank.

The other part of Lloyds' new strategy was its exit from investment banking. Again, in contrast to its clearing competitors, Lloyds' senior management and board disproportionately emphasized the negatives about that business, a perspective that Barclays and NatWest only came to address a decade later, in 1997 – and then only in response to strong investor pressures and years of low performance. 'We saw investment banking as a very crowded field – very volatile – with margins being cut to ribbons. Also, it involved managing alien people who made huge salary demands and who didn't like to be managed. And it was a bad cultural fit. Our culture was to maximize shareholder value, and the investment bankers' culture was their getting rich. So that was not for us and we got out,' recalled a senior manager.

While some of this may be retrospective rationalization (imputing more logic to Lloyds' withdrawal from these businesses than may have been the case), much of this thinking probably did take place at the time. Indeed, when I asked a senior Lloyds manager why the bank had exited from investment banking in the 1980s, he insisted that Pitman and his colleagues were acutely aware at the time of the above-mentioned risks in that business.

The fact is that all UK clearing banks faced these competitive conditions and only Lloyds both retreated from global wholesale and investment banking and intensified its focus on UK retail. While its tremendous losses in international banking contributed, the others had big losses there as well, suggesting that Lloyds' leadership was a key factor in the bank's actions.

What was there about Pitman, then, relating to his own experiences and character, that led him in this direction? In terms of the former, after joining the bank in 1952, some of Pitman's most formative early assignments were in its international division. He saw first-hand how the bank kept incurring big losses there, all the while bleeding away profits from its cash cow (or money machine), the UK retail bank. He commented in an interview in 1994 that a year in Europe, when he managed some of Lloyds international operations, gave him much insight into the vulnerabilities of those businesses.[15]

Other aspects of his international experience were his extensive contacts with US management consulting firms and their increasing interest in strategic analysis, particularly in their 'portfolio' approach to managing large, multiproduct corporations. One prevailing idea among them was the importance of strategic focus and concentrating on one's areas of core competence.

In addition, Pitman came into contact with some US firms whose strategies fitted that approach. One such firm was Wells Fargo, long regarded worldwide as one of the best-managed commercial banks. It had gained that reputation largely because of its success in exiting from international banking and concentrating on what it did best as a regional bank: maintaining deposit services for individuals and small and medium-sized businesses; providing loans for these clients; and doing all this in increasingly efficient ways. BancOne and Nations Bank were reportedly other supra-regional banks that Pitman admired for having a similarly focused strategy.

Pitman's horizons were broader than banking, however. He was interested in high-performing firms, wherever they appeared. Coca-Cola and GE, for example, were two firms that also served as positive models for him, because of their approach to maximizing shareholder value and retailing.

Still another contributing factor from Pitman's international experience may well have been the fact that it gave him more opportunity to be innovative than working exclusively in the more prosaic operations of a retail bank. As one of his colleagues pointed out: 'The international business he was in was more entrepreneurial and free-spirited and fostered more independent-mindedness and innovation than retail banking. He used that experience to develop his creative approach to banking and then applied it to retail.'

Despite coming from the same lower-middle-class, non-university background as his senior banking contemporaries, Pitman thus transcended that background in ways that many of them did not. Though not formally trained in strategic analysis and management, he apparently had such a natural curiosity about numbers and about understanding how and why high-performance firms worked that he was able to apply it in restructuring Lloyds. He had, in a word, an astute, inquiring mind that he put to productive use in interpreting trends in banking and other industries. These interpretations then became the basis for his strategy at Lloyds.

Pitman had a particular interest in the US and kept learning a lot from his contacts with US consulting firms and from his continued observations of US companies. 'Even though he felt there was no revenue here for us, he was an admirer of the US,' reported one of Pitman's colleagues. 'He loves to go to the US to look at leading-edge banks and at retail and consumer industries.'

An interview with Pitman published in the *Financial Times* of 23 April 1994 captured these qualities. It referred to his 'formidable capacity for strategic thought', as exemplified by such actions as pulling out of overseas retail banking and holding onto third-world debt while it rose in price. Pitman attributed his strategic wisdom and skills to a year spent working in Europe in his early twenties and another in the US. 'I was surrounded by strategic thinking in US banks,' he said, 'at a time when British ones did not even have budgets, and did not disclose profits.'

Otherwise, financial reporters, consultants, colleagues, competitors, and other 'bank watchers' in the UK characterized Pitman in terms of traits often ascribed to highly effective leaders. He was seen particularly as a person of *vision*, as reflected in his keen understanding of how the industry was evolving and how Lloyds might best position itself with that in mind. Related to his vision, he was seen as *iconoclastic*, in the positive sense of having an irreverence for traditional frames of thinking. A big part of that iconoclasm was his willingness to speak bluntly in public about how banking worldwide and in the UK was undergoing radical restructuring, requiring much downsizing and likely to require much more in the future. While those were not words that bank employees and their unions wanted to hear, he was willing to express them.

In that sense, he was seen as *tenacious*, often referred to as having bulldog-like qualities of being determined to move ahead with strategies he believed in, regardless of perceived opposition. Related to that, he was clearly seen as a *doer* – an *action person* – who would follow up on his strategic initiatives by pressing continuously on the details of their implementation. One senior manager noted, for example, that Pitman only required four or five hours of sleep a night, comparing him in this regard with Margaret Thatcher, another tireless change manager. The implication was that both of them had more time to pursue their causes than their competitors and opponents.

Finally, Pitman was seen as a man of much *discipline, nerve, ambition,* and *boldness*. He was bent on relentlessly pursuing his strategies. This was not a leader, then, who was formulating bold new directions and leaving to others their implementation. He was both a visionary and a so-called 'hands-on' manager, who almost single-handedly moved Lloyds from being a highly vulnerable, low-performing clearing bank in the 1970s and early 1980s to having become UK banking's highest performer in the late 1990s. Indeed, one consultant referred to Lloyds under Pitman as an important test of the Big Baron theory, that strong personalities do in fact find the best profit streams.

Were there any downsides to the Pitman style, notwithstanding his successes? The answer is 'yes', based on what we know about strong-minded, entrepreneurial leaders and about developments affecting British banking in the mid- and late-1990s. One problem that strong leaders pose for organizations, even while they may still be effective change managers, is that they often do not do enough succession planning, leaving many doubts about what will happen when they leave. That took place at Lloyds, with many observers noting that the very management style that had made Pitman so successful had limited his efforts at developing effective CEO-calibre senior managers who might succeed him.

At his board's request, Pitman stayed as CEO several years beyond the compulsory retirement age of 62. He then became board Chairman in 1996, at age 65, in which capacity he was still the leader in setting Lloyds' strategy. His successor as CEO, Peter Ellwood, former CEO of TSB, has played a more secondary role in that position than Pitman did, still leaving open the question of Lloyds' future direction after Pitman retires and whether his initiatives will be sustained.

The school leaver and the patrician: an effective if unlikely duo

I referred above to Pitman's having transformed Lloyds 'almost single-handedly'. While he was the major figure in this development, reportedly running the bank much like a centralized monarchy, he wasn't alone. Indeed, he had an important partner in this change effort, namely Sir Jeremy Morse, who was a remarkable leader and intellect in his own right and who both supported and at times tempered Pitman's leadership.

Morse had been on Lloyds' board since the 1970s and was Chair when Pitman became CEO in 1983. He was in many respects the antithesis of Pitman. Despite that, they collaborated well, due in large part to their agreeing on some fundamental strategy directions for the bank.

As for their differences, while Pitman was an activist change manager, with many 'street smarts' and impatient to move ahead quickly on each new strategy, Morse was an erudite intellectual, a deep conceptualizer and strategic analyst of financial services, and a self-professed conservative by temperament. Pitman wanted to scale down considerably Lloyds' international businesses, having seen first-hand how they were bleeding the bank, while Morse argued for maintaining a strong commitment to international activities and to investment banking. His background was in that arena, having served previously at the Bank of England and having worked with the International Monetary Fund. He also commanded an intimate knowledge of central banks. 'He had a lingering affection for the international side of the bank,' reported a Lloyds manager. In fact, when he retired, Morse reportedly visited the 13-odd nations where Lloyds still had a significant business, to celebrate their continued viability. There was widespread consensus among Lloyds' senior managers that Morse fought vigorously to make sure the bank didn't cut back its international business too far.

The press would print, over the years when they served together, that Pitman and Morse were having big differences.[16] While they certainly did have different points of view at times, they worked well together. Morse delegated to Pitman the responsibility of running the bank and developing its strategy, although he made continuous inputs in discussions between them on the substance and viability of that strategy.

Morse, an Oxford-educated, upper-class intellectual, had arrived at Lloyds in 1975 as Deputy Chair, became Chair in 1977, and retired from that position and the bank in 1993. All four clearers – Lloyds included – had followed a long tradition of only selecting as board chairmen members of the British Establishment, that is, people of upper-class background, who would represent it well to outside groups in banking, government, and business.

Morse, however, had many more credentials than that. He had earned so much respect among bankers worldwide that he was elected President of the International Conference of Commercial Banks in the 1980s and chaired their meeting in Boston in 1986. He gave a significant speech on banking strategy at that meeting, characterizing the highly competitive global environment of the industry, and arguing for the importance of scaling down and focusing more in that environment. 'He stated that not even the biggest bank (referring to Citicorp though not mentioning it by name) could afford not to pull out of losing businesses in that environment,' reported a senior banker present at the meeting. 'He felt strongly that the Citicorp view at the time that it could accelerate out of trouble was not viable and that Citicorp could not do that.'

In this basic respect, then, Morse and Pitman converged around the view that a focused UK retail strategy made the most sense for Lloyds. 'They both agreed that diversification was yesterday's game and that Lloyds should look for honey in personal and small business loans,' explained a senior Lloyds banker.

Where they disagreed, with Morse tempering some of Pitman's views, was in the importance of wholesale global banking. Morse did not want to pull out of wholesale banking to the same degree as Pitman did. He believed more in maintaining a balance between wholesale and retail and in shifting priorities without getting out of the corporate business completely. In brief, he wanted to make sure that Lloyds did not limit itself too much. Even in the 1990s, he felt strongly that Lloyds' businesses in Latin America, New Zealand and some other nations outside the UK still fitted its style and long-term goals. Their differences, then, were more ones of degree than of kind.

Future Lloyds leadership?

If leadership and management make a difference, it is not clear what Lloyds' future will be. In the immediate future, Pitman is likely to remain its leader as Chairman of the board, since he is not obliged to retire from that position until age 70. His ascendance to the chair position was unprecedented in Lloyds' history, allowing him to break the mould once more.

British banks, as class-ridden institutions, had traditionally chosen outsiders from upper-class origins.[17] It is conceivable, then, that Pitman may break with tradition still one more time, by staying on as Chair beyond 70. Regardless of his future status at Lloyds, however, the bank must engage in more succession planning to ensure its survival as a leading UK bank in an industry that is increasingly competitive. This is particularly the case in the UK retail banking niche, where Lloyds has chosen to concentrate.

In the past, Lloyds, like the other clearers, had never picked a chair from its own management, choosing instead those from the aristocracy. Not surprisingly, there was some rationale given for this practice: namely, that banks as institutions needed statesmenlike figures who were well connected in government, business and financial circles.

Given Pitman's strategic astuteness in directing Lloyds to ever higher performance, his UK and worldwide reputation, and his increasingly public role as a statesman for the industry, this appointment certainly matched the bank's interests. Despite his limited formal education, Pitman had demonstrated considerable capability as a strategist, conceptualizer of financial and business trends, and therefore as the kind of statesman the bank needed in that position. And, as many observers had noted, he was a man of considerable charisma, likely to play a strongly effective role in representing the bank to such outside stakeholders as institutional investors, regulators, central banks worldwide, and large wholesale customers.

Over the short term, then, Lloyds can most likely count on Pitman for strong leadership in its continuing trajectory as a leading UK retail bank. Meanwhile, his successor as CEO, Peter Ellwood, must manage many complex organizational and operations problems – for which he is well suited. Among Lloyds' most significant problems are those of effectively absorbing and sorting out its recent acquisitions, particularly TSB. There are many issues of consolidation and down-sizing, the merging of the different cultures, and managing redun-dancies of product lines and back-office systems. Such a division of labour between Pitman, the grand strategist, and Ellwood, the skilled administrator and operations manager, is likely to serve Lloyds well over the next 4–5 years.

The bank also needs a longer-term strategy, however, of grooming talented successors. Perhaps, over time, Ellwood will play more of a role as a strategic thinker; or perhaps a CEO or board chairman of another financial services institution that Lloyds might acquire in the near future would emerge as a possible candidate. If Lloyds is to keep its momentum as a leading UK financial services institution, it must build into its operation such succession management, with a full leadership-development process.

Entrepreneurial leaders like Pitman sometimes fail to put enough resources and creativity into that task, thereby risking that their institution lose momentum when they depart. Since Pitman has positioned Lloyds in a particularly competitive niche that is likely to become only more so in the future, with electronic banking and 'virtual banking' looming on the horizon, the bank must focus on this task.

Heretofore, Lloyds' financial performance has made it the leading British commercial bank. It has been widely acclaimed in that regard, with Pitman getting much of the credit.[18] Success is increasingly ephemeral, however, in hypercompetitive industries such as financial services, and developing a strong leadership group to carry on when Pitman finally retires is critical to maintaining the performance and reputation that Lloyds has achieved in the last decade.

Lessons from the Lloyds configuration

In addition to the theme that management – and particularly leadership – count in contributing to an industry's adaptive capability, I discussed in Chapter 1 the issue of organizational configuration. I mean by that the combination of strategy and supportive organizational infrastructure required to survive in the competitive environment that financial services institutions face today. Since Lloyds has been so successful, it is important to examine its profile or configuration of characteristics associated with that success. Many of them flow from the leadership that Pitman and Morse provided.

At the same time, what contributed to success in the past may not do so in the future. Given how quickly market conditions are changing in banking – for instance, the rise of electronic banking – many new competitive challenges are likely in the coming years. Assuming, however, that there may be at least some carry-over of challenges from the past, we will now analyse in depth the main characteristics of Lloyds that contributed to its success.

A first-mover, prospector strategy

It should be clear from the above discussion of Pitman's style that Lloyds has increasingly pursued a first-mover strategy since the mid-1980s. Management theorists Miles and Snow refer to this strategy as a 'prospector' one, characterized by a firm constantly analysing its competitive environment and just as constantly making changes – in products, in customers, in geographic markets – in order to adapt to that environment.[19] We might best describe Lloyds, in Miles and Snow terms, as a *focused* prospector, concentrating on one major market and making many acquisitions and innovations in the context of that market.

Thus, Lloyds was the first of the clearers to emphasize shareholder value and strategic portfolio analysis, leading to a drastic simplification and reduction of its businesses, and constituting a more focused approach to financial services. Lloyds was, in that sense, the first to question the 'big is beautiful' paradigm and the supposed benefits of diversification. In many respects, Lloyds could be characterized as 'advancing by retreating', with Pitman becoming known as the master of selling off losing businesses. More substantively, it was the first to concentrate so heavily on retail–domestic as opposed to wholesale–international banking. It was the first to recognize the complexities of having to manage both together; it was certainly the first to see the extraordinary difficulties of managing investment and commercial banking under the same organizational holding company. Finally, it was the first to acquire building societies. And so, in all of these respects, one could point to Lloyds' strategy as a potentially effective way to position a British bank for a hypercompetitive future.

One might take a different view, however. Some sceptics have argued that Lloyds' strategy may have become *too* focused and that it now risks 'drowning in its own fundaments'. Some refer to it as just another 'glorified building society'. They assert that having a more balanced portfolio of wholesale and retail businesses and of domestic and international businesses would make Lloyds less vulnerable to competitive threats in the future than would a continuation of its concentration on UK retail banking. Growth opportunities in the latter are probably limited, especially since it has become more competitive. New non-banks and foreign banks are invading UK retail banking in greater numbers – and more effectively than in the past.

At the same time, Lloyds' focused UK retail banking strategy may have more sustainability than its critics realize. Within this segmented market, Lloyds has diversified its product base to make it less vulnerable to intrusions of new competitors than would otherwise be the case. British bank watchers have thus consistently hailed all three of its main acquisitions as contributing strongly to its future prospects. That of Abbey Life in 1988, for example, made Lloyds a significant player in the UK life assurance industry, and at a significantly low cost. The acquisition of Cheltenham & Gloucester (C&G) in 1995 gave Lloyds marked strengths in the home-mortgage industry, and through a financial services institution that was the most efficient in its field. Indeed, at the time of transfer C&G had a cost:income ratio of 25 per cent, the lowest of any British building society.[20]

Most recently, the merger with TSB gave Lloyds both a strong bancassurance capability and a broader customer base. While Lloyds had traditionally served a more upper-class clientele, to the south and east of London, and was sometimes referred to as 'the Tories' bank', TSB's main clientele as a former mutual bank was blue-collar workers and university students in the north of England and in Scotland. In brief, each acquisition involved broadening the product and/or customer base and, in that sense, Lloyds has solidified its position within UK retail banking and reduced its vulnerability to market swings.

There are other aspects of the Lloyds strategy, in addition to its focus on UK retail banking, that give it a sustainable potential. Perhaps most important in that regard has been its relentless cost-reduction emphasis accompanying its acquisitions. Pitman had emphasized for years the importance of banks following a low-cost, low-price strategy, and each of his acquisitions was accompanied by much consolidation of branches, back-office systems, headquarters administrative-support operations, and product divisions. Continuously wringing costs out of the institution was one of his highest priorities, and Lloyds' success at maintaining a lower cost:income ratio than those of its clearing bank competitors has been yet another basis for its leading market position in UK retail banking.

Should such formidable high-tech outsiders such as Citicorp begin to invade this market in the next several years, Lloyds may be able to hold its own by virtue of the strategies it has followed since the mid-1980s. In addition, it may get itself into a position where it can transfer core competencies previously developed in UK retail banking to various European nations. Banks there are not as advanced in technology, products and infrastructures as Lloyds has become by its being focused so much in that market. In that sense, just as Citicorp is successfully pursuing a global retail banking strategy, so might Lloyds do so on a pan-European basis. Since the UK is likely to become much more integrated into the EU in the next several years, this may be a productive next step for Lloyds. Such a development is particularly likely in view of Pitman's having adopted a similar branding and retailing strategy as Citicorp.

In brief, a continuation of Lloyds' past successes may best be understood in the context of a kind of a cyclical scenario that has characterized its evolution in recent decades. The first stage was to become an international bank, as opportunities for growth and geographic diversification seemed to be opening in the 1960s and 1970s. There was no coherent vision underlying this international growth strategy other than the desire to gain representation in many parts of the world. Bigness and market share in different geographic areas seemed to be the only larger goals and were equated with strength.

When that approach led to huge losses, a second-stage strategy emerged, starting as an exercise in retrenchment from international banking and an intensified emphasis on domestic business. This was developed as a way of concentrating on the goal of enhancing shareholder value and only competing in markets where Lloyds had some underlying core competencies.

Having built up that domestic business and established a strong and perhaps sustainable market position there, Lloyds might conceivably move to a third-stage strategy of selectively exporting its UK retail banking franchise to various European markets. That would be a very different kind of international banking from what Lloyds had pursued in the seventies and eighties, in that it would involve exporting an established and successful set of core businesses to newly emerging markets in Eastern Europe and selective ones within Central and Western Europe.

A Salomon-type culture

Such a first-mover–prospector type of strategy is likely only to succeed if supported by an appropriate organizational infrastructure. Pitman, in his relentless push for effective implementation, seemed to have achieved that. The Lloyds culture under Pitman reflected his personality in basic ways. A senior Lloyds manager referred to it as 'results-driven, ruthless in our pursuit of excellence and performance, very much a Salomon-type culture. We don't want to lose and we won't,' he continued.

Other aspects of the culture often mentioned are its emphasis on cost cutting, efficiency, and employee productivity, all the while pursued by aggressive downsizing, even at the possible expense of low employee morale and much anxiety about the future. Basically, it is a culture in which the bank is run as a business for shareholder value, with minimal priority on people. A study by human resource management researchers from the London Business School, for example, seemed to corroborate this characterization of the Lloyds culture. Their interviews with Lloyds' branch employees in 1995 and 1996 indicated that those emplyees saw management as wanting more productivity for less pay, as having abandoned a paternalistic old culture that had provided a lifetime career at the bank, and as not providing anything in its place. Downsizing and new technology (eliminating branch jobs) were seen as shrinking opportunities, and yet with the bank providing few resources for training and development for alternative careers.

In brief, this was a results-dominated, 'lean and mean' culture that placed much emphasis on shareholder value through serving customers, but at the seeming expense of employee interests. In that sense, meeting employees' needs was seen as having lower priority than maximizing shareholder value through new strategies and systems. As we will discuss below in the chapters on Barclays, NatWest and Midland, these culture changes were not unique to Lloyds. However, they may well have been more accentuated there.

A flat structure

A still further aspect of the infrastructure Pitman established to implement his strategy was Lloyds' very flat organizational structure.

When knowledgeable informants, including Lloyds senior managers, were asked to describe its structure, they usually mentioned two related characteristics. One was that Lloyds under Pitman as CEO revolved almost completely around him and was seen as having no formal structure. As one long-time UK bank watcher explained: 'Pitman absolutely dominates that bank. Its organization chart looks like the solar system, with Pitman in the middle and everybody reporting to him.'[21]

The other observation relates to Lloyds' extreme flatness. 'We are so atypical in being so flat,' reported a senior manager in wholesale banking. 'We are immensely flatter than the other banks. Two people in wholesale banking are the only ones not assuming trading tasks in front of the screen. And in retail banking there is only one senior general manager, and that person has four other general managers, and the rest are seeing customers. We are so flat, we may have to temper our enthusiasm for our flatness. Because we are still so big, we couldn't be any flatter.'

This characterization of Lloyds as having a fluid, flat structure certainly matches its aggressive, opportunistic strategy of being an innovator in its market niche. It also fits the observation Mintzberg has made that organizations that see themselves in crisis often centralize power in a strong leader, who then develops a flat organization and bypasses levels to ensure that his or her policies are implemented.[22]

A new organizational structure issue has emerged as a result of Lloyds' domestic acquisitions. It relates to the importance of co-ordination across product groups as a way of serving better the consumer and enhancing profits. For example, before Lloyds' acquisitions of Cheltenham & Gloucester and of TSB, it maintained high levels of autonomy for such product groups as home mortgages, credit cards, insurance, and the like. Furthermore, bank observers referred to its incremental additions of new retail products as 'a strategy of sprawl'; and they characterized its branches as 'enormous buckets'.[23]

TSB, however, had a different organizational style, with one of its core competences being its close linkages across product groups, particularly insurance services and deposit and loan services, thereby facilitating cross-selling. The challenge for Lloyds was not only to merge the TSB style with its own, but to enhance revenue and service by incorporating TSB's successes in this regard and by breaking down barriers within its traditional structure.

Performance profile of a winner

I have referred throughout the chapter to Lloyds being by far the top performer of the UK's four clearing banks. It may well be one of the top-performing banks *worldwide*, as indicated above in our reference to Lloyds as having the largest market capitalization of any commercial bank in the world. Many other performance indicators as well point to its being a top performer.

One commonly used measure of financial performance is *return on equity* (ROE). Lloyds has far outperformed the other three clearers on this dimension in recent years. Thus, during 1990–5, Lloyds averaged a 21.5 per cent ROE against 12.8 per cent for the average of the five largest UK commercial banks.[24]

One of Pitman's stated goals is to increasingly outperform his British competitors. That is certainly the case with regard to ROE. And it is likely that Lloyds' impressive numbers (an ROE of 41 per cent in 1997) are not that time-bound. Given Lloyds' strategy of only staying in businesses that generate significant profits, the numbers are not at all surprising.

A critical measure of banks' efficiency is their *cost/income ratio*. They can only be strong competitors in retail banking by driving their costs down below those of other players in that market. One of the vulnerabilities that the clearing banks have had in competing with the building societies, for example, is that the latter have had much lower costs than the clearers. The comparison isn't completely appropriate, however, in that the clearers must maintain services in their branches for small and middle-sized business clients as well as for retail consumers (unlike the building societies), thereby driving up their costs. Nevertheless, the disparity allows the building societies to undercut the clearers on price.

Thus, in 1997, three building societies – Halifax, Abbey National and Woolwich – had ratios of 40.8 per cent, 43.3 per cent and 45.1 per cent respectively. Meanwhile, as may be seen in Table 2 of the Appendix, the clearers do considerably worse than the building societies, with Lloyds being the best of the clearers. Moreover, Lloyds has been on a consistently downward trend for many years. Pitman's recent claim that Lloyds is well on the road to his goal of getting into the 40 per cent range may well be realized. Moreover, he has set a target for the bank to eventually get down below 40 per cent. Given his strong push toward relentless cost cutting, it is likely that Lloyds will make considerable progress in that direction. With each major acquisition, it has been able to consolidate headquarters and branch operations, thereby squeezing considerable costs out of the newly enlarged bank.

Market capitalization is yet another measure widely used in the industry, and there again Lloyds far surpasses its competitors. While Midland's capitalization was £15.6 billion in 1997 and NatWest's and Barclay's was £17.5 billion and £24.7 billion respectively in the same year, Lloyds was £42.1 billion.[25]

Since maximizing shareholder value is such a critical aspect of Lloyds' strategy and is a goal to which its clearing competitors give increasingly high priority, one may compare its *relative share price performance* with that of its clearing bank competitors. Trend data on this for Lloyds, Barclays and NatWest during the period 1980–95 indicate outstandingly superior results for Lloyds relative to the other two.[26] With all three starting from parity in 1980, Lloyds' improvement was more than twice that of the other two.

Still other measures are the banks' *price/book value* and their *relative market-price/equity ratio*. On the former, Lloyds' price/book value in 1997 was 377 per cent, compared with 167 per cent for Barclays and 166 per cent for NatWest. And on the relative market-price/equity ratio, Lloyds led again in 1997 with 79.8 per cent, compared with 62.7 per cent for Barclays and 57.5 per cent for NatWest.

On a wide range of financial performance indicators, then, Lloyds is by far the best-performing British bank and has been since the mid-1980s. Moreover, given its continued success in cutting costs, its getting out of loss-making businesses, and its acquiring new businesses that broaden the product line and customer base, all the while maintaining a focus on UK retail banking, Lloyds is likely to have a sustainable financial performance for several years to come. Of particular note is the fact that Lloyds has not had a rights issue since 1976, compared with NatWest and Barclays, both of whom had them during the late 1980s.

Given this superior performance, it is little wonder that Lloyds keeps getting mentioned as the leading commercial bank in Britain. It continues to engage in effective cost cutting, while at the same time pursuing profitable business expansion through well timed and executed acquisitions. It is also not surprising that the Salomon Brothers' European Equity Research group characterized Lloyds' acquisition of TSB as 'moving from strength to strength'.[27] Lloyds has much momentum in its core business lines and can be expected to maintain that in the coming years.

A product/business mix that works

Positioning one's firm in the most appropriate product, geographic, and customer markets may not in itself lead to high performance, but without such positioning it is unlikely that the firm will be effective. It is useful to recall that the earnings profile for Lloyds since the early 1980s has been to change from 70 per cent wholesale and 30 per cent retail to its opposite. More specifically, the following product mix characterizes the bank in 1997: retail banking 25.9 per cent, home mortgages 21.5 per cent, insurance 16.4 per cent, wholesale markets 20.3 per cent, and international banking 13.2 per cent.[28]

Moreover, Pitman announced in October 1997 that Lloyds is continuing to reduce its business in wholesale markets, concentrating more and more of its resources in the retail sector where, he indicated, the most growth opportunities lie and where there is less risk. To illustrate his point, he noted that Lloyds had then recently sold its German investment bank as not fitting either its strategy or culture.

Ultimately, the configuration is what counts

High-performing companies need more than just an appropriate strategy. They also need a configuration of organizational characteristics that supports the strategy, providing for what might be called its *implementation intensity*. It should be clear from the discussion in this chapter that Pitman and Lloyds have that configuration – not without some accompanying stresses and strains, but meshing well with the strategy nevertheless.

Given the bank's relentless goals of maximizing shareholder value, doubling its profits every three years, and being a leader in its chosen markets, it has an appropriate infrastructure. The culture is one emphasizing cost efficiencies, being results driven, and being a leader in the markets it chooses. The organization is one of being extremely flexible, non-bureaucratic, flat, and decentralized, devolving authority to product managers and directors at lower levels, as long as they meet ambitious target goals for profitability. Managerial compensation and rewards all the way down the line are based on how performance measures up to company standards of efficiency, ROE, and the like. And the human resource management approaches are the antithesis of the industry's traditionally paternalistic ones of providing lifetime employment and salary increments based mainly on seniority. Pay-for-performance, a relentless pursuit of cost cutting and efficiency through applying new technology to administration and service delivery, and continuing consolidation and downsizing of operations replace the old, paternalistic, lifetime contract policies of the past.

One of the main stresses of this style is an inevitable alienation of lower-level employees in the branches. Many may feel that their career interests are of little or secondary importance to the bank. And many see the merger, restructuring, and downsizing programmes as proceeding in a top-down fashion, with little input from them.

From Pitman's and the bank's perspective, this is one of the prices of moving from being a paternalistic, status-quo-oriented institution, providing lifetime employment to branch employees, to being a rationally managed business. The latter involves a commitment to continual and, at times, radical change to survive. Just as Citicorp and Walter Wriston broke the mould in the US as they changed the paradigm of banks from public utilities to growth stocks, so did Lloyds and Sir Brian Pitman do likewise in UK banking. Pitman's argument was that the banks could not survive unless they ruthlessly modernized and rationalized their operations, were highly selective in the businesses they were in, and downsized as part of that process.

Having now described the highest performer in the industry, we move on to examining what happened to the others. All these case histories are designed to enhance our understanding of what strategies and organizational configurations are required to succeed in the increasingly hypercompetitive world of UK banking and beyond.

Notes and references

1. From Bloomberg, *Financial Markets* (online).
2. Lehman Brothers, *UK Clearing Banks: 1998 Annual Review*, 23 July 1998, p. 107.
3. *The Economist*, 17 January 1998, pp. 65–6.
4. Lehman Brothers, *op. cit.*
5. J.R. Winston, *Lloyds Bank*, Oxford University Press, Oxford, 1982, p. 28ff.
6. Steven I. Davis, *Leadership in Financial Services*, Macmillan Business, Basingstoke and London, 1997, pp. 94–8.
7. *The Economist*, 17 January 1998, p. 65.
8. *Financial Times*, 21 September 1996; and *The Economist*, 19 September 1997.
9. R.S. Sayers, *Lloyds Bank in the History of English Banking*, Oxford University Press, Oxford, 1957.
10. *The Economist*, 19 September 1987.
11. *The Economist*, 17 January 1988, p. 65.
12. *Financial Times*, 11 February 1994. For a discussion of bancassurance in France and its twin, *Allfinanz* in Germany, and of the potential synergy of combining banking and insurance, see Roy Smith, *Comeback*, Harvard Business School Press, Boston, 1993, pp. 181–3.
13. *The Economist*, 16 October 1995.
14. *The Economist*, 19 April 1978 and 2 July 1988.
15. *Financial Times*, 23 April 1994.
16. An example is *The Economist*, 17 September 1987.
17. *Financial Times*, 25 March 1992.
18. Steven I. Davis, *op. cit.*, pp. 94–8.
19. Raymond E. Miles and Charles C. Snow, *Organizational Strategy, Structure, and Process*, McGraw-Hill, New York, 1978.
20. *The Economist*, 23 April 1994.
21. This was similar to the structure that Jack Welch instituted at GE, one of the US firms that Pitman reportedly admired. A description appears in *General Electric: Jack Welch's Second Wave (A)*, Harvard Business School, 9-391-248, 1 April 1993.
22. Henry Mintzberg, *The Structuring of Organizations*, Prentice Hall, Englewood Cliffs NJ, 1979, p. 308.
23. *The Economist*, 22 July 1995.
24. Steven I. Davis, *op. cit.*, pp 94–5

25. Most of the data in this section come from Lehman Brothers, *op. cit.*, or Bloomberg financial analysis unless otherwise indicated.
26. Salomon Brothers, *Lloyds Bank Plc – Momentum Returns*, European Equity Research, 3 March 1995, p. 3.
27. Salomon Brothers, *Lloyds TSB Group – From Strength to Strength*, European Equity Research, 2 March 1997.
28. Lehman Brothers, *op. cit.*, p. 107.

5 Barclays: the Quaker Squirearchy of UK Banking

Barclays was a family bank, formed through regional mergers, and some families hung on for a long time. It had an almost military style, with many faceless, grey types amongst the employees. And it was lacking in vision and an awareness of outside forces. Centralized, bureaucratic and hierarchical, with a command-and-control style, it had been in many respects a metaphor for British institutional public life. And the bank was badly burned as a result.

Bank journalist

Their international division was the flagship bank for them, and it was proud of all the dots on the map all over the world, where Barclays' branches were located. On strategy, there was none. They were a classic bankers' bank that did things because they had always been done that way. And they went from unthinking expansion, with weak strategic thinking, reflecting their concern with size, to their infamous rights issue in 1988, to their purge in 1992.

Economist at a London University

It is very institution-minded, and they think of themselves as at the top in the industry. It is a culture of higher-class gentlemen, having formed as an amalgamation of family banks. They want to be always leading the way, to be first movers, much like Citicorp. They go for new directions in a big way.

Bank analyst

OUR NEXT case, Barclays, is in many respects the polar opposite from Lloyds. While Lloyds is a prototype of the focused, specialist bank, Barclays had become a conglomerate, universal bank after the 1986 Big Bang. Often referred to as the bank of the empire, because of its large overseas business since World War I, Barclays had emerged in recent decades as one of the biggest, most diversified, and by far the most international of the British banks. Until the 1950s, Midland had been the UK's largest bank, but Barclays displaced it after that, alternating at times with NatWest, its arch-competitor.

Barclays has operations in the world's main financial centres and, as a big wholesale and retail bank, it has significant businesses in insurance, asset management and investment banking, in addition to its large UK retail banking. Chosen in the mid-1980s by a panel of experts as the only British bank in a list of the 16 best-managed world-wide, Barclays had – until the 1980s – an international reputation as one of best of the UK clearers.[1] 'When we made lists of the top global banks,' explained a banking expert, 'we always included some of the European universal banks like Deutsche, UBS, and Swiss Bank – and we included Barclays. It had been a highly regarded global bank for decades.'

The story of Barclays' recent evolution, like that of NatWest in later chapters, contains important lessons about the viability of universal banking in the UK. It also throws light on whether a large commercial bank can ever develop an organizational infrastructure to support an effective investment bank.

An additional, related aspect of the Barclays case is that, unlike Lloyds, Barclays was not only committed to universal and investment banking but it has also struggled increasingly since the late 1980s to define just what that entailed. It has reorganized many times over the past decade, but that has not helped clarify its larger strategy as a financial services institution. 'The Barclays people too often confused reorganizing with strategic change,' explained a bank analyst, 'and that didn't help them move ahead in deciding where they might best position themselves as a bank and what kind of universal bank they wanted to be.'

This struggle for self-definition and a coherent strategy has intensified since Barclays' then CEO, Martin Taylor, announced late in October 1997 that Barclays was formally abandoning its ambitions to build a full-scale global investment bank. The decision came after the bank had committed huge sums to build that business and had moved many of its back-office and trading operations to new facilities in Canary Wharf in London's Docklands only a few months before, at considerable expense.[2] John Aitken, bank analyst formerly with Switzerland's UBS, estimated that since 1984 Barclays had (in his words) squandered at least £750 million on investment banking.[3]

Responding in part to pressure from institutional investors after Barclays' investment bank, BZW, had suffered huge losses, and to the implications of a recent merger in the US of Travelers with Salomon Brothers, creating yet another investment banking giant with which it would be hard to compete, Taylor decided that Barclays should exit from much of that business. He concluded that the business would not contribute enough to shareholder value to make it worth the continued commitment of required resources.

This decision, mirroring a similar one that NatWest had made two months earlier, constituted a significant turning point in British banking.[4] In Barclays' case, the exit decision was announced publicly before finding a buyer – an unlikely way of selling at a favourable price and thereby enhancing shareholder value. The decisions of both NatWest and Barclays raised serious questions about the future strategy of these banks and about the viability of universal banking in Britain. At the very least, they raised questions about the way the British banks had implemented that strategy.

If the exit in late 1997 from investment banking was a dramatic turning point for Barclays,[5] a series of events in late 1998, culminating in Taylor's sudden resignation in late November of that year, proved at least as dramatic. The main developments included:

(1) a messy implementation of the 1987 exit plan, with Barclays selling off BZW, its investment bank, piecemeal;

(2) the development out of the ashes of BZW of a reconfigured investment bank, Barclays Capital, concentrating on debt market businesses;

(3) substantial losses, both from the sale and in completely unanticipated ways from Barclays Capital trading, including £250 million in Russia and another in the Long-Term Capital Management hedge fund;

(4) increasing frustrations for Taylor throughout the year at his inability to implement needed changes in the bank's culture and strategies, accompanied by escalating conflicts with his board on the bank's direction;

(5) Taylor's sudden announcement in late October 1998 of a major reorganization, splitting the bank into separate wholesale and retail operations.

To understand how and why Taylor made that last decision and its larger implications in terms of future prospects for British banking, it is useful to provide the same kind of interpretive history as we did for

Lloyds. In the Lloyds case, the historical analysis indicated the many benefits of developing a strategic focus. Conversely, for Barclays it will highlight the many possible costs of moving in the opposite direction, toward becoming a highly diversified, conglomerate bank.

The Quaker squires' amalgamation

Founded as a joint stock bank in 1896, amalgamating 20 private, country banks to the north and east of London, Barclays had many characteristics that distinguished it from the other clearers. Most stem from the fact that it was by far the most family-dominated of the group. Each of its 20 constituent banks was a family enterprise whose autonomy was to be preserved in the consolidation. As a result, Barclays was for many decades the most decentralized and loosely organized of the clearers.[6]

Also reflecting the families' role, Barclays had more of a partnership and entrepreneurial culture than the others, making it seemingly more compatible in the 1980s and 1990s with the performance demands of investment banking. And it clearly had more of a first-mover, high-risk, innovation-minded culture than the others. While this was not always to be the case, it was true throughout most of Barclays' history, thereby making it a UK leader in international banking, in the credit card business, in investment banking, and, like Lloyds, in closing down operations in many parts of the world where it was experiencing significant losses.[7]

Finally, and also reflecting the dominance of the bank's founding families, there existed what British bank watchers often referred to as a 'Barclays' diaspora'. Thus several outstanding, non-family, senior managers, having experienced blocked upward mobility to top positions at Barclays, left in the eighties and nineties to become CEOs elsewhere. They included such well known figures in recent British banking history as Sir Brian Pearse (who became CEO of Midland in 1991), Peter Ellwood (CEO of TSB), Malcolm Williamson (CEO of Standard Chartered), and Peter Wood (CEO of Abbey National). In addition, Deryk VanderWeyer, Vice Chair of Barclays 1978–83, was passed over for the chair position in favour of Timothy Bevan, a descendant of an old Barclays family. This took place even though VanderWeyer was widely regarded both inside and outside the bank as the person most qualified for the position.

Validating this collective judgment, Bevan then provided minimal leadership during his term as Chair, as Barclays drifted through the early and mid-1980s with few initiatives and little coherent direction.[8] The top-16 rating it was to receive around the time of his departure was a likely result of the bank's earlier achievements and of the promise of his successor, Sir John Quinton, who vowed to get the bank moving again after many sleepy years.

The amalgamation of privately held, country banks in 1896 to form the modern Barclays is often characterized as a defensive merger, to resist takeover attempts, at a time when many of Barclays' competitors were also consolidating as joint stock companies.[9] Each country bank was family-owned and family-managed, serving primarily the fishing and farming communities nearby, and was associated with a particular town or region. In addition to the Barclay family, there were the Tukes, Buxtons, Bevans, Birkbecks, Gurneys, Trittons, Backhouses, Seebohms, Ransoms and Bouveries. Clearly, these are not household names to outsiders unfamiliar with the history of British banking; but to people familiar with it, they have much significance.

The families were all Quakers as well as being country landholders or squires, and highly respected members of their local communities. Indeed, as Quakers, they had well deserved reputations for high levels of probity and honesty, epitomizing the best qualities of private, family banks in eighteenth and nineteenth century rural Britain. As an upper-middle-class landowner group, representing in many respects the Establishment of British banking, many of Barclays' family bankers were, in addition, Etonians and graduates of Cambridge and Oxford. Though not quite aristocracy, they were nevertheless the élite group of the industry.

Not surprisingly, these country bankers had an intimate knowledge of their customers, having done business with them and their families for generations. Indeed, in many of their communities, the only cheques that were accepted, after cheques began to gain wide usage in Britain, were those with the Barclays name. In all these respects, Barclays' country banks were similar to the many community banks in the US, some 8000 of which still exist.

After the amalgamation, Barclays deliberately preserved the autonomy of the individual family banks. It ran for many decades as if it were 20 mini-banks, each with its own separate board. Meanwhile, the heads of the 20 individual bank boards were usually given seats on the central Barclays board. Thus, in 1900 that body included a Bevan as chairman, a Buxton as vice-chairman, two Barclay family members, two Birkbecks, a Seebohm and a Tritton.[10]

Even as late as 1970, although the families owned a small and shrinking portion of Barclays' shares, they were still a dominant force. At that time, for example, the board included three Bevans, two Tukes, a Barclay, a Burney, a Birkbeck, and a Seebohm. Still carrying on in the family tradition, Timothy Bevan was chair from 1980 until 1987, and Andrew Buxton, one of the last of the family grandees, has been Chair since 1992. Conversely, there have been only two non-family chairmen since 1896, the year of Barclays' founding.[11]

The UK's most expansionist international bank

Almost from its inception, Barclays had large domestic and international businesses. The international part of Barclays followed the British empire, with its name reflecting that policy. Thus, it established its Colonial Bank in 1917 and its Dominion, Colonial and Overseas (DCO) unit in 1925.[12] DCO was Britain's first global bank and as such was severely frowned upon by the Bank of England. True to the latter's non-interventionist style, however, it never prevented Barclays from continuing the overseas expansion. A former senior manager at Barclays recalled the Bank of England's regulatory role relative to this international banking initiative: 'The closest the Bank of England came to acting on its concerns,' he said, 'was when one of its governors asked "How is your madcap colonial venture going?".'

Barclays' international expansion involved two main waves: an early one, starting in the 1920s, in developing nations; and a later one, dating from the mid-1960s, in industrial nations.[13] The sites of Barclays' early overseas businesses were some of Britain's main colonial outposts around the world. They included South Africa, Nigeria, Ghana, East and Central Africa, Libya, Egypt, Sudan, Palestine, Jamaica and other British dependencies in the Caribbean. Barclays' approach was to build a full branch-banking system in these nations. Most of the early branches in these colonies were opened in the mid–1920s, under the aegis of DCO, which operated largely as a separate bank within Barclays.

The strategy – if it could be called that – was to set up replicas or imitations of the bank all over the world, especially in the colonies. As a former international banker from Barclays explained:

> Barclays' international strategy was driven by a sense of manifest destiny.
> It wanted its flags on maps all over the world. It was ludicrous. There

was no sense of the value of these businesses, but only to have the flag there. There were too many disasters from following that strategy.

As the old colonial system broke down in the late 1960s, Barclays either withdrew or converted to local ownership and control. Its largest overseas banking was in South Africa, and it finally pulled out of there in the 1980s, as the fight against apartheid gained momentum. The bank was committed to helping get rid of apartheid, but it finally left when the politics escalated. A Barclays banker who had served there recalled the way in which, in his judgment, the bank had mismanaged its exit:

> They said they would originally stay to lobby for change there, and in fact they stayed because their business there was quite profitable. The real reason they left was that they couldn't take the heat there any more. But they got out at precisely the wrong time. Three years before they left, their operation in South Africa was worth twice book value. It was worth only a fraction of that when they sold it. It took them several years to smell a dead rat, when it was sitting there under their noses.

The other international strategy by Barclays began in the mid-1960s, when banks from several industrial nations, including the US, Japan and some European countries, embarked on overseas operations. Barclays was one of them, concentrating its areas of expansion in the major financial centres of the US, Europe and Asia.[14] While these ventures experienced varying degrees of success, several suffered tremendous losses. A US banking scholar has suggested: 'This Barclays experience reflected a larger pattern. None of the British banks knew how to make much money elsewhere in the world.'

The US was one such financial centre, with Barclays eventually developing a US-in-Transition division to sell off most of its branches there. The initial expansion in the US, in the seventies and eighties, was extensive. It was not supported, however, either by a coherent strategy or by an organizational infrastructure, having been developed in a top-down way with little consideration for its profitability. Again, size, market share, and geographic coverage formed the logic that drove the expansion, rather than that of enhancing shareholder value. A Barclays manager involved in US operations during those years recalled:

> I was in New York City for the first time in 1968. We had only three branches there and that was it. By 1979, we had 8000 employees in the US. New York then had 85 branches, California had 50, and we had wholesale branches in Miami, Pittsburgh, Cleveland, Chicago, San Francisco, Seattle, Houston, Dallas and many other cities. But we were

highly fragmented. For example, the head of American Credit – one bank we bought – cut his own deal, and we were only allowed to send one person to oversee that operation. We had a general policy that the wholesale branches would be headed by locals.

The basic approach, then, was one of aggressive expansion without much consideration for its likely impacts on profitability. I mentioned in Chapter 4 the importance of having an implementation intensity, meaning by that the maintaining of close attention to the details of how one's strategies get carried out. Barclays' international expansion in the US and Europe was marked by little attention to these matters. Rather, it constituted a prime example of overreach. 'We became extremely deficient in systems and controls,' reported another senior manager in the US at that time. 'We had been overly optimistic about our prospects for success in an expansion strategy without such controls. The fault was strategy: it came from the top, and it was unusual for such a conservative, tradition-bound bank to do that.' This banker thus summarized Barclays' US banking as involving many separate aquisitions, pushed from senior management in London, and unsupported by any infrastructure.

Barclays had other international businesses as well – particularly in Europe – and many turned out in the same way as had those in the US. In the early 1980s, Barclays developed a profitable business in Spain, but the bank suffered huge losses from later acquisitions in France and Germany. As part of an expansionist push in the late 1980s, it bought Compagnie Européenne de Banque in France and Merck Fink in Germany when both were at the top of the market. The value of both has reduced significantly since then.[15]

In addition, Barclays became involved in commercial property loans in France that it later had to write off. A Barclays international manager explained: 'They tried to branch *de novo* in Paris, feeling that their name had cachet there. But that was not enough. Their own numbers should have told them that was no good. They wanted to be like French banks, but French banks are very volatile. Add that to Merck Fink in Germany, a bad purchase, and you have Barclays involved in putting cash from profitable UK business into the most unprofitable France-and-other continental business. The bank had been bleeding shareholder value in both the US and continental Europe.' A US banking scholar further suggested: 'This Barclays experience reflected a larger pattern. None of the British banks knew how to make much money elsewhere in the world.'

Indeed, the Barclays international losses sound much like the Lloyds experience, which in fact they were. It should also be pointed out, however, that many big US banks, including BankAmerica, Chemical, and Chase, experienced similar losses in their international businesses.

A key reason for these poorly performing international ventures was, again, the absence of a developed strategy other than to gain geographic representation and market share. The poor performance was also a result of failure to develop an infrastructure to support the businesses. One former Barclays international manager suggested: 'The sad thing is that Barclays' management recognized the absurdity of the US and European businesses but nevertheless carried on with them. In that sense, they were not intelligent businessmen.'

One interpretation he and some others gave was that Barclays was following Citicorp as its role model. Since some Barclays managers correctly saw Citicorp as an effective global bank, they were determined to go in the same direction. Citicorp, however, had a much larger cadre of senior management talent than Barclays, for Citicorp had developed an impressive meritocracy since the late 1950s through its aggressive recruiting of MBAs and graduates of international studies programmes.[16]

These people constituted its global management group, many of whom spent years running branches around the world before returning to headquarters in senior positions. Citicorp also had strong headquarters leadership for a global strategy that was much more developed than anything Barclays had. Though Barclays had some highly regarded senior managers, it did not have nearly the numbers or depth of talented people that Citicorp had. Neither did it have the articulated global strategy of Citicorp. As a former Barclays banker explained: 'They saw Citicorp as the model of a global bank, but Citicorp was a *unique* global bank because it had people and a vision that it stayed with. Barclays was not nearly as strong.'

A dual strategy: high street and international

Barclays' strategy, however, went way beyond its international operations. It was also a major UK retail or 'high street' bank; and, much like Lloyds and the other clearers, Barclays' domestic banking was a big revenue source. Continuing the Lloyds comparison, Barclays' domestic bank was the 'cash cow' that generated much of the capital used to finance its international operations.

In 1997, for example, UK Banking Services, which includes both personal and business banking, accounted for roughly 70 per cent of operating profits.[17] While the number of Barclays' domestic branches has decreased steadily from 2842 in 1986 to 1737 in 1996, following industry-wide trends, it remains one of the two biggest banks, along with NatWest.[18] It was the leader in credit cards, having 30 per cent of that market through its Barclaycard subsidiary, and was also strong in small and medium-sized business loans, where its reputation historically had been very good.[19] In recent years, it had made forays into the market for home mortgage loans, insurance, and asset management (where it was traditionally weaker).

Much of Barclays' UK retail banking is not particularly unique. In common with the other three clearers, and in the face of increasing competition, particularly from non-bank outsiders, Barclays is engaged in a concerted effort to cut costs by restructuring its branches and developing alternative delivery systems. The branch restructurings have involved outsourcing both the back-office (data and cheque) processing and the so-called middle-office vaults for securities. There are many more ATMs and fewer cashiers in the branches, and the staff who remain function increasingly as salespeople rather than bank tellers and clerks.

A major reform has been the conversion of branches from a processing to a sales operation. This has required a massive culture change, in directions quite alien to traditional British values. A Barclays retail manager explained:

> Our people regard sales as cheap and dirty. A sales-and-service culture is not part of our national legacy in banking. Many of our staff feel they came here to do clerking and don't want to dirty themselves with customer contact around sales. It was particularly hard on the older staff, who took on the attitude that they joined to be a clerk and have a nice back-office job, not be in sales.

Barclays' version of developing such a sales culture has been its 'new retail approach' in its pilot 'Eagle' programme in Tunbridge Wells, a suburban community south-west of London. 'It involves the use of focus groups and qualitative interviews with customers,' stated a retail manager, 'to understand their needs – particularly the whole of their financial situation. We are working to develop a model for the bank of the future.'

This new bottom-up, grass-roots model, as Barclays' retail bankers refer to it, involves having customers indicate their financial needs, developing close relationships with them based on that, trusting the branch staff closest to the customer to provide that information, and then customizing products based on it. Barclays has been using this model in every sector: in the retail sector; amongst business customers as well as personal; in operations; and in product groups. 'We hope that, through this approach, trust and loyalty develop, we build a good reputation with customers, and we get one-stop shopping,' reported a Barclays' programme manager.

The approach in reconfiguring the branches involves becoming a much lower-cost provider than before, through outsourcing and reducing the number of people in the branches, all the while increasing their productivity and doing more cross-selling. At the same time, Barclays, like the other clearers, is moving ahead with alternative delivery systems through electronic banking. The latter includes telephone banking, pc banking, interactive TV, and the Internet.

In early 1995, Barclays developed a joint venture with VISA to pilot pc banking with 2500 of its customers.[20] It has done extensive market research to determine which populations are likely to be most receptive. The early adopters tended to be people in a higher income bracket, otherwise engaged in pc use in their jobs, holding both business and personal accounts with Barclays, and seeing control and convenience as the biggest perceived benefits from it. Barclays has gathered much information on these people: their income, occupation, accounts at Barclays, lifestyle and consumption patterns, and what they would like to do on the computer. As one member of staff explained: 'These are people who travel all over the world on their jobs and have to use alarm clocks to do their transactions. That is no longer necessary, since this is a 24-hour-a-day service.'

From two businesses to four business clusters

For many years, and certainly from the 1970s through to the mid-1980s, Barclays' strategy had two main divisions: domestic, UK retail banking; and international, predominantly wholesale banking. After Martin Taylor became CEO in January 1994, Barclays' senior management characterized the bank increasingly as having four business clusters:

(1) UK retail, which encompassed individual and small and medium-sized business banking;

(2) asset management, a growing business involving institutionalized savings products for individuals (for example, pensions, trusts and mutual funds), as well as services for institutional clients;
(3) investment banking; and
(4) large corporate banking.[21]

The first two focused primarily on individual customers, with the second two on institutional clients (corporations and government). Viewed another way, asset management and investment banking – the second and third clusters of the four – dealt mainly with capital-markets-related (securities) products, while UK retail and large corporate banking dealt more with traditional banking services.

I use the past tense in describing these four business clusters because Barclays has kept reorganizing since this structure was established in 1995. At that time, it looked like it would last for several years, with appropriate fine tuning. There were many more structures to come, however, suggesting either Barclays' continuing adaptiveness or some basic confusion about its direction, depending on one's point of view.

Big Bang changes the equation

Barclays' move from two legs to four in its business was driven at the time by deregulation and the rise of capital markets. After Big Bang in 1986, Barclays made a strong commitment to investment banking as the biggest of the four clearers.

It bought both a broker (de Zoete & Bevan) and a trading or market-making firm (Wedd Durlacher), and it paid a big price for each. Later, in 1995, with Barclays' purchase of a fund management firm, Nikko, from Wells Fargo, it separated out asset management as a distinct business entity or division.

The establishing of four such business clusters did not constitute a coherent strategy, however, unless there was a developed rationale for the clusters. One senior manager from Barclays agreed: 'We have no strategy,' he said at the time. 'What we *do* have is a concept of what we are doing in terms of the four business clusters, two by customers and two by products. We have no strategy here or in any of the other British banks – except for perhaps Lloyds, with its shareholder value emphasis.'

Some of this judgment as to whether Barclays and its clearing competitors have a strategy depends on what is meant by that term. The Barclays senior manager just cited was using it to mean positioning the firm in product, customer, and geographic markets in ways that matched its core competences and thereby would enhance profitability or shareholder value. None of the clearing banks could be construed as having had a viable strategy before the 1980s, and perhaps only Lloyds after that.

Since January, 1994, however, when Martin Taylor arrived as CEO, Barclays has begun moving in that direction. For the first three years, Taylor argued that Barclays' strategy was to maintain a balance between being a universal bank and developing more focus. He agreed that it should do fewer things and do them better than before; but he also argued that banking must be a multiproduct, multifunction business to survive and perform well. The question remains for Barclays, after Taylor's 1998 departure, as to what kind of multi-product business it should be.

While Taylor was CEO, there was also the question of how he could balance Barclays' continued high levels of diversification while also emphasizing its being more focused. He did so in part through his policy that the different businesses must reinforce each other. He relentlessly emphasized the importance of developing collaborative linkages across the business clusters, thereby achieving the kinds of synergies that conglomerates are in theory supposed to have. One senior manager explained: 'He kept making sure that the bank had doors in the walls for their business and he let all his managers know that nobody could have their wall without doors and windows.'

A manager in strategic planning emphasized how the headquarters group was particularly directed to those tasks:

> A critical question for us is: Where can the centre (HQ) add value? We do look for lots of value-adding linkages across businesses and push for them every chance we get. For example, individual and smaller business banking share a branch network. We are putting asset management products into the branches. And our corporate and investment banking arms service the same institutions.

Taylor and his HQ senior managers promoted such linkages by using the same techniques commonly used in other multiproduct corporations. This included bonuses to facilitate co-operation, issuing Barclays shares to managers to encourage them to identify with the total organization rather than just their particular business, requiring cross-product contacts, and public commendations for doing so.

It is not clear to Barclays' senior managers, however, that these actions have achieved their desired results. One explained:

Our concern is that all the things we do reinforce each other, but it does take an enormous amount of managerial skill to make that happen. We have let all our managers know that nobody can have their business 'without doors and windows'. In addition, we have aligned incentive structures so that people are paid to co-operate. It is a mistake to require synergy everywhere, and there have been huge amounts of time wasted as people attempted to get co-operation when it made no sense. But we have made sure that people get good marks for working together, and incentives are supposed to make it worth their while to work together. We have a separate bonus pool to reward people for collaboration. Also, we have management training where managers from different businesses come together and get to know and understand one another.

Enter investment banking

More needs to be said, however, regarding how these business clusters came into existence and what their rationale is. Perhaps the most significant driving forces were the deregulation of investment banking in 1986 with Big Bang, and the consequent rise of capital markets products, replacing traditional banking products. Barclays responded to Big Bang much more aggressively than did NatWest or Midland, reflecting cultural differences between Barclays and its clearing competitors.

Due in part to Barclays' informal, family culture that emphasized partnership values and led to its being a first-mover, entrepreneurial bank, Barclays moved into investment banking with more alacrity than its competitors. It paid heavily for one of the leading London brokers, de Zoete & Bevan, and one of the leading jobbers, Wedd Durlacher. The new investment bank was soon given the acronym, BZW.

A bold early step was to recruit Sir Martin Jacomb, an investment banker from Kleinwort Benson, an old-line British merchant bank, as BZW's first chairman. Jacomb, a vice-chairman of Kleinwort, had been trained as a tax barrister and had much wisdom and experience as an investment banking strategist. He had already served on key policy committees of the Bank of England, including one on regulatory reform of the financial markets. The Bank of England had also chosen him to become the first chairman of the Securities and Investments Board, the watchdog agency created to supervise the industry after Big Bang.[22] He turned down the offer. Yet, the offer further reinforced his reputation as a significant British figure in financial services.

Jacomb was thus a member of the financial services industry Establishment, recruited by perhaps the most élite of the British banks to head its new investment banking division. In that sense, the fit between Barclays and Jacomb was very good. To ensure that he and BZW had as much power as possible within Barclays, Jacomb requested that he be made Vice Chair of the whole bank, and it was immediately granted. 'All the senior Barclays managers trusted and had confidence in Jacomb,' explained a board member. 'That included Bevan, a family person who was leaving as CEO; Quinton, a non-family outsider, who was Bevan's successor; and Buxton, who later became CEO and Chairman.'

Barclays' definition of BZW's role within the bank is critical to an understanding of how BZW fared. Of importance are the following:[23]

(1) BZW's substantial independence within the bank in the early years;
(2) severe conflicts that immediately developed between it and the corporate division, requiring much sensitivity and skill in managing;
(3) BZW's absorption over time of virtually all of Barclays' wholesale banking business; and
(4) its emergence in the late 1990s as one of the last remaining British-owned investment banks.

This was the case until Taylor sold it off in late 1997. The fact that Barclays had been the bank of the empire and later became the last hope of British-owned and controlled investment banking made Taylor's decision particularly painful to some in the British banking Establishment.

BZW's independence from the rest of Barclays was explicitly agreed on by senior management from its inception in 1985. The two parts of Barclays were to operate at arm's length. The rationale for this decision included several arguments. First, the new investment banking firms that Barclays had bought wanted much flexibility, so that they would not be held back by the more risk-averse, control-minded culture of the clearing bank. Given the high volatility in their securities markets, requiring much faster action than was commonly practised in commercial banking, such flexibility was important. Also, it would be easier for BZW to keep attracting talented investment bankers (brokers, traders and corporate finance specialists) if these people knew in advance that they would have considerable autonomy.

Finally, with the huge difference in compensation between investment and commercial (clearing) bankers, to insulate them from one another might possibly limit the jealousies that the latter would inevitably feel. Commercial bankers regarded investment bankers as Barclays' prodigal son, resenting deeply the latter's large base salaries and bonuses. One senior commercial manager at Barclays bemoaned in 1995: 'There were a dozen or so in BZW this year who were into seven figures on their compensation. Compare that with my paltry salary and bonus. And, let me tell you, I contribute a lot more to the bottom line here relative to them than the difference in our compensation would suggest.'

Later, in October 1990, Barclays' CEO Sir John Quinton formalized this separateness by announcing a new divisional structure based on what he labelled 'culture' or 'ethos'.[24] He identified two main cultures within Barclays, one in the investment bank and one in the clearing bank, and he built two divisions around them. This was with the help of a banking consultancy group from McKinsey.

Jacomb was to head one division, called Markets and Investment Banking (MIB) and containing global treasury functions and BZW securities businesses. The other division, to be headed by a Barclays clearing banker, Alastair Robinson, was to contain traditional commercial banking businesses. Quinton emphasized in his public announcement that investment banking could only succeed in a commercial bank by preserving its autonomy. He went on to predict that European universal banks would have to follow that model if their investment banking was to be successful. He noted further that the Barclays model was different from the ones that NatWest and Midland followed, implying that it would be more effective as a result.

Over time, investment and corporate banking became much more integrated, but BZW functioned as a separate entity throughout most of its existence. Having reviewed some of the arguments for maintaining its autonomy, it is important to acknowledge the costs. One was that both divisions dealt with many of the same corporate customers, and there was the risk that both would be calling on these customers with overlapping services. This was particularly the case after clearing bankers had been given training in providing new capital markets products. Both felt they owned the customers, resulting in many turf struggles around the world over who had what rights.

The struggles were intensified in the absence of any clear policies from headquarters about which division was responsible for what. A BZW international investment banker explained how it worked:

There was much tension between BZW and the corporate people in London, and it was even worse overseas. The most exciting opportunities for the bank were investment-banking-related, and the clearing branch managers in places like Japan felt it was their area. But BZW was set up as an autonomous divison that reported to nobody, and it was extremely difficult to manage the conflicts that arose. I was in Tokyo, and we in BZW were *at war* with the head of the Barclays branch there. We were a huge threat to him; we never reported to him; his boss and mine were not on good terms; and there was no coherent strategy from London. The result was that enormous energy was wasted fighting over turf. I then went from Tokyo to Hong Kong, where we had a prominent stockbroking and corporate finance operation, and again the conflict was intense.

I know it works much better now, because I keep in touch with them. But it took a lot of strife to get to that point. Immense energy was spent in management discussions arguing for territory. It was such a waste, but there seemed no other way.

One area of strong overlap was corporate underwriting. Each party felt it was their jurisdiction, and there was much duplication. This confused customers and took up much managerial time within Barclays. The problems were most pronounced during the first 4–5 years of BZW's existence. After that, they got sorted out, with BZW taking on more and more of the wholesale business.[25]

A prime example of how BZW took on Barclays' previously failing wholesale banking was its operations in the US. Taylor announced, in November 1994, that since New York City is a capital-markets centre of the world, he wanted BZW to have a significant presence there. He also characterized the 1980s as an era of 'extreme promiscuity' in Barclays' international wholesale banking, indicating his intention of grafting an investment banking business onto what was left of it. The approach in the US, he continued, was to have fewer and deeper relationships with big corporations, shrinking the number of customers from 900 to 200 and pulling out completely from US retail and small business finance.[26]

Jacomb's successor as chairman of BZW, Sir Peter Middleton, who arrived in late 1991, said of the US strategy: 'We took it over almost in total – all the corporate lending – with an idea of making it a more integrated corporate business. Although everything in the US isn't BZW, it all came under the general BZW umbrella.' After that, BZW followed the same strategy of taking over the large corporate business in Asia and Europe.[27]

Summary of 'two into four'

In summary, the Barclays strategy with regard to incorporating investment banking into its large clearing bank was first to have BZW as a free-standing division and later to integrate it by having it take over and absorb corporate banking. The original separatist approach was justified in large part through the differences between the businesses. Since the bank's traditional banking culture was a conventional and measured one, in contrast to with the more glamorous but risky one of investment banking, the rationale was that it would be very difficult to manage both without smothering the entrepreneurial strengths of investment banking.

By 1992, a new strategy and organizational design had emerged, namely to integrate or unify most of Barclays' wholesale banking under BZW.[28] This made sense from many perspectives. First, profit margins in the traditional corporate loan business had become low or non-existent, as new capital markets products were replacing it. And Barclays needed a major overhaul of its international wholesale banking anyway, for reasons already discussed. There was also an obvious need, in particular, to manage the duplication between investment and corporate banking, since it was annoying to customers and the internal conflicts were consuming valuable managerial time.

The integration involved BZW taking over Barclays' treasury operations, along with other corporate loan and advisory-related businesses. This also included building a corporate-finance capability within BZW, something that it had not as yet done – nor was it effective in doing so for several years after that.

Integrating the investment bank with commercial banking was no easy task. As one BZW executive said: 'We had always been regarded as a rather precocious and spoiled child by a lot of people, so delivering a large amount of the family silver to us was controversial. It looked as though this cuckoo was grabbing everything. It highlighted the divisiveness within the Barclays stable. Barclays had to reap the whirlwind internally, because of the non-hierarchical nature of BZW and because the pay differentials were so pronounced.'[29]

Managing recent conflicts

Barclays' handling of the recent conflicts between its investment and commercial bankers may provide some guidelines for the many other commercial banks worldwide, including those in the US, that incorporate an investment bank. Several of Barclays' initiatives, both planned and unplanned, helped in managing the conflict, although it remained a source of bad feeling for many on both sides.

A first lesson stems from its hiring of Jacomb as Chair of BZW. As an outsider to Barclays, not initially aligned with either the commercial or investment bankers, he had early legitimacy with both. Though he had been associated before with an investment bank and had been trained as a tax barrister, he could play a third-party, mediator role between the sides more credibly than if he had been identified professionally as either a commercial or an investment banker.

Beyond that, he had further credibility because of his broader policy role and reputation in London as a leading figure in financial services regulation. Moreover, as a senior manager at Kleinwort Benson, he was seen as a strong strategist, having just previously played a leading role in the privatization of British Telecom. And, within Barclays, the fact that he was immediately made Vice Chair also enhanced his standing. In brief, having a strong, highly regarded leader, whom both sides respected and trusted, provided a good start in managing such a high-conflict situation.

Jacomb's position was also enhanced by having as his associate, his number two, a strong ally in Lord Camoys, who also had experience and credibility within Barclays. Lord Camoys had been the CEO of Barclays' Merchant Bank since 1978. He had orchestrated the executive search that resulted in Jacomb's appointment, and they worked together very closely. 'Camoys in the early years was good to work with,' recalled a senior Barclays manager. 'He was there all the way through as a credible ally, and that also helped. His background was as a banker, originally at Rothschild and then at American Express International.'

Fortuitous developments also helped ease the conflicts. One was BZW's big losses in the stockmarket crash of 1987 – it lost £75 million in one day. This was a humbling experience for the investment bankers and minimized their arrogance at an early stage. 'We got a mixture of both sympathy and superiority from the clearing bankers on that one,' recalled a BZW banker. Most importantly, senior managers at Barclays reaffirmed their support for BZW, while its separate groups came together more. As Lorenz reported in his historical account: 'We blinked about 42 times and thought, "God, what have we got into?",' recalled Buxton. 'But there was never a serious, "Let's get out."' [30]

Later, during 1989–92, while the clearing bank side of Barclays suffered, big revenues from BZW helped keep Barclays somewhat intact, and that also improved the relationship. As a bank analyst stated:

> Corporate banking absolutely haemorrhaged money for many years, and it wasn't until 1992 that Barclays realized how much. It slashed the corporate lending and selling businesses. BZW began doing better, and Barclays got BZW, with its new CEO, Sir Peter Middleton, to take over the mess. This was the first example of BZW taking over all large corporate lending, first in the US and then in Europe and Asia.

Beginning in 1992, relations between BZW and Barclays' clearing bank improved somewhat. The main development was to transfer more and more of commercial banking – Treasury and corporate loans – to BZW. The conflict was still intense, however, making it very difficult to manage notwithstanding the credibility of Jacomb and Lord Camoys, their skills, and the fortuitous events described above.

Cultural differences

One reason this conflict continued related to sharp differences between the investment and clearing bankers in culture, in career commitments, and in compensation. They were not at all unique to Barclays, but they were very intense there. Even leaders with Jacomb's and Middleton's skills were not going to be able to eliminate mutual hostilities of these groups from at least occasionally erupting and affecting their performance.

The culture conflict relates to sharp social class and educational differences between the two. Quite consistently, the investment bankers had university training and regarded themselves as several cuts above the clearing bankers, the vast majority of whom were still non-university. The head of NatWest's investment bank reported, for example, in late 1995, that he had a hundred PhDs and five hundred MAs among his six thousand investment bankers, with over 90 per cent university-trained. By contrast, the numbers in the retail bank were roughly the reverse, with around 10 per cent being university graduates.

Traders and corporate finance bankers regarded the clearing bankers as risk-averse, rigid and bureaucratic in their work habits, uncultured, and ignorant of new capital markets products. Clearing bankers returned the favour with their own negative stereotypes: they saw investment bankers as undisciplined, loose cannons, often out of control, as making enormous bonus and salary demands, as holding the bank hostage if it didn't meet those demands, and as having little or no loyalty to the bank.

Differences in career aspirations

Differences in careers, labour markets, and organizational loyalty were also sources of conflict. The vast majority of clearing bankers entered the bank in an era when there was an implicit psychological contract for lifetime employment and when a 'no-poaching' rule prevailed. They had been employed at one bank all their working lives and could be characterized as extreme 'locals' in career orientation.

The investment bankers operate in different labour markets and with different career orientations. Their primary reference group of colleagues are not so much others within the bank of their present employment, but rather their peers elsewhere in investment banking. They are thus 'cosmopolitans' in career orientation. If they are unhappy about their compensation or working conditions within a commercial bank, they often either leave or threaten to leave – in each instance with the understanding that their team – of swaps specialists or derivatives traders, say – might leave with them.

Differences in the levels of control

Investment bankers also like a lot of autonomy, making them difficult to manage. Efforts to build collaborative teams with other product specialists and with commercial bankers thus face big obstacles.

Furthermore, the fact that their tasks are more non-routine and require much creativity – for example in putting together deals, providing advisory services, or structuring new hedging products – make investment bankers' contributions very different from those of clearing bankers. Investment banking operates much like a 'professional bureaucracy', such as a law firm or a hospital, where the professionals carry out the main production activities and are subject to minimal managerial controls. They like to operate in flat, decentralized organizations with minimum constraints on what they do. And many equate management with oppressive interference, making it even more difficult to monitor and regulate their behaviour.

Managing the differences

Managing conflicts, then, between bankers living in these two separate worlds was extremely difficult. Tensions consistently erupted over compensation. Jacomb and his colleagues used a wide array of arguments. One was to point out to the clearing bankers that external labour-market forces was the determining factor in compensation differences and that the clearing bankers should not take it personally. A senior manager at BZW recalled: 'We were able to communicate to the clearing bankers that the pay of the investment bankers was the market's fault, not ours. The clearing bankers got to understand the market rules. There was no way of completely eliminating this problem of jealousy, since envy is a powerful force, but we were able to manage it. We had industrialists on our board who couldn't understand the huge bonuses and compensation demands of our investment bankers. And we did lose people who felt we weren't paying them enough.'

One action Barclays *did* take was to raise the compensation for the clearers above market rates. That seemed to help their morale. On the other side, it exercised some controls over the investment bankers. It developed various tie-in policies whereby some of the investment bankers' bonuses were a function of the extent of their teamwork activity and some to Barclays' overall profits. Also, some of the investment bankers' compensation was in bank shares rather than cash. 'We did get more institutional loyalty from some investment bankers as a result of these policies,' explained a senior manager in BZW, who went on:

> Also, once people saw we were winners or possible winners, we were able to get more loyalty. Our early success and our commitment of capital to investment banking helped win over some investment bankers. They had a fear of being swept away by the clearing bankers, and now they know it will not happen and that Barclays is a strong and great institution to be affiliated with. The fact that we did not cower in the face of our losses at the end of the eighties and in the early nineties also helped.

Other tactics that the BZW leadership used included finding moderates on each side who were more tolerant of the other side than many of their colleagues. It then built coalitions of support through those people, and that further helped bridge the gap, even encouraging some collaboration.

Finally, if all these tactics didn't help, Barclays' senior management used a blunt and more direct approach, particularly in managing the commercial bankers' jealousies. A senior manager went over the arguments: 'First, we tell the commercial bankers that their job is less stressful, less susceptible to burnout than for investment bankers. Then we tell the commercial bankers that if any of them want to be traders, they are welcome to try it. They never take us up on it. And, third, they know we are paying more than market to many of our good commercial bankers and firing the bad investment bankers, and that helps. The commercial bankers see more justice in that, because there is more justice.'

Ultimately, the leadership that Jacomb, Camoys, Middleton and their colleagues provided could only be judged by BZW's financial performance. The first four years, which included the stockmarket crash of 1987 and many start-up costs, were almost by definition not going to be big revenue-producing ones. They were perhaps best summarized in the *Financial Times* thus: 'By any normal test of performance, its [BZW's] first four years seem a very expensive mistake for Barclays. Rather than a success, the best that can be said for it is that BZW has not been as big a failure as others.'[31]

Starting in 1992, when BZW absorbed much of Barclays' wholesale business, its contribution to the bottom line started to pick up. Global investment banking, however, was increasingly consolidated and competitive, and there was the serious question as to whether BZW could break in. It was not at all clear whether there was in fact a market niche that it could fill, at the same time boosting its financial performance to a level that would justify its continued existence. Competing with top universal banks of Germany and Switzerland, the hope was that Barclays might become become, in Middleton's words, 'the pre-eminent European investment bank'.

Acknowledging that BZW could not compete with US giants raised serious questions as to its capability to be a serious player in Europe. That in itself was a challenging goal, particularly in view of the investment requirements in compensation, technology, facilities and client building. Moreover, none of the European universal banks had done that well in investment banking, suggesting that either they did not have the management capability to develop an appropriate infrastructure, including maintaining some minimal cost controls, or they lacked other core competences associated with having the right investment banking products.[32]

Thus, notwithstanding the leadership and many seemingly effective efforts of Barclays' and BZW's management in handling internal process problems around the conflicts and jealousies mentioned above, BZW continued to pull down the bank's bottom line in the middle and late 1990s. It still involved enormous compensation costs, along with those of technology investment, to build an international presence so that it could compete. And maintaining its presence as the last of Britain's locally owned investment banks seemed a dubious distinction.

In any event, if Barclays were to continue with BZW, it was going to take many more years to catch up in market share with the big US investment banks, if that were ever a possibility.

In that context, it seemed a particularly appropriate decision for CEO Martin Taylor to sell off many parts of BZW. While he was not necessarily making Barclays just a high street bank, he was now heading in that direction. He was behaving in that respect much like Sir Brian Pitman had with Lloyds, starting in 1983. It was, however, a bit late for Barclays to be reversing course, since Taylor had only been at Barclays for just under four years – and one can make a compelling argument that it takes at least that long to begin to turn around a large, bureaucratic, encrusted institution such as Barclays.

Notes and references

1. Steven I. Davis, *Excellence in Banking*, St Martins, New York, 1985, Ch. 1.
2. *Financial Times*, 3 October 1997.
3. *The Economist*, 8 November 1997.
4. Interviews with bank analysts.
5. *Financial Times*, 28 November 1997.
6. See 'Family Vault', *Independent*, 24 January 1993, pp. 12–14; Derek F. Channon, *Cases in Bank Strategic Management and Marketing*, Wiley, New York, 1986, pp. 291–8.
7. From interviews with bank analysts.
8. In 1984, Steven Davis's panel of distinguished bank watchers, while selecting Barclays among its top 16 international banks, indicated that Barclays had lost its leadership position of several years before. Davis, *Excellence in Banking*, St Martin's, New York, 1985, p. 12. In Davis's next book, *Managing Change in the Excellent Banks*, St. Martin's, New York, 1989, the same panel had selected NatWest but not Barclays among its top 16. He concluded (p. 7): 'National Westminster Bank was beginning to overtake Barclays in most performance indicators when the panel voted in 1985, and relative performance since then has confirmed National Westminster – at least until now! – as the choice of analysts looking primarily at the numbers.'
9. Michael Collins, *Money and Banking in the UK*: a History, Croom Helm, London, 1988, pp. 75–9.
10. *Independent*, 24 January 1993, p. 13.
11. Interviews with Professor Leslie Hannah, City University, London.
12. Channon, *op. cit.*, pp. 272ff.
13. *Ibid.*, p. 281–7.
14. Derek F. Channon, *British Banking Strategy*, Macmillan, London and Basingstoke, 1977, pp. 126–9.
15. Lehman Brothers, *UK Clearing Banks, 1996 Annual Review*, 29 April 1996, pp. 60–1.

16. Harold Van B. Cleveland and Thomas E. Huertas, *Citibank: 1812–1970*, Harvard University Press, Cambridge MA, 1985, pp. 284–5.
17. Lehman Brothers, *UK Clearing Banks, 1998 Annual Review*, 23 July 1998, p. 66.
18. *Annual Abstract of Banking Statistics*, Vol. 14, 1997, British Bankers' Association, p. 66.
19. Lehman Brothers, *UK Clearing Banks, 1998 Annual Review*, pp. 70–1.
20. From interviews for this book.
21. A version of this structure as it existed in 1995 appears in Lehman Brothers, *UK Clearing Banks, 1996 Annual Review*, 29 April 1996, p. 58.
22. Andrew Lorenz, *BZW: The First Ten Years*, published as a book by BZW, October 1996, p. 26.
23. *Ibid.*
24. *Financial Times*, 1 November 1990.
25. Lorenz, *op. cit.*, Ch. 7.
26. *Financial Times*, 10 November 1990.
27. Lorenz, *op. cit.*, p. 132.
28. *Ibid.*, Ch. 6.
29. *Ibid.*, p. 87.
30. *Ibid.*, p. 46.
31. *Financial Times*, 18 April 1991.
32. *The Economist*, 21 June 1997, pp. 71–3; and 13 December 1997, pp. 61–3.

6 Leadership: from Vision to Implementation

HAVING ANALYSED Barclays' evolution in the 1980s and 1990s as a universal bank and its withdrawal in late 1997 from investment banking, we turn now to the critical role of leadership. I use that term in two senses: First, having the vision to understand what strategies are likely to be successful in the turbulent environment of financial services; and, second, developing the organizational infrastructure to implement those strategies.

It was a much more complex challenge to provide effective leadership at Barclays than at Lloyds. Barclays was bigger and more diverse than Lloyds, and because of both these factors it has had many more vested interests and fiefdoms. Furthermore, Barclays has had the singular tradition of the founding families. Institutions bear the stamp of their origins and history, and that is particularly true in nations that emphasize tradition as much as Britain does.

We have discussed the benefits and costs of Barclays' family traditions. While it was true that this influence contributed to the bank's partnership culture and its often entrepreneurial, first-mover strategy, there was a potential downside to that influence as well. The families had the power, and they usually exercised it to exclude outsiders from becoming CEO. This not only limited the access of outstanding people to that position, but it contributed as well to the exodus of some potential leaders, thereby depleting the bank of a critical resource. While that may have been irrelevant by the time Martin Taylor arrived in 1994, it had sometimes denied Barclays the leadership so badly needed since the 1970s, in the increasingly competitive environment of financial services.

Barclays had another characteristic that reinforced its family dominance. It combined the authority and power of the CEO and board chair in one position. Moreover, from its founding in 1896 until

1987, it had only one outsider in the position. This was during and just after World War II, and the incumbent was regarded both inside and outside the bank as an interim leader, filling the post for a family member until he could return.[1]

Pulling in the reins

1981 marked the first problematic selection of a family member as chairman. At that time, an outstanding non-family candidate, Deryk VanderWeyer, was available. Instead, a family insider, Sir Timothy Bevan, was chosen. VanderWeyer had risen to become head of Group Finance and Planning within Barclays and was widely regarded within Barclays and outside as one of its most innovative bankers; many regarded him as a logical choice for the position.[2] However, family and non-family insiders felt that he did not have the depth of contacts within financial and related institutions in the City that Bevan had. There were also questions about his openly expressed antagonism to the families and to particular individuals such as Bevan.

It is not at all clear, however, that he would have been chosen had he been less outspoken in the years leading up to the decision. One top member of staff recalled: 'Deryk VanderWeyer was quite creative and brilliant about everything. He knew he would never become chair, and he could not get on with Bevan. So that was it for him. He was also outspoken and wanted to cut down the family fiefdoms. He was right, but that did not endear him with the family.' Another senior manager at Barclays, even closer to the decision, had a vivid recollection of the events:

> Yes, it is true that some exceptional people left senior management because they were non-family and did not expect to go any higher. VanderWeyer was the one I knew best, since he brought me in. I don't mean to be disrespectful to the others to say that he was by far the best and miles better than anybody else for the position. And he should have been made chairman.

Bevan was Chairman from 1981 until 1987, when he reached retirement age, though he stayed on as a board member. While the end of that period marked Barclays' bold foray into investment banking, Bevan's administration is widely regarded as a time when Barclays lost its momentum as a leading UK bank. One staff person noted: 'Bevan had held Barclays back in the 1980s, largely because we had previously suffered such losses in property loans. So he pursued a policy of selective and limited loans after that, and he was tight-fisted.' A senior manager was more critical: 'It is true that a lot of people left – for example, Deryk VanderWeyer. Had he become chairman, the bank would have been much stronger. Bevan was terribly cautious, and we were slipping badly in the early 1980s.'

Expansion under Quinton

Sir John Quinton, a non-family banker, became Chairman in 1987. He was intent on restoring Barclays to its former position of leadership in British banking. As Quinton was quoted at the time:[3]

> We have found our competitive position coming under pressure to the point where we lost our long-established position as Britain's biggest and most profitable bank. I know from the recent staff attitude survey that our staff like it as little as I do.

Quinton and some of his senior colleagues thus saw Barclays as needing to re-establish itself as a leading British bank. In the 1980s, NatWest had passed Barclays in asset size, profits and reputation. A major article at that time in *The Economist* referred to NatWest as the 'top British bank', noting it was the only one rated triple-A by Standard & Poor.[4]

Thus, 'Number One in '91' became a motto of Quinton's administration. A Cambridge graduate and son of a Barclays banker, Quinton's appointment was greeted with much optimism within the bank. He had joined it in 1953 and had particularly strong support in the branches and in the UK retailing group. For such a person to be selected as combined CEO and Chair meant that he had exceptional qualities. Indeed, Quinton was often lumped with VanderWeyer as one of Barclays' ablest bankers of his generation.[5]

Quinton was a person of enormous energy, bent on promoting Barclays' expansion into investment banking and particularly into wholesale and retail banking in Europe. In addition, Quinton was a person with a strong sense of social responsibility, genuinely interested in how Barclays' financial services had historically helped improve economic opportunities for minorities – particularly the black population in various African nations and the immigrant Jews in the East End of London.[6]

Reflecting these qualities, Quinton was dedicated to having Barclays become more customer-friendly in its retail branches. Barclays under Quinton's leadership became the first clearing bank to keep its branches open on Saturdays. That leadership was reported to have been one main reason that he won the Chair position in May 1987.[7]

The dominant motifs of Quinton's years were those of loan growth and expansion – particularly in global wholesale banking – and in investment banking, and of cutting costs and improving marketing in UK retail banking. The latter brought an emphasis on having the branches develop more of a sales culture and cultivating a more responsive relationship with customers. All of these goals were designed to restore Barclays to its past eminence. Unfortunately, for Barclays and for Quinton, he did not succeed in his cost-cutting goals. Indeed, the loan growth and expansion were at cross purposes with cost cutting.

Some of Quinton's specific actions in his push for growth were a massive £920 million rights issue in late 1988, followed by a vast expansion of loan volume and acquisitions. The biggest concentration of new loans was in commercial real-estate development projects, while the main acquisitions were of Merck Finck, a private, family bank in Germany, and of Compagnie Européenne de Banque in France. As summarized in *The Economist* in 1988: 'After keeping tight control of its loan book from 1983 to 1986, Barclays is now lending money hand over fist.'[8]

The financial press described Quinton's strategy in both positive and negative terms, with the latter increasing as the recession deepened and as Barclays' financial performance deteriorated. As late as 18 February 1991, however, several years into the recession, he was still portrayed as 'breathing new life into a sleepy bank'.[9] Starting a few months earlier, however, there were also increasing references to his 'dash for growth', and to his having a 'voracious appetite for European growth'.[10] Given Britain's deepening recession at the time, the implication of these descriptions was that Barclays' expansionism was ill-timed.

Throughout 1990, Quinton had sounded optimistic about his strategy, referring to Barclays as one of the most strongly capitalized banks in the world.[11] But the bank was steadily declining in financial performance. By early 1991, he acknowledged an 'overexpansion of lending', and in April 1991, the bank issued a curious statement to the effect that Quinton would continue as Chair for several more years.[12] This was reportedly to quell rumours that Sir Peter Middleton, a highly publicized recruit from Britain's Treasury Department, was soon to be next in line for the position.

Several fortuitous developments came together to make Quinton's situation as chairman increasingly tenuous. One was the poor timing of his expansionist strategy. Barclays was in many respects replicating in more extreme form a common practice of commercial banks around the world. This was to book more loans at the end of an economic expansion cycle, only to get caught holding them and having them turn sour when a recession set in soon afterwards. The UK experienced a severe recession from 1988 until early 1992, and Barclays' dismal financial performance in those years reflected how ill-advised this loan expansion strategy had been. For example, its return on equity after taxes averaged just under 4 per cent per annum from 1989 until 1992, and it was −6.3 per cent in 1992 itself.[13]

Meanwhile, Barclays' senior managers were late in understanding and acknowledging the problems. Andrew Buxton, for example, who was to become Quinton's successor as Chair in 1992, stated in March 1990: 'We are not worried by our exposure to the property market.'[14] In retrospect, he and his colleagues should have been very worried.

A second critical event was Quinton's heart bypass surgery in early 1990, followed by complications. He soon regained much of his energy and returned to work, but the health problem kept him away at a critical time when major decisions were being made as to what Barclays should do with its big infusion of capital from the rights issue.

Although Quinton did return full time to the bank soon after his surgery, Barclays' performance in 1990 and 1991 was poor. Its cost/income ratio went up from 64 per cent in 1990 to 66 per cent in 1991, and its return on equity was dropping steadily. Meanwhile, Barclays was referred to as 'the most expansionist of the UK's biggest banks',[15] and by early Spring 1992 as engaged in 'overzealous property lending, ill judged', with Quinton nevertheless quoted as stressing the bank's relatively cautious approach to the property sector.[16]

Then, suddenly, in late April 1992, Quinton resigned. He had planned to retire within the next year or two, but the financial press reported that his board pushed him out.[17] Knowledgeable observers inside and outside the bank generally concurred that he was pushed to early retirement. One former Barclays member of staff recalled: 'Quinton was badly treated. He was sacked. There were always other signatures besides his on those loans that turned sour, and Buxton in particular was just as instrumental as he. It was a small gang of five directors who literally pushed him out. He was not only a decent man, but he was a quite competent banker.'

Though Quinton denied that he had been pushed out, one non-executive director explained that a fresh team was needed at the top as soon as possible. This director went on to say that the board felt changes were needed – sooner than Quinton had envisaged – to address problems of escalating costs.[18] Quinton's resignation was most unexpected and sudden, even though the board identified his management style as contributing to Barclays' poor performance. They commented, for example, on how its costs had risen more rapidly than those of its main rivals.

In retrospect, there are varying interpretations of Quinton's role in Barclays' poor performance. His supporters argue that he was made the scapegoat for systemic weaknesses within the bank and for decisions that some of his senior management colleagues had made. His critics meanwhile argue that these problems took place during his tenure and that he should be held accountable.

Perhaps in part to shape future historical judgements on these events, Quinton identified Buxton as an active participant in Barclays' go-for-growth policies. In an interview for the 3 December 1992 issue of *European Banker*, he also went on to describe how Barclays 'went off the rails' in the late 1980s because of poor communications between HQ and regional offices, where commercial property lending took place.

Some observers, including staff within Barclays, reported that Quinton was ill-served by a relatively weak senior management group who reassured him that the commercial real-estate loans were sound. Recall, for example, the quote from Buxton in March 1990 that Barclays was not worried by its exposure to the property market.[19]

The argument citing weak senior management gains credibility when juxtaposed with board members' comments six months after Quinton's stepping down as Chair that they were looking actively for outside rather than inside candidates to replace him. As the *Financial Times* reported: 'Several board members believe that a vacuum of talent exists near the top of Barclays and are looking around outside for a new CEO.' Later in the same article, there is reference to the 'weak management culture' at Barclays that generated the lending binge from 1986 until 1990.[20]

A return to family

Quinton's immediate successor, Andrew Buxton, was the last of the old family grandees. Since he had participated actively in the commercial real-estate lending and had signed off some of the bigger loans, the board's rewarding him with this appointment gave at least an appearance of family favouritism. It was not clear to many observers why he should be spared while Quinton was not. The Lex column in the *Financial Times* of 25 April 1992 thus refers to Buxton's promotion as 'perplexing', arguing that 'he must take a share of the blame for the lax cost control which has been a substantial part of Barclays problem'.

Though not known as a charismatic or visionary leader, Buxton had gained respect within Barclays as a solid, capable banker, notwithstanding its poor performance in the late eighties and early nineties.[21] He had joined the bank in 1963, after graduating from Oxford, and started as a clerk in a West London branch. He made a fast rise in the 1980s, to head a new corporate banking division and as temporary acting CEO at BZW in 1987, when Lord Camoys suffered a stroke.[22] A year later, he became Group Managing Director, and in April 1992, when Quinton resigned, he was appointed CEO and Chair.

Though the board gave Buxton a vote of confidence by appointing him, he nevertheless came under continued attack from the institutional shareholders for holding both the chair and CEO positions. The board defended the arrangement, with Sir Peter Middleton arguing that, in fact, the bank had one chairman and three CEOs – one for each of its three main divisions. However, some large shareholders remained unconvinced.[23]

The famous Cadbury Committee on corporate governance published a report at that time, arguing strongly that the two positions should be separate in all large institutions. Its rationale was that there should be checks and balances in top management, rather than centralizing so much power in one person.[24] At the end of 1992, Buxton gave up the CEO position and settled for being solely Chairman.

Throughout these succession decisions, from the appointment in 1981 of the insider Bevan over VanderWeyer, to the appointment in 1987 of the outsider Quinton, to that of Buxton as Quinton's successor in 1992, there were continual allusions to the role of the Barclays families in the decisions. Reference was made to the families' exclusivity, Quinton's ascendance being the exception.[25]

When Buxton was appointed Chair and CEO, family dominance was seen once more as a driving force. He was referred to as having been passed over for the chairmanship in 1987 only because of his youth. It was reported as 'common gossip in the bank that Sir John Quinton was only supposed to be "keeping the seat warm for Andrew".'[26] Furthermore, VanderWeyer's son, then a banking reporter for *The*

Spectator, wrote a strong article shortly after Buxton was appointed to the effect that family favouritism still prevailed at Barclays.

Enter Martin Taylor

In late 1992, Barclays began a search for an outsider to fill the CEO position that Buxton had been occupying. Just as this search got underway, senior managers engaged in an unprecedented act of public hand-wringing. Given the bank's past pride and reputation, this was an unusual display. 'We are not doing well, we are not giving our shareholders value, and we have got to do better,' said Buxton. 'We must learn from the mistakes of the past, and improve substantially,' said Alastair Robinson, director of the banking division. 'I don't know if we were dumber than others, but we were certainly dumb,' said Joseph DeFeo, director of service businesses.[27]

Since the major shareholders had expressed much anger about the bank's performance and about Buxton's holding both the CEO and chair positions, these public statements seemed designed to provide re-assurance that Barclays had indeed embarked on a radical break with the past. 'If results do not improve in time, I would sack us all, and rightly so,' said DeFeo.

The selection of Martin Taylor may well have marked such a significant break with Barclays' past. At first glance, his background and skills did not appear particularly appropriate to providing the kind of transformational leadership that the bank needed. One board member active in the search had the following recollection of how Taylor compared with the other candidates on the short-list: 'We had people on that list who were able investment bankers but knew little about commercial banking. And we had others who were leading commercial bankers but knew little about investment banking. Martin Taylor didn't have any direct experience in either field.'

Despite such inexperience, Taylor had many qualities that made him an ideal choice. A Mandarin scholar and Oxford graduate, only 41 years old, he had already had two successful careers. His first was as a journalist for the *Financial Times*, where he was widely regarded as a 'brilliant' writer and analyst and where he had much initial contact with financial services. He often wrote about the banks in that paper's respected Lex column. His second sucessful career was as Chairman and CEO since 1987 of a large conglomerate, Courtaulds Textiles, where he was regarded as a 'brilliant hands-on manager'.[28]

Taylor's particularly positive qualifications for the position at Barclays included his extensive managerial experience at Courtaulds and his charismatic personality, the latter contributing to his ability while there to charm shareholders, analysts and journalists alike.[29] The job at Courtaulds involved transforming a fragmented conglomerate into a much more focused corporation, including in the effort the closing down of 20 of the company's 23 UK spinning mills, the divestment of non-core businesses, and the elimination of levels in the chain of command. Also, nearly a third of Courtaulds sales went to Marks & Spencer, and Taylor had worked closely with that firm, thereby learning much about retailing, a major part of Barclays business.

In brief, as banking evolved from a protected and highly regulated business to a much more competitive one, it needed the managerial skills of people who had experience in the latter. And Barclays was no exception. Given its particularly erratic performance in the eighties and nineties, it needed a CEO with management skills in strategic analysis to help focus on core business competencies, possibly to divest itself of businesses peripheral to that core, and to develop the organizational infrastructure needed for effective implementation. One might argue that CEOs from large manufacturing organizations in mature industries were ideally suited to managing these issues in financial services firms, especially given that the latter were facing similar competitive threats that manufacturers had at an earlier time.

Moreover, banking is in many respects a reputational business, and Martin Taylor's skills in dealing with the analysts, the institutional shareholders, and the media were invaluable for Barclays at the time he became CEO. The bank had gone through a period when its reputation had been seriously damaged by bad loans and questionable acquisitions. Indeed, Martin Taylor was soon regarded as a 'breath of fresh air' among the British clearing banks. 'He was a refreshing person in a closed world,' remarked one banking writer. 'He developed a large fan club, of which I am obviously a member.'

Many observers characterized Taylor's public presentations to these groups as 'electric' in quality, reflecting a combination of analytical brilliance, charm and grace that made him by far one of the most celebrated CEOs in Britain. 'His great public profile gives Barclays an extra fifty basis points,' stated a bank analyst, 'and that's not to be taken lightly.'

The future of Barclays was to depend heavily on the leadership that Taylor provided. It would most likely have to be transformational, given Barclays' particularly poor performance in the years leading up to his appointment and given the increasingly competitive threats that the British banks faced.

When he was appointed, Taylor indicated that 'if at the end of two years – and two years is a deliberate time frame – the business has no direction, then that will be my fault.'[30] In retrospect, this was asking a lot of himself, given what we know about the difficulties of turning around a large, encrusted institution such as Barclays.

Taylor also made many forthright and provocative statements about Barclays in his first few months as CEO that indicated both his keen analytical skills and the fact that his appointment had brought to the bank a seemingly fresh and new perspective. In brief, he looked well qualified for the task.

One of Taylor's most compelling early observations related to what he described as the limited management sophistication in financial services firms. Although he referred in his remarks to the industry at large, he was most likely commenting on Barclays as well, since his most direct experiences were there. 'I am absolutely astonished,' he observed 'that what seem to me to be ordinary management principles are not yet established in this industry.'[31]

He then went on to describe Barclays in particular as 'stuffy, pompous, and snobbish', with 'no strong group identity', 'far too status-conscious for [his] taste', and having 'old-fashioned military traditions'. It was comments such as these, highlighting the over-bureaucratic and stultifying aspects of British banks in general – and of Barclays in particular – that endeared Taylor to many knowledge-able outside observers who were impatient with the bank's decline in recent years. The comments were also reportedly welcomed among many staff within Barclays, who felt unduly constrained by its traditions and whose morale went up when they heard their new leader identifying with their concerns.

Over time, as was his style, Taylor made other compelling observations. With regard to Barclays developing more focus – one of his strong concerns – he characterized the 1980s as an era of 'extreme promiscuity', in referring to Barclays' global expansion.[32] Yet, he also indicated the importance of maintaining a strong commitment to investment banking as an inevitable part of being a leading global wholesale bank. He referred, for example, to world financial centres, such as New York City, as places where Barclays should have a significant presence. He was in that sense giving his support to BZW, even to the point of later committing substantial resources to a new London facility at Canary Wharf.

Nevertheless, Taylor acknowledged, in prescient remarks that were to perhaps come back to haunt him in his last year as CEO, that no British bank had yet discovered the full secret of managing a securities business. 'These are relatively new kinds of organization, and there's no template for them,' he said, shortly before taking office.[33]

Is transformational leadership possible at Barclays?

In November 1998 Taylor resigned, just short of five years in office. At the time of writing, soon after, an initial assessment of his leadership can be made. This assessment should also include discussion as to whether any single leader, regardless of his or her skills, can transform an institution such as Barclays at this point in its history and in the turbulent market environment of financial services.

Until his last year as CEO, Taylor did well on many counts. Barclays' post-tax return on equity rose from 5.9 per cent in 1993, just before he took office, to 22.9 per cent in 1996. It then declined to 15.2 per cent in 1997, reflecting in large part the bank's losses in investment banking and in the sale of various parts of BZW. Other indicators were equally strong. Profits before taxes rose from £647 million in 1993 to £2.31 billion in 1996, with a decline to £1.72 billion in 1997. Earnings per share rose in that period more than fivefold, from 19.2 pence in 1993 to 104.2 pence in 1996. The decline to 74.4 pence per share in 1997 still represented a quadrupling from 1993.[34]

A negative marker was the cost/income ratio, which rose from 62.3 per cent in 1993 to 68.5 per cent in 1997.[35] Nevertheless, the authors of Lehman Brothers' annual review concluded in 1998: 'Barclays' financial performance over the past five years has been impressive.'[36] They also noted: 'Barclays is generating an ROE at least equal to the sector average.'[37]

Clearly, Britain's economic recovery after 1992 contributed to Barclays' improved performance, just as the world capital markets' increased volatility and investment banks' consequently large trading losses in 1997 affected its decline.

One point of comparison is between Martin Taylor and Sir Brian Pitman, Lloyds' CEO from 1984 to 1986. Pitman had radically transformed Lloyds during his tenure. The fact that Lloyds far outperformed the other clearing banks on virtually every financial effectiveness indicator and was described in 1998 as having 'established itself as the UK's most profitable and best-positioned retail financial services group' is an indication of the quality of Pitman's leadership.[38]

Pitman had 13 years in which to establish these results, however, in contrast to five for Taylor. Also, Pitman was dealing with a much smaller and more manageable organization than was Taylor, and it operated in a less turbulent market. Lloyds did not have the huge international businesses, the history of families (however attenuated they had become by 1994) and the many baronies spread throughout its wholesale and retail businesses. As one banking consultant observed: 'Turning around these huge, supertanker institutions like Barclays and NatWest is a daunting task. Martin Taylor says so many of the right things, but carrying through on what he says is another matter.'

A review of Taylor's early actions suggests many positive changes and at least one unusual omission. Taking the omission first, Taylor made few appointments of outsiders to senior management positions during his first year, and the pattern continued throughout most of his tenure. Turnaround managers in large institutions whose recent performance was as poor as Barclays usually bring in at least *some* new people in senior management positions. In Taylor's case, his not doing so fitted with his expressed intention of maintaining the best of Barclays' managers and culture while still sweeping away some of its unproductive past.[39] It probably also reflected his confidence in the capabilities of many of Barclays' senior managers, as well as his desire to maintain morale within the institution. In any event, there seemed a significant gap between his incisive public statements criticizing the bank and his limited personnel changes in senior management.

The actions that Taylor took tended to be incremental, save his sudden October 1997 decision to sell off much of Barclays' investment bank and his equally sudden resignation in November 1998. Overall, the direction of many of his decisions was similar to that of Pitman at Lloyds. There were no more rights issues; there was much emphasis on gaining more strategic focus, by divesting the bank of loss-making businesses (or at least not growing them); and he instituted an important risk-analysis control system in order to assess the costs and performances of all businesses, helping to make capital allocation decisions more rational.

In addition, Taylor streamlined the headquarters bureaucracy that he found very 'encrusted', shrinking the number of managers there, having the various divisions report directly to him, and revamping the divisions based on the different sets of customers they served. And as

Barclays' profits increased significantly after 1994, Taylor was the first of the clearing bank CEOs to institute shareholder buybacks, rather than simply using the capital to make more loans and acquisitions.

In brief, Barclays became more focused and streamlined than it had been before and less prone to unthinking expansion. Under Taylor, it withdrew from losing commercial real estate and small and medium-sized business loans in France, completed its exit from corporate lending in the US, and replaced the latter by fewer and deeper relationships managed by BZW.

One big difference between Taylor and Pitman was Taylor's continued reluctance to scale down investment banking when its losses started escalating over a period of a year or two and when he was unable to curb them. It was not surprising, then, that as late as August 1997, almost four years into Taylor's term, *The Economist* saw Barclays as an overdiversified firm: 'Far from running the sort of sharply focused firm that tends to please shareholders these days, Mr Taylor's bank looks suspiciously like a doddery old conglomerate.' It concluded that such conglomerates may yet prove to be relics of the past.[40]

Taylor seemed caught, throughout his first three-and-a-half years as CEO, between focusing the bank more on businesses where it had core competences and pursuing global investment banking, where its core competences were uneven at best. He was not alone. NatWest had a similar dilemma; and several European banks (Deutsche, Dredsner, Commerzbank, UBS) were similarly intent on retaining their poorly performing, second-tier investment banks. As one senior manager explained:

> Taylor felt that the two were consistent, making the bank more focused but still pursuing a universal banking strategy. He saw that in the past we were weakly spread all over the world, were far too complex to manage, and [that] we had to do fewer things and do them better. But he still regarded banking as a multiproduct, wholesale and retail business and was not cutting out investment banking.

One way that Taylor tried to make Barclays' multiproduct, wholesale and retail strategy work was to emphasize that all businesses had to reinforce one another. As already discussed, he was convinced there were many synergies in having so many diverse businesses, and he was deeply involved in encouraging them. Many of his presentations to analysts, shareholders, the media and his board were couched in terms of this theme. 'He pushed hard on this and made it very clear that businesses that did not relate to others, and that were instead stand-alone businesses, would be dropped,' explained a senior manager in late 1995.

Abandoning full-scale global investment banking

It was in Taylor's fifth year that, despite his emphasis on synergies and integration across businesses, Barclays still appeared to many outsiders, including *The Economist* writer(s) cited above, as a 'doddery conglomerate', with the investment bank not carrying its weight – and in fact draining shareholder value. Shortly after that negative commentary in *The Economist* in August 1997, Taylor took perhaps his most significant action since arriving at Barclays. On 3 October 1997, he announced Barclays' withdrawal from many aspects of investment banking and his intention to sell off BZW. Although there had been rumours for several months that this might happen, the timing was unexpected and had significant repercussions in Britain and around the world.[41]

Events leading up to this momentous decision included the continued poor performance of BZW over the previous couple of years, accompanied by increasing pressure from institutional shareholders to improve that performance or get out of the business. Rising payroll and technology costs that were required to keep BZW competitive in global investment banking and waves of consolidation that occurred among investment banks made it increasingly difficult to compete. A trigger event may well have been the 1997 merger in the United States of Travelers with Salomon Brothers, sending shock waves around the world. Taylor publicly acknowledged that it had an impact on his exit decision, although it was only the latest of several such mergers. These consolidations often brought increased competition, squeezed fees of all investment banks, and forced increases in the staff costs of second-tier players such as BZW as they competed to hire expensive talent.[42]

It is important to note the differences between the British and the continental European banks in the way that they handled these big losses. The European banks had the same negative results – for instance single-digit ROEs – but their shareholders and boards were much more willing to continue (and even expand) those businesses. Deutschebank's acquisition in late 1998 of Bankers Trust and rumours that Commerzbank and Dredsner Bank may soon be buying investment banks abroad are examples. Part of their willingness to persist in this volatile business is that their domestic retail banking revenues are not nearly as high as those of British banks. More factors are involved, however, and we discuss them in the last chapter of this book.

Stuck in the middle

Before providing our concluding assessment of Martin Taylor's service as Barclays' CEO and its larger implications for the future of British banking, it is important to put his problems with investment banking in a broader perspective. While it is easy in retrospect to criticize Barclays' 13-year effort in investment banking, it had experienced a problem common to many large financial services firms: it was caught up in an industry myth that one had to be a conglomerate wholesale and retail bank to survive and be a world leader.

Given the tremendous rise of capital markets worldwide, as well as declining margins and opportunities in the corporate loan business, any continuation in wholesale financial services seemed to require that one became an investment bank. That industry, however, was highly competitive and produced only very volatile revenues. Moreover, the American 'bulge bracket' (leading) investment banks already had a significant head start and, given that reality along with the wave of recent consolidations, it was becoming increasingly difficult to break in with a catch-up strategy.[43]

Economist and strategy theorist Michael Porter of Harvard Business School has coined the term 'stuck in the middle' to characterize firms like Barclays as it pursued its investment banking strategy.[44] To Porter, 'being "all things to all people" is a recipe for strategic mediocrity and below-average performance'. Porter's notion is that evolutionary market trends limit the number of niches that firms in an industry can fill as high performers, given their core competences and the cost of growing or buying their way in. This, in turn, leads to a shake-out process, resulting in a decreasing number of successful firms that fit particular niches. Many others then 'fall between the cracks' and eventually leave the industry. If they stay, they enter huge mergers to acquire needed competences, they form strategic alliances, or they undertake joint ventures to do so.

A staff writer for the *Financial Times*, arguing in terms analogous to Porter's, referred to Barclays as finding itself in the 'muddled middle' in investment banking. It was too big to be a niche player in some specialized markets such as M&A, underwriting, or trading; but it was also too small to be a global player competing against the big US investment bankers – Merrill Lynch, Morgan Stanley, Goldman Sachs, and now Travelers Salomon. Given such poor positioning and the huge investment required to improve it, one might well argue that Taylor and Barclays made a most appropriate decision to exit.[45]

Moreover, before condemning Barclays for its lack of foresight in failing to exit investment banking earlier, one must hasten to add that it was not alone in its increasingly disadvantaged positioning; many of the second- and third-tier European universal banks already mentioned were in a similar situation. Eventually they may have to make the hard choices that Barclays made, just as its rival, NatWest, did. In the US, Lehman Brothers was in a similar position in the early 1980s, eventually being acquired by Shearson.[46] More recently, Bankers Trust and JP Morgan have had to face that problem: Bankers Trust sold out to Deutschebank, while JP Morgan may face a similar fate, despite its professed goal of remaining independent.

While one may be critical of the senior management of firms that do not make hard exit choices, it happens often enough to suggest a more multifaceted explanation than simply 'bad management'. One part of such an explanation is that even seemingly well managed organizations have much inertia, which causes a pursuance of particular strategies long after a rational assessment of their merits suggests their abandonment.[47] Industry myths supporting the strategies, including a desire to save face by not admitting past mistakes, contribute to such inertia.

The phenomenon is sometimes referred to in academic writings as 'the escalation of commitment',[48] and involves persisting with a strategy despite continuing poor results. Sometimes the stakes may be very high, as in NASA's space shuttle *Challenger*, where scientists went on with the project even as they had increasing evidence that it could lead to the disaster that later took place.

Beyond that, in industries facing turbulent environments, market changes are often difficult to read, and they may be radical and sudden, increasing the number of 'stuck in the middle' firms. Many firms do not have the capability to anticipate such market changes in advance. As one writer on organizations has noted: 'It isn't as though these environmental trends are like a thousand-pound gorilla knocking at the door. They are often hard to understand and interpret.'[49]

Firms capable of adapting must transform themselves quickly if they are to survive and/or become major players in the future in niches that match their core competences. Barclays now faces that challenge – one that many of its competitors face as well.

The decline of Martin Taylor: explanations

How does the previous discussion bear on a summary assessment of Martin Taylor? Not surprisingly, a wide array of views prevails, from continuing admirers on one side to strong critics on the other, and various gradations in between.

Admirers see him as having provided strong leadership and as having been increasingly victimized by a recalcitrant board and institutional culture and bureaucracy that blocked the implementation of sound ideas that would have made Barclays more competitive. Critics acknowledge his many strengths – vision, analytical skills and charisma – but they see him as responsible in large part for the many problems that the bank is facing in early 1999, particularly that of strategic confusion. My main argument is that Taylor was both victim and initiator of the bank's declining performance in his last year as Barclays CEO.

Taylor's last year may best be characterized as one of reputational decline, increasing frustrations at being unable to move his board and the bank in directions he felt would be productive, and an increase in seemingly radical and rapidly introduced proposals to which his board was not as receptive as he wanted. There was at times an appearance of burnout and despair in his public presentations, alternating at other times with the optimistic and unflappable demeanour that were so characteristic of his first four years.

Set out below are some of the explanations that might apply to Martin Taylor's final year as CEO.

Raising the white flag in investment banking

The reputational decline, the frustrations and the thwarted proposals of Taylor's last year are traceable to several key events. The first was managing the exit from investment banking. As difficult and complex as that series of actions was, Taylor's reputation was diminished by the way he handled it. He went public before he had found a buyer, either for the entire BZW (his stated preference) or for particular parts. This was widely interpreted as lowering BZW's market value in at least two ways: first, individuals or entire teams might leave for another firm, obliging him to provide them with early and generous bonuses to retain them;[50] second, prospective buyers might cherry pick rather than buy the entire business.

For the first time since he became Barclays CEO, Taylor's reputation visibly diminished in financial services circles. *The Economist* carried an article entitled 'How Not to Sell Your Bank', referring to the exit from investment banking of both Barclays and NatWest, but with most of its references to the former.[51] One well regarded banking reporter said: 'Martin Taylor lost much esteem with this move. To spend what he did on the new Canary Wharf facilities and on Harrison and senior hires and then pull out like this is not a sign of good management. And Barclays' lower share price reflects this.' A bank analyst was even more critical:

> Taylor's announcing this without yet having a buyer diminishes shareholder value if many demoralized people leave. He hired Goldman Sachs to do the sale and they will then know about the backlog of deals BZW people had. And the timing was terrible, given the costs from the Canary Wharf move.

John Aitken, a leading bank analyst then with Switzerland's UBS, estimated that Barclays had squandered £750 million on investment banking.[52] As he commented at the time: 'Barclays paid a huge premium to get into the business and now it is paying a huge premium to get out again ... quite a feat.'

Some informed observers felt that Taylor's decision to exit parts of investment banking was a betrayal of British national interests. They saw BZW as one of the last British-owned investment banks, with NatWest having already declared its intention to exit, and most of the others having been bought by European universal banks. Taylor's decision was thus seen as representing the end of an era and, for some, as a further step in the decline of British economic power.

In Martin Taylor's defence, once he and his board decided to exit investment banking he may have had few options other than to publicly announce Barclays' intention to do so. So many inside investment bankers knew about it that Taylor may be seen as having had no choice but to go public. Rumours had already begun circulating inside and outside the bank that a sale was imminent, and there was considerable concern that Barclays would lose many investment bankers as a result. In brief, Taylor was between the proverbial 'rock and a hard place'. On balance, however, he and

Barclays would have been better served had he not gone public before finding a buyer.

The press coverage a month after Taylor's announcement conveys the complexities and the high stakes in the decision. The *Financial Times* thus referred to Taylor trying for a hard sell of the entire BZW and not being successful in selling it as a single entity. He was described as appearing exhausted, with the mechanics of break-up as complicated and protracted. His need to keep the staff of the equities and advisory businesses that he planned on selling was seen as hard to carry out. Finally, his and Goldman Sachs' reputations were seen as dented.[53]

By mid-November 1997, Barclays had sold its UK and European equities and corporate advisory businesses to Credit Suisse First Boston (CSFB) and it disposed of its US business and Asian arm some months later. Even the sale to CSFB had some negative commentary: Taylor was quoted as saying he was happy with the deal but wished he had sold all of BZW as well; John Aitken said it was an awful deal for Barclays, selling far below asset value.[54]

Out of the ashes: Barclays Capital

Rather than exit completely from investment banking, Taylor decided to build a new business in debt capital markets so as to retain the momentum lost in the original sale of BZW's equities and M&A businesses. Called Barclays Capital and headed by Bob Diamond, a highly regarded American investment banker from First Boston, it was set up in October 1997 with some fanfare. It was designed to be the cutting edge of the corporate bank. Diamond claimed that with European Monetary Union there would be major growth opportunities for corporate finance in Europe and that Barclays Capital would also do well in proprietary trading there.[55]

By April 1998, after six months in business, Diamond was announcing that Barclays could gain a dominant position in fast-growing European corporate bond markets. He characterized Barclays Capital as having the financial resources of the US bulge-bracket firms but with far more focus, and he forecast ROEs of 20 per cent in the 'very near future'.[56]

Unfortunately, 1998 was a rough year for global investment bankers, and Barclays Capital soon shared in the losses. Taylor announced in September that Barclays was taking a £320 million before-tax charge on its exposure in Russia, one of the biggest charges of any bank. He said, however, that the size of the exposure in Russia was not out of line with that in other emerging markets and that he was still hugely encouraged by the progress of Barclays Capital. Appearing relaxed at a press conference, he stated: 'We're in the risk business. We take positions. We lend money. We get most of it back.'[57]

Within a month, there was yet another hit of £300 million in the Long-Term Capital Market hedge fund, accompanied by a dramatic bail-out, with Barclays Capital closing its proprietary trading operation and scaling down plans to expand rapidly in emerging markets.

Again, many other big global banks took losses, as they had in Russia but the timing was poor for Barclays, given its messy bail-out from BZW and the announced hopes earlier in the year for Barclays Capital. One of the things that was particularly frustrating for Taylor was that the risk models and management controls that he had instituted had not been sophisticated enough to enable Barclays to cope with these global shocks. A difficult exit from BZW was thus compounded by big, unanticipated losses from Barclays Capital. Obviously, models are not adequate substitutes for sound judgement.

Actually, Taylor was reported to have wanted to exit from all of BZW, but his board had prevailed on him to set up Barclays Capital. Sir Peter Middleton, Taylor's temporary successor after he resigned in late November 1988, quickly announced that the bank was reviewing Barclays Capital and that the latter might well be reconfigured or shrunk in a short time.[58] Ironically, Taylor had himself asked for such a strategic review following the Russian crisis and his board members were reported to have resisted his effort, interpreting it as a sign that he was panic-stricken.[59]

Taylor's last stand: reorganization

On 20 January 1998, Taylor had announced a big shake-up to split personal and business banking, integrating all international businesses with their counterparts in the UK. Thus, retail financial services would be responsible for all retail banking throughout the world, with the same holding for Barclays Capital, and two other divisions, namely Barclays Global Investors and Business Banking. While this made sense, it was not necessarily clarifying a long-term strategy.[60]

The denouement for Taylor took place at a dramatic October 1998 board meeting in New York, in which he presented yet another structural reorganization. This one involved splitting the bank into two separate segments – retail and wholesale – to stop the volatility of the latter from tainting the high rating and performance of the former. Furthermore, he argued, each could then be merged more readily – the retail bank with possible UK prospects to further solidify Barclays' position in that market, and the wholesale perhaps with European firms. The plan made much sense, to a point where several institutional investors have commented favourably about it since then and urged its strong consideration.

The board's response was reportedly quite negative. Two objections were registered: first, some board members were 'furious that Taylor presented no data to back up his plan, yet he kept moving ahead on it'; second, there was the expressed board concern that this might make Barclays vulnerable to a hostile take-over, especially in view of its big losses of the past year.[61]

An impasse with the board?

This confrontation between Taylor and his board on his last reorganization plan finally led to his sudden and unanticipated resignation in late November 1998. As various interpretations have emerged, both from recent press coverage and from interviews with participants and knowledgeable observers, what appears is a story of increasing conflict between Taylor and some members of his board.

The trust that seemed to exist between them for much of Taylor's tenure as Barclays' CEO declined increasingly over his final year. Like Pitman, Taylor was a strong CEO, bent on moving ahead on his own. Since board members regarded Taylor's actions after the sale of BZW as increasingly impulsive and erratic, some lost confidence in his judgements. His relationship with them had likely been deteriorating since then, as indicated by the fact that he had threatened to resign on several occasions before he finally did.[62]

At a minimum, the board increasingly resented what they regarded as his unilateral style of moving ahead on key strategic decisions. They wanted to be consulted much more, and he was not managing them in a way that satisfied that need. He was probably doing himself, the board, and the larger bank a favour, then, by resigning when he did, since it did not seem likely that trust could easily be restored.

Where does that leave the assessment of Taylor? He will always be remembered for his analytical skills, his charisma, and his ability to deal with most key stakeholders. Some observers feel he will be seen as effective in wringing more efficiency out of losing businesses and mature markets than in building new ones. Some will see him, as one astute observer reported, as more of a 'sparkling' but not always a 'clicking' CEO, meaning he was much better at articulating than at implementing visions.

Given the difficulty of the leadership task of transforming an institution such as Barclays in these recent years, these judgements seem to this observer as unduly harsh. Taylor was in many respects a victim of having to choose between at least two competing strategies, in an economic environment where it was unclear which would have the biggest pay-off. One was the strategy that Pitman and Lloyds chose and that worked so well there. From this perspective, the assessment would be that while Taylor deserves much credit for having improved tremendously Barclays' credit quality, for selling off many losing businesses in Europe and the US, and for eventually tripling the stock price, his development of the investment bank was the wrong strategy. Had he concentrated much more on retail than wholesale banking a few years ago, instead of beginning to do so in late 1997, Barclays would be much farther along the road to recovery.[63]

The other strategy is to get scale and diversity in both wholesale and retail banking. Taylor was trying to do that, only in an extremely volatile economic environment and an increasingly hostile political one inside his own institution. From this perspective, he is seen as pursuing a radical strategy with mixed success. He seemingly wanted to compete with the biggest and the best – the Merrill Lynches and Goldman Sachs – but he felt thwarted by an unresponsive board, an old guard among the management ranks, and too little time in which to carry out this strategy.

I conclude these assessments with the observation that managing one's board and building broad-based coalitions within the institution are indispensible for the success of any manager of change.[64] Developing a far-reaching vision is important and difficult. But without managing the politics of its implementation, failure follows. Comparing Barclays with Lloyds in this regard, Pitman was able to be both a visionary and an effective implementor; Taylor was not – but his task was much more complex.

Barclays after 1997

The developments at Barclays since late 1997 may signal a move toward the strategy that Sir Brian Pitman had established earlier at Lloyds. A profile of Barclays' configuration or main organization characteristics helps support that direction.

A first-mover, expansionist strategy, now chastened

Historically, British bankers and bank watchers saw Barclays as similar in some respects to Citicorp in its strategy. Thus, with the recent exception of Lloyds TSB, Barclays has been the most entrepreneurial, the quickest first mover of all the British banks. Lloyds can only claim that distinction since the mid-1980s, while Barclays had been an industry leader for over 70 years.

Consider the following: Barclays was the first British bank to develop a large international business in the 1920s; it was the first to develop a big credit-card business, Barclaycard, in the 1960s; it was the first and boldest to diversify into investment banking in the mid-1980s; it was the first to institute a shareholder buyback programme in 1995; and, since late 1997, it has been one of the first of the European universal banks seriously to question the viability of that strategy by exiting from many parts of its investment bank.

While there are inconsistencies in Barclays' first-mover strategy – for example, its periodic demonstrations of risk-aversion in the early and mid-1980s and then again in the late 1990s, and while it did have a bureaucratic, quasi-militaristic structure – it still remains an example, overall, of one of the most entrepreneurial of the British commercial banks.

Other similarities with Citicorp are equally striking. Not only did Barclays and Citicorp both have an innovative bent; they both also pursued an injudicious expansion in the late 1980s and early 1990s that had devastatingly negative effects on their financial performance. Just as Citicorp staged a dramatic turnaround in the early and mid-nineties by exiting from loss-making businesses (such as investment banking and information services) and by restoring its credit culture, Barclays has engaged in similar efforts.

Obviously, being a first mover does not automatically lead to high performance, as both Citicorp and Barclays demonstrate. When the first-mover approach leads to uncontrollable growth, with more emphasis on asset size, market share and geographic coverage than on profitability, it clearly detracts from shareholder value, as both banks also demonstrate.

An anomaly of this first-mover strategy in Barclays' case is that the bank was dominated throughout much of its history by family interests. The conventional wisdom of many economic and business historians is that family domination limits a firm's development and rationalization. However, in the case of Barclays, one can argue there has been a positive side to family domination.

Professor Leslie Hannah, economic historian and now Dean of the City University Business School in London, states in his forthcoming book on Barclays that nepotism is known to have contributed to a meritocracy.[65] A key reason is that the sons of Barclays families were university-trained, unlike most senior managers in other clearing banks. Only the best among them were then promoted to senior positions in the bank. Hannah refers to this phenomenon at Barclays as 'competitive nepotism'. 'They were clearly a cut above their counterparts in the other banks in education and social background,' explained a bank analyst, 'and this undoubtedly helped make some of them strong managers.'

A family culture

Barclays' culture is clearly distinguishable from that of other British clearing banks, even though the families on which it is based are nearly extinct in their impact. Historically, the senior Barclays bankers and board members contained a disproportionate number of upper-middle-class, old-style British gentry. They went to boarding school and universities – particularly Cambridge and Oxford – and as Quakers they valued probity and austerity. They also had a lifestyle appropriate to their station, with its emphasis on such leisure pursuits as hunting and high culture.

Despite the failures of BZW, Barclays' family-based culture was ironically more attuned to investment banking than the more risk-averse and cost-control-based ones of some of the other clearing banks. Reflecting the family dominance, Barclays developed a partnership orientation that seemed ideally suited to investment banking. Even the outsiders it brought in at the start to head BZW, Sir Martin Jacomb and Lord Camoys, were upper-class, partnership-oriented people who epitomized the investment banking culture.

A complex structure with many turfs

Barclays has gone through many structural changes – perhaps more than any of the other clearing banks. That is still another way in which it resembles Citicorp. One explanation was that Barclays had always regarded reorganization as a substitute for developing a new strategy.

The changes have often taken place in cycles. In the first several decades of Barclays' existence, it was quite decentralized, with much autonomy given to the separate family banks in the regions. In the 1960s and 1970s, it then became much more centralized, to a point where Sir John Quinton was concerned in the late eighties with making headquarters more responsive to customer concerns through the branches.

In addition, there were constant reorganizations of the divisions over the years, alternating between a customer, product or geographic market base. Taylor gave at least as much emphasis to the integration issue during much of his administration – that is, to securing linkages across businesses – as he did to their original design or differentiation.

The role of headquarters has also been a focus of change in recent years. Devolution and delegation have been emphasized more. This has involved a big reduction in staff at headquarters and giving more responsibility to each business division and to product groups within each.

The bank has paid much more attention than before to how headquarters can best add value in a quasi-parental role in relation to the various divisions.[66] It has emphasized helping the divisions and product groups develop linkages with one another, promoting more focus for the entire bank by reducing the portfolio, cost cutting, and applying risk-management techniques as a basis for allocating capital across businesses.

The central thrust of these developments has been gradually to streamline and focus the bank so that it could become more agile, more efficient, and thereby compete more effectively in the future. The bank was always entrepreneurial and always had a flair for innovation and early action, despite its bureaucratic, centralized, and even militaristic structure by the seventies and early eighties. Under Taylor, it had become both more flexibly decentralized and with a stronger centre.

The future?

In many respects, the changes under Taylor, culminating in Barclays' exiting from many aspects of its investment banking, suggest a move toward the paradigm that Pitman established at Lloyds TSB much earlier. Barclays will never become a clone of Lloyds, however. But Pitman instituted some fundamental reforms at Lloyds, a variant of which Taylor began implementing at Barclays. It may always have more of a wholesale global banking business than Lloyds, but competitive pressures that all the British banks face are forcing them into making a number of similar changes.

They must all cut costs, gain more focus, rationalize their operations, and only compete where they have some core competence and can become significant players. Lloyds was able to make these changes earlier, because of its leadership. It was also smaller and more manageable. Barclays, in its own style, seems to have followed suit.

Does this portend that Barclays will become a high-street bank and largely shed itself of wholesale banking? That seems doubtful, given its long history in wholesale businesses. Instead, Barclays may more likely intensify its efforts to develop a more focused wholesale banking strategy around areas of greatest core competence, while continuing to cut costs and rationalize its retail banking. Some sharper self-definition may then emerge that Barclays never had before.

For Barclays, the motto for the future will not be so much 'grow or die' as 'focus and establish clear niches' or be doomed to second-tier and second-rate status. Given the pace of consolidation, technological change and increasing competition on both the wholesale and retail sides, Barclays will have to develop its identity and focus quite rapidly.

The outlines of Barclays' future direction may be indicated in its choice of a successor to Taylor. The skills and vision of that person will suggest what the Barclays board liked and disliked about the directions that Taylor followed and, depending on his or her longevity, may well influence its development for some years to come. As of late April 1999, that successor had not been chosen.

Notes and references

1. From interviews with senior, old-line Barclays managers.
2. Much of this recent history comes from interviews with senior managers who were in the bank in these years.
3. *Banking World*, January 1988.
4. *The Economist*, 25 June 1988.
5. *Financial Times*, 14 August 1992.
6. Interviews for this book.
7. *Financial Times*, 14 August 1992.
8. *The Economist*, 25 June 1988.
9. *Financial Times*, 18 February 1991.
10. *Financial Times*, 13 December 1990.

11. *Financial Times*, 22 October 1990.
12. *Financial Times*, 19 April 1991.
13. From Bloomberg, *Financial Markets* (online).
14. *Financial Times*, 2 March 1990.
15. *Financial Times*, 27 February 1992.
16. *Financial Times*, 13 April 1992.
17. *Financial Times*, 25 April 1992.
18. *Financial Times*, 29 April 1992.
19. *Financial Times*, 2 March 1990.
20. *Financial Times*, 12 December 1992.
21. Interviews for this book.
22. *Financial Times*, 21 November 1992.
23. *Financial Times*, 6 August 1992.
24. *Financial Times*, 21 November 1992.
25. *Independent*, 'Family Vault', 24 January 1993.
26. *Financial Times*, 11 December 1992.
27. *Financial Times*, 14 December 1992.
28. *Financial Times*, 20 August 1993.
29. *Financial Times*, 2 September 1993.
30. *Financial Times*, 2 December 1993.
31. *Financial Times*, 11 March 1994.
32. *Financial Times*, 10 November 1994.
33. *Financial Times*, 20 August 1993.
34. From Bloomber,g *Financial Markets* (online).
35. Lehman Brothers, *UK Clearing Banks, 1998 Annual Review*, 23 July 1998, p. 76.
36. *Ibid.*, p. 70.
37. *Ibid.*, p. 63.
38. *Ibid.*, p. 103.
39. *Financial Times*, 11 March 1994.
40. *The Economist*, 16 August 1997, p. 53.
41. *Financial Timess*, 3 October 1997.
42. *The Economist*, 13 December 1997.
43. *The Economist*, 21 June 1997 and 13 December 1997.
44. Michael Porter, *Competitive Advantage*, Free Press, New York, 1985, p. 16.
45. *Financial Times*, 5 October 1997, p. 24.
46. Ken Auletta, *Greed and Glory on Wall Street*, Warner Books, New York, 1986.
47. Danny Miller and P.H. Friesen, *Organizations*, Prentice Hall, Englewood Cliffs NJ, 1984.
48. For an insightful analysis of the dynamics of this process, see Barry M. Staw and Jerry Ross, 'Understanding Behavior in Escalation Situations', in Staw (ed.), *Psychological Dimensions of Organizational Behavior*, Prentice-Hall, Englewood Cliffs NJ, 1991, pp. 228–36.
49. Stephen Robbins, *Organization Theory*, 3rd edn, Prentice Hall, Englewood Cliffs NJ, 1990, p. 200.
50. *Independent*, 8 October 1997, p. 25.
51. *The Economist*, 'How Not to Sell Your Bank', 8 November 1997.

52. *The Economist*, 8 November 1997.
53. *Financial Times*, 7 November 1997.
54. *Financial Times*, 13 November 1997.
55. *Financial Times*, 23 October 1997.
56. *Financial Times*, 14 April 1998.
57. *Financial Times*, 2 September 1998.
58. *Guardian*, 30 November 1998.
59. *Financial Times*, 30 November 1998.
60. *Financial Times*, 20 January 1998
61. *Guardian*, 28 November 1998.
62. Interviews for this book.
63. *Guardian*, 30 November 1998.
64. See in that regard Jeffrey Pfeffer, *Managing with Power*, Harvard Business School Press, Boston MA, 1992. A witty yet sympathetic (to Taylor) discussion of Taylor's exit is Christopher Fildes' article in the *Daily Telegraph*, 14 December 1998.
65. Interview with Professor Hannah.
66. For a thoughtful discussion of these issues, which has had an impact on many large corporations, see Michael Goold, Andrew Campbell and Marcus Alexander, *Corporate-Level Strategy*, Wiley, New York, 1994.

7 NatWest: Another Global Bank Gone Home

NatWest has what I would call a Masonic culture. They have a strong sense of Christian fellowship there. By 'Christian' I mean that they are very fair, humane, and honest in their dealings. And 'Masonic' means that they see it as a club and that we buddies stick together. The idea of a club is a very British one, more there than elsewhere. No meritocracy traditionally existed at NatWest or Barclays. Their people at the top were good politicians, not necessarily great bankers, managers, or decision makers.

Bank Analyst

Culturally, they are the bank of the people, ordinary grey people – solid, conventional, steady, non-risk-taking. Over time, they have done quite well, in contrast to Barclays that also did well but was always erratic. The NatWest culture clearly comes through, and it says that solidity and stability pay off.

Banking Reporter

They are like the Russian army in World War II. They just keep marching on. Sometimes they experience dreadful casualties, but they will get there. They will arrive in Berlin. They are the infantry, while Barclays are the cavalry.

Banking Reporter

A second supertanker of British banking

OUR NEXT case is NatWest, the British bank often described as most similar to Barclays in size and strategy. Some observers have characterized both as the supertankers of British banking, alluding to the great difficulty of repositioning the large, bureaucratic and complex institutions that they have become, at a time when rapid adaptation is so necessary.

Barclays and NatWest, more than any of the other British banks, have engaged in intense rivalry over the past couple of decades, as the most diversified and biggest of the four clearers. Their rivalry resembled that of Citicorp and Chase, New York City's cross-town rivals of a previous era, including as well some similar cultural contrasts between each pair. NatWest and Barclays had become British banks with strong domestic as well as international franchises, until they faced a series of setbacks in the late eighties and nineties. From 1989 until 1992, for example, NatWest had an average return on equity of 3.5 per cent, similar to Barclays' 3.3 per cent.[1]

NatWest, like Barclays, had pursued a universal banking strategy from the 1986 Big Bang through to the late 1990s, maintaining:

(1) a large domestic retail bank, NatWest UK;
(2) a global wholesale investment bank, NatWest Markets; and
(3) wealth management, a new sector, established in April 1997, that included long-term savings-and-investment management, institutional fund management, and international private banking for the very rich.

NatWest had pursued this wide range of financial and related activities in the UK and in 29 other nations.[2]

To give some indication of NatWest's size, it can be stated that at the end of 1997 it had a staff of roughly 70 000, 1750 branches, and total assets of £185 billion.[3] This was after NatWest had begun downsizing in recent years, to cut costs and achieve more focus. (In 1986, for example – a time of peak expansion – NatWest had employed 102 400 people and had 3133 branches.)[4]

As of the end of 1997, NatWest UK was the cash cow of the bank. It accounted for virtually all the bank's after-tax profits, with an after-tax return of 27.6 per cent in ROE, generated through six main product groups in personal and business sectors. NatWest Markets, by contrast, organized into debt, equities, advisory, and traditional money-market activities such as foreign exchange, lost £499 million and posted an ROE of –22.4 per cent. The new Wealth Management group, including Coutts (a private bank), Lombard (the UK's leading finance house), Ulster (providing a range of wholesale and retail services in Ireland), and fund and asset management businesses, accounted for most of NatWest's remaining profits, with an after-tax return of 5.6 per cent.[5]

This broad array of business indicates NatWest's intention of becoming a top-tier, highly diversified, global player. That was not easy to accomplish, however. Although NatWest had made strong commitments in the eighties and nineties to retail banking in the US and Europe, and to global investment banking, it then exited from them in each instance. The most recent withdrawal was from investment banking. Since late 1997, NatWest, like Barclays, sold off much of its investment bank after experiencing escalating costs and consistently low performance.[6]

These aborted global initiatives in investment and retail banking hurt shareholder value, just as they did at Barclays. Many also speculate that NatWest, like Barclays, may well end up in the coming years with a strategy similar in many respects to Lloyds, with a strong emphasis on domestic retail banking as its core business. A big question is why it took so long for NatWest and Barclays to see the benefits of following the Lloyds strategy.

NatWest and Barclays: twins or not?

A comparison of NatWest and Barclays in size and product mix indicates just how similar they have been. While NatWest was bigger in the late 1980s, Barclays overtook it by 1997, in total assets (£234 million against £185 million), number of employees (83 200 to 70 000), and branches.[7] They have both remained, however, as the giants of British banking.

Moreover, they have had a similar product mix. Thus, UK retail banking was the core business for both, along with global investment and corporate banking, wealth or asset management, and private banking. Much of the latter was also international. Each has thus had the same three sets of financial services in its portfolio.

In addition, both banks have traditionally maintained a high-cost, bureaucratic structure in their retail branches, staffed primarily by non-university-trained people. They have also had a much more loosely structured investment bank, staffed mainly by university graduates, many with advanced degrees. At the same time, both have been actively restructuring their retail operations to cut costs as markets become more competitive.

Most importantly, by the 1980s both had developed a reputation as leading UK and international banks. They had become landmark institutions, particularly in the UK, much like Citicorp and Chase had become in the US. NatWest, even though only formed in 1970, quickly attained this status through melding its three constituent banks (Westminster, District and National Provincial), each of which had its own distinguished history.[8] NatWest in particular was seen as having a 'sureness of touch', with the 1980s as its Golden Years, culminating in its attaining market leadership in 1988 when it surpassed Barclays both in asset size and profits.[9] Serious lapses in judgement, however, led to major financial losses for both NatWest and Barclays in the late eighties and early nineties that harmed their reputations considerably.

Notwithstanding their similarities, NatWest and Barclays differed significantly in culture, leadership, style and, in recent years, performance. Those differences are a central theme of this chapter. As poorly as Barclays' performance was in the late eighties and early nineties, its recovery up to 1998 had been stronger than NatWest's – a likely result of its greater emphasis on strategic consolidation and downsizing. For example, Barclays' ROE averaged 20.1 per cent over 1994–7, the recovery years, while NatWest's averaged only 12.8 per cent. Moreover, while Barclays' share price more than quadrupled during 1990–6, NatWest's slightly more than doubled.[10]

Indeed, NatWest had emerged at the end of 1997 as the lowest performer of the Big Four, with the implication that it suffered from broader leadership weaknesses that needed correcting. The *Financial Times* reported, for example, in August 1997: 'For the last three years, NatWest has been the laggard of UK banking, disappointing shareholders with a series of strategic about-turns and mishaps.'[11] Lehman Brothers' *Annual Review* for 1997 reached a similar conclusion: 'NatWest's underlying performance still appears to be disappointing by sector standards ... Moreover, far from showing an improvement, the commercial banking ROE and cost/income ratios actually deteriorated in 1997.'[12] The remainder of this chapter provides an analysis of NatWest's problems, then indicates how and why they developed, and, as a result, what its future options may be.

1997: poor results for NatWest and deepening gloom

Publicly traded corporations throughout the industrial world participate in the annual ritual of reporting and interpreting the previous year's results for shareholders. In line with what students of organizational behaviour call 'attribution theory', there is much managing of appearances on such occasions.[13] If the results are good, spokespeople for a corporation attribute the results to far-sighted initiatives by the senior management. Poor results, by contrast, are often attributed to external events over which the corporation had limited control – 'general economic conditions', for example. In those instances, the firm's spokespeople refer to its 'satisfactory' performance and highlight its profitable businesses. This is sometimes characterized in common parlance as 'spin control' and 'corporate speak'. The exercise is particularly important in financial services, which is a strongly reputation-driven business.

1997 was a difficult year for NatWest. Instead of following the script that attribution theory suggests and externalizing the blame, senior management at NatWest forthrightly acknowledged the problems and at least implicitly blamed themselves. They referred to the results as 'disappointing'. Lord Alexander, NatWest's chairman was quoted as saying: '1997 was a difficult year and our overall results were poor.'[14] At the same time, the bank announced a new recovery strategy, focusing on domestic UK retail banking, wealth management, and very selective wholesale banking.[15]

NatWest's comparative decline in performance had been accelerating since the mid-1990s. Early signs were evident in the disappointing 1996 results. Its 5.8 per cent ROE (after taxes), was considerably below Barclays (23 per cent), Midland (24.5 per cent) and Lloyds (33.5 per cent).[16] As a result, NatWest shareholders expressed concern, particularly in such a bull market.

Based on these results, Lehman Brothers' 1997 and 1998 annual reviews of UK clearing banks attributed NatWest's recent problems to a series of events:

(1) The sale, in December 1995, of its large US retail bank at well below market price;
(2) using the bulk of the proceeds for several investment banking acquisitions that did not add anticipated market value;
(3) the late discovery of an £85 million loss from a NatWest derivative trader's mispricing of interest-rate options; and

(4) the negative financial and reputational impacts of these events, raising serious questions about how the bank had been managed and its future prospects.

The sale of NatWest's US retail bank was prudent in view of competitive threats posed by the increasing consolidation of US super-regional competitors. But its handling and aftermath raised 'doubts about [NatWest] management's genuine commitment to value.'[17] The sale price of roughly $3.5 billion was seen as well below those obtained in similar US bank sales at the time.[18] It then used the bulk of the proceeds for several investment banking acquisitions. While these made sense in theory, NatWest's investment bank had other problems, which were to make the acquisitions highly questionable.

Furthermore, a week after presenting its poor 1996 results, NatWest acknowledged an £85 million loss from the mispricing of interest-rate options.[19] The loss raised immediate concern about NatWest's seeming lack of internal controls. Martin Owen, the head of NatWest Markets, the investment bank where the loss took place, admitted it could only have resulted from a chain of failures, rather than a single lapse.[20]

The question then was how this situation could have gone on for the more than the two years that it did (late 1994 through to the end of 1996) and be undetected. Why weren't NatWest's senior management monitoring these trading decisions and taking corrective actions? 'Two years is a hell of a long time to keep fooling somebody when systems are supposed to discover it,' said Richard Coleman, a bank analyst at Merrill Lynch.[21]

Little wonder, then, that both Lord Alexander, NatWest's Chair, and Derek Wanless, its CEO, acknowledged mismanagement. An article in *The Economist* characterized CEO Wanless as 'the beleaguered boss of NatWest who "continues to reel from one sucker-punch to the next".' It referred to the NatWest board as 'in some disarray' and questioned the quality of management at the top.[22]

Martin Owen, NatWest Market's CEO, referred to the investment bank acquisitions, along with other product groups within NWM, as a 'family of cultures' that he and his senior colleagues would weave together.[23] That integration did not happen; instead, he ran NWM as a loose confederation of autonomous businesses, much like most investment banks, and never developed the management controls required to assess the risks that their traders were taking.

With this loose management style, it was not surprising that the options mispricing occurred. But the question was raised as to why

Lord Alexander and Wanless had not detected it before they did. Even more damaging to NatWest's reputation was the fact that the problems were only discovered after the rogue trader involved in these actions left the firm. As Richard Coleman, bank analyst of Merrill Lynch stated: 'It's disturbing that the mispricing was only discovered because an individual left.'[24]

One answer is that Wanless's management style, as CEO and the person most responsible for the bank's operating performance, may have had elements in common with Owen's. While Wanless should have been closer to the situation some years before and introduced tighter risk-management controls so as to protect the bank against derivatives mispricing (or at least limited its duration), that obviously did not happen. This sounded like an earlier version of what Martin Taylor was to face in his handing of Barclays' investment banking. A banking writer generally supportive of NatWest concluded: 'Wanless is intelligent, professional and a genuinely decent man, but he has not been enough of a hands-on manager. He now says that he will be running the bank very closely, but it is rather late in the day for that.'

Another issue for NatWest related to its cash cow, the UK retail bank. While NatWest UK was the bank's best-performing business, its profitability in recent years had been below that of the other three clearers.[25] Thus, NatWest UK's cost/income ratio in 1996 of 66.7 per cent, while on a par with Barclays UK, was well above that of Lloyds and Midland let alone of many of its new competitors amongst the building societies, supermarkets, department stores, Virgin Airlines, and British Telecom.

As part of its recovery strategy, NatWest is now in the midst of a series of critical changes: 'getting it right in retail banking'; completing the sale of its investment bank; gaining more focus as an institution; reconstituting its board; and restoring its reputation.[26] Until the past couple of years, with a few notable exceptions, that reputation had been as a prudently managed, consistent, and reliable franchise, committed to high-quality services to its customers. A fuller understanding of what contributed to NatWest's rise and recent decline is discussed in the remainder of this chapter.

How it all happened

Recall that, unlike Barclays, which had been a consolidated bank since 1896, NatWest has been so only since January 1970. Nevertheless its member banks, which amalgamated at this time, were among the most venerable in British banking history. They included National Provincial (founded in 1833), District (formed in 1829 but later acquired by National Provincial) and Westminster (the first joint stock bank in England, and also formed in 1833).[27]

There was much geographic complementarity among the three, with National Provincial prominent in Wales and north-east England, District in the North- West, and Westminster in London and the South-East.[28] Several other banks were also part of the 1970 merger, although they maintained their autonomy and separate boards: Ulster Bank, founded in Belfast (now Northern Ireland) in 1836, was providing a wide array of retail and wholesale banking services, as part of Westminster; Coutts, a prestigious, family-owned private bank, was servicing the very rich; Isle of Man Bank, based in Ireland, offered retail banking services; and Lombard North Central did so for leasing and automobile finance services.[29]

After 1970, NatWest pursued several broad goals (taken from annual reports of the time and from interviews for this book):

(1) to become a premier global bank, with a broad mix of domestic and international businesses, similar to that of its British banking competitors, particularly Barclays;

(2) to develop a reputation for high standards of integrity and quality in its relations with all major stakeholders – customers, employees, shareholders, and the wider community – and to proceed with a cohesiveness and unity of purpose in doing so;

(3) to maintain a strong commitment to social responsibility and community development – perhaps unique among British banks and reflected, for example, in the fact that its CEO of the late 1980s, Tom Frost, was chair of a Task Force on Business and Urban Regeneration in the inner cities; and

(4) to provide extensive staff training, as part of its pursuit of excellence, accompanied by the development of physical facilities off-site for such purposes.

On the first item in this list, Barclays and Lloyds were the most international British banks when NatWest was formed. NatWest was particularly eager to join that group, even as Lloyds was just as eager, starting in the early 1980s, to leave it. Recognizing that Barclays and other competitors were well ahead in global banking, NatWest pursued from its early years intensive catch-up efforts. Building on NatWest's well established relationships with big corporations, the bank's actions included opening branch offices in Europe, the US, Canada, Mexico, the USSR, and the Far East.[30]

The effective pursuit of these goals resulted in NatWest gaining by the late 1980s the reputation as Britain's top clearing bank. It had become the largest in assets, and it had achieved a consistent record of profit growth and expansion, both domestically and overseas. It also developed an enviable reputation for cohesiveness and sense of purpose among its top executives that was seen as contributing to these achievements.

Rationalization and Global Expansion

Two purposes of NatWest's 1970 merger were, first, to rationalize the branch networks of the previously separate banks, creating economies of scale and a broad coverage of the United Kingdom, and, second, to ride the crest of expanding international banking. A senior manager from that time recalled:

> We had McKinsey consultants in here to advise us in 1970, and they said we were too small to survive in a global economy and that we could only maintain our leadership by creating a bigger, more viable bank. And that is what we did.

The rationalization involved introducing common management systems throughout the branches, shrinking the number of branches, and yet ensuring a geographic spread by offsetting branch closures with new ones in previously unrepresented areas. By the end of the 1970s, NatWest had gained representation in all major population centres of the UK, including Edinburgh, Glasgow and Aberdeen, where it opened new branches.[31]

NatWest had a related commitment to major investments in technology. This increased over the years and was designed to improve productivity and efficiency in retail banking and to enhance its corporate and investment banking capabilities.

The international growth in Europe, North America, the USSR, and the Far East was extensive. The development of a quasi-pan-European strategy, with Britain's entry into the European Economic Community in 1973, was marked – as was the opening in 1979 of a significant presence in New York City and New York State through the acquisition of National Bank of North America.

Not surprisingly, NatWest was acutely aware of the need to catch up with its main competitor, Barclays, and that awareness gave some impetus to the international expansion. As one very senior manager explained:

> In 1970, we were just a UK bank and we had only three people abroad, all in New York City. To make up for all those years when Barclays was a global bank before we were, we got involved in sovereign loans. We wanted to become global instead of being just parochial to the UK.

At least two other considerations drove that growth. One was to leverage NatWest's corporate customer base; another was to spread risk. A former NatWest manager recalled: 'We were leveraging our wholesale strength and making money. And we had a concern to have balance in our businesses and lending, where we would not be subject to single-country risks or product risks. Being balanced seemed to us an appropriate vision.'

The NatWest strategy, then, starting in 1970, was to be a diversified international bank, with a significant presence in global wholesale and retail banking, in UK retail banking, and in private banking. 'We entered the era of global banking when we were formed,' explained a senior NatWest banker. There were no major differences, then, between the NatWest strategy and that pursued by Barclays – and even by Lloyds until Pitman's becoming its CEO in 1984.

After the 1986 Big Bang, NatWest, like Barclays, moved into investment banking. Then, in the early 1990s, NatWest started its own insurance company. It had thus become a universal bank by the 1990s, having diversified into many new areas of financial services.

The expansion into the US was quite dramatic, and a fast-rising senior banker, Tom Frost, was sent over in the late 1970s to manage that operation. 'Frost was given no notice,' recalled one old-time NatWest banker, 'and he was there through 1981, when he hired Bill Knowles – who had done a great job as head of retail banking at Bankers Trust – to succeed him. Frost wanted to bail out and return to England, to resume his life and NatWest career in London.'

Meanwhile, there was a similar expansion of NatWest into Europe, through branches in Spain, France, Holland, Belgium, Germany, Greece and the USSR. Like Barclays' international expansion, however, there was no coherent strategy behind the expansion other than to have representation. 'They followed Barclays down a path they should not have taken,' remarked a bank analyst. 'They were just involved in putting flags up in different countries, to show they were there.'

Was there a NatWest strategy?

Since its inception in 1970, NatWest's strategy was very similar to Barclays': pursue asset size, market share, global presence, and product and market diversity. It could be encapsulated in the adage 'big is beautiful', with the addition of 'beating Barclays is beautiful'. Numerous senior bankers at both Barclays and NatWest acknowledged that an intense competitive rivalry between the two banks certainly drove many of their decisions.

Was this a viable strategy for NatWest and, more to the point, was it a strategy at all? Some NatWest senior managers and staff agreed that it was neither. They often hastened to add, however, that the bank had changed significantly since the early nineties and had replaced its less reflective drift of the past with a coherent and sophisticated strategic planning process for the future. One senior NatWest banker explained: 'Until recently, we had no articulated strategy. We were all things to all people. You could make a long list of non-meaningful activities we had all over the world. It made no sense.' Another acknowledged: 'We are unbelievably diverse. We have some 300 products, many companies in many countries, and using diverse delivery channels. We are all over the map, and sometimes it is hard to keep track. In the past, we had been in far too many businesses going nowhere. We had a flags-on-the-map legacy, just like Barclays.'

Performance jolts and turning points

Perhaps as a part-reflection of NatWest's unthinking drift and limited strategic analysis in the first two decades of its existence, it has experienced several jolts since the late 1980s, from which it is still recovering. Prior to that time, NatWest had maintained both its financial performance and its reputation as a leading UK and world bank. It then faced major débâcles in the late 1980s in both its investment bank and its US retail bank; a few years later in its European retail banks; and, again, in its investment bank in 1997, as already discussed. All involved serious financial losses, but the ones in investment banking brought with them serious damage as well to NatWest's reputation for effective, prudent management and integrity. In retrospect, all four jolted NatWest into a series of changes in management, strategy and organization in order to reposition itself as a leading UK and world bank. As at the time of writing, it is unclear how successful it will be in those efforts.

Investment banking and Blue Arrow

One of the first jolts that NatWest faced in the late 1980s was in investment banking. It had established an investment banking division, County NatWest, in 1984, but it still had a limited presence in those businesses until Big Bang in 1986. Even after that, NatWest moved into investment banking in a much more cautious, risk-averse fashion than Barclays, which pursued an aggressive acquisition strategy. 'We did not have the first-mover approach that Barclays did,' explained a senior investment banker at NatWest. 'Barclays paid a huge price for a broker and a jobber. Though both were well regarded, I felt the goodwill they paid for had little value – and they did pay a fortune. We went smaller, and felt we could pick up good people that way. We also felt that when the blood was on the floor and people had been fired or resigned from those banks, like Barclays that went first with this, we could pick them up.'

NatWest did not always follow a risk-averse strategy, however, lurching periodically into aggressive deals for which it was not well prepared, perhaps in part to compensate for the slow start that its more cautious approach entailed. The most dramatic of those lurches was underwriting an £837 million rights issue in 1987 for Blue Arrow, a large British employment agency. Blue Arrow needed the financing in order to acquire a rival American firm, Manpower, and this transaction provided an opportunity for County NatWest to become a more significant player in securities underwriting.[32]

Unfortunately for NatWest, the rights issue was substantially undersubscribed, with only 38 per cent of the shares being sold.[33] In its understandable concern that the share price would fall, if that information became public, County NatWest proceeded to absorb another 11 per cent of shares in some of its own divisions and in Union Bank of Switzerland.[34] These additional holdings, however, were in potential violation of the Companies Act 1985, which required disclosure of any holding of more than five per cent. County NatWest's senior managers met several times with their lawyers and with Bank of England officials to determine whether it had broken these disclosure requirements and concluded that it had not.

Had the stockmarket crash of 19 October 1987 not taken place, this secret might never have got out. The crash, however, halved Blue Arrow's share price and made it extremely unlikely that County NatWest could sell off the remaining shares in a rising market. Events then escalated after the crash, resulting in an unprecedented court case in 1988, in which the Department of Trade and Industry (DTI) instituted an inquiry in connection with NatWest's non-disclosure in handling the rights issue. The inquiry related to a charge of NatWest's creating a false market, concealing the failure of the Blue Arrow placement, and thereby deceiving or misleading the investors.

In an attempt at damage control, NatWest first did an internal investigation and issued a report. However, one year later the DTI, not satisfied with NatWest's version of events, initiated its own investigation. A court case suing several individuals at NatWest for fraud then followed. It was unprecedented in the history of British banking for senior staff to be prosecuted like this, and the case cost over £40 million of taxpayers' money. Moreover, the proceedings were covered in detail in the press and damaged NatWest's reputation considerably.

The trial took place in two instalments. The first was limited to probing the actions of senior managers and board members at County NatWest. This phase culminated in a lengthy report, issued in December 1989, charging some of these managers and board members with illegal activities. It led to several resignations (forced and voluntary), arrests and criminal charges.[35]

That was damaging enough to NatWest's reputation, but at least it seemed limited to County NatWest, with Tom Frost, NatWest's CEO, not charged with any crimes. He claimed that he had delegated authority to senior management at County NatWest and was unaware of these practices. A lengthy article in *The Economist*, however, more than two years after the DTI report, sugggested otherwise.[36] It accused Frost of both knowing about the Blue Arrow events and participating in a deliberate cover-up and whitewash. It charged him with misleading DTI inspectors and concealing documents containing his notes that indicated his involvement and a possible active concealment. It even referred to him in the article as 'Teflon Tom', implying that he had consistently removed himself from any accountability for what happened. In addition, it implicated the Bank of England as implicitly colluding with NatWest by providing its senior management with advice on handling the matter and trying hard to persuade the DTI not to conduct any formal inquiry.

The charges were obviously so serious and potentially damaging that NatWest's new Chair, Lord Alexander, immediately asked the DTI to reopen the inquiry. The second investigation cleared both Frost and NatWest from any charges of wrongdoing, and *The Economist* then apologized profusely to NatWest, Frost, other senior managers and the

Bank of England, and publicly retracted the charges of cover-up in its previous article.[37] But the damage to NatWest's reputation had already been done.

There were undoubtedly many lessons for NatWest from the Blue Arrow episode. One that stands out is that underbuying – as NatWest did in its cautious entry into investment banking – can have significant costs. Another, related lesson is that the bank had reached well beyond its expertise in leading the rights issue. A London investment banker close to the situation observed: 'When you are on the edge of the industry, as NatWest was in 1987 with its start-up caution, and are just beginning, you feel compelled to demonstrate an early success. And when you have limited expertise to do it, the Blue Arrow sort of thing can happen.'

In addition to the reputational impact on NatWest from Blue Arrow, County NatWest had anyway been performing poorly for a long time. It had lost money every year from 1985 to 1990, losing $95 million in 1990 alone, for a six-year total of over $450 million.[38] The situation was grave enough for Lord Alexander to announce in early 1991 that he gave County NatWest one year to show profits or be closed. An article at the time in *The Economist* referred to Alexander's statement as the investment bank's 'death warrant! Talented people do not rush to join or stay with someone two cells from the scaffold. Nor do clients.'[39] Within months, however, County Natwest did start to show profits, and Lord Alexander announced on November 30 of that year that 'leading banks should have an investment banking arm' and that NatWest was willing to wait five years for County to hit a profit target of at least 17.5 per cent for its ROE.

The 'black hole' in the US

Another failure in these years was NatWest Bancorp, its US retail bank. Opened in 1979, it had expanded considerably in the 1980s as part of a strategy to build a major regional bank in the north-east US. By the end of 1991, however, the bank was estimated to have incurred $2.5 billion in acquisition costs and capital injections and to have experienced net losses of $745.5 million. It had paid top-of-the-market prices for the acquisition of two New Jersey retail banks in the late eighties. And its $352 million deficit reported for 1990 was the largest ever suffered by a British bank in the US, surpassing the $324 million loss suffered in 1984 by Midland Bank through Crocker.[40]

The NatWest losses in the US came from a combination of Latin

American loans, US project finance, and commercial real-estate loans, with the latter being the most damaging. The recession in that market had hit the north-east US particularly hard, and NatWest Bancorp, along with many US banks, had taken big losses. Some, like Bank of New England and MidAtlantic, did not survive.

By the early 1990s, bank analysts and reporters in the British financial press began to refer to the US retail banking market as a 'black hole' for foreign banks. These people kept referring to a classic pattern that the British banks and those from other nations consistently followed: they would first hire US managers to run their branches there and give them much autonomy, on the theory that locals knew the market best; then, as losses mounted, the foreign parent would assert much tougher control, although by that time it was often too late; eventually, they would close the branches and exit the US retail business.[41]

NatWest had followed a similar strategy in the US, as had Barclays and Lloyds. But the latter two had cut their losses and closed down their US retail branches by the early 1990s, while NatWest marched on. 'We had the guts to keep on in the US,' a senior NatWest banker recalled in late 1995, 'which is more than Barclays did.' The costs of keeping on, however, had obviously mounted.

In an effort to reverse the losses, NatWest fired in 1991 the US manager, William Knowles, who had run its bank there for ten years, and replaced him with John Tugwell, then head of its international division. Knowles had come to NatWest in 1981, after a successful career as head of Bankers Trust's retail bank. Tugwell was one of its top bankers, often mentioned on the short-list as Frost's possible successor as NatWest CEO. He acknowledged that this was so and that the personal stakes for him in taking such an assignment were high.[42]

The financial press, hard on Frost in the Blue Arrow case, was equally critical of him in regard to NatWest's US operations. The *Financial Times* thus referred to the US strategy as 'the brainchild of Mr Tom Frost', in the same article where it recited the enormous losses that the US arm of the bank had incurred.[43]

Tugwell did an outstanding job in turning around this business. Indeed, the results of 1992–4 contrasted sharply with those of earlier years.[44] At the same time, the experience since 1979 constituted another dent in NatWest's reputation, and this business, along with NatWest's investment bank, were often cited as two of its biggest strategic errors.

By 1994, an increasing faction of senior managers and board members within NatWest argued for selling the entire US retail banking operation. Given the increasing consolidation among US regional and super-regional banks, NatWest's main competitors there, this group argued that continuing contributed little, if anything, to shareholder value. Strategic analysis scenarios of CEO Derek Wanless pointed both to the diminished attractiveness of that market and to NatWest's falling market share. Moreover, there were additional arguments that no synergies existed between that business and NatWest's other operations.

Tugwell was not part of that faction, arguing that not only had he turned NatWest Bancorp around, but that its prospects for future expansion were promising.[45] One meeting of senior management in late 1994 came close to recommending the sale, but Tugwell reportedly arrived late and got a reprieve, after not being initially informed that the meeting was to take place.

The next year, however, witnessed the repeal of the McCarran Act in the US, thus opening opportunities for interstate branching and more bank mergers; and that development made NatWest's competitive prospects even more doubtful, short of its making a huge investment in acquisitions to keep up. The board and senior management were not prepared to make such an investment, and they announced in December 1995 that they had sold NatWest Bancorp to Fleet Financial, a fast-growing super-regional bank, based in New England.[46]

Wanless confirmed the sale with a public statement acknowledging past losses. He was quoted as saying: 'The story of Bancorp over 16 years is an awful story for shareholders, and we have never hidden that.'[47] By contrast, barely a year earlier, in NatWest's annual review and summary statement for 1994 (p. 14), he had indicated considerable optimism regarding the US operation.

> In the US we have acquired Citizens First and Central Jersey banks within Bancorp's area of operation, creating the largest non-US-owned retail bank, with nearly 350 branches. We gain three particular benefits: a leading position in New Jersey, one of the most attractive state markets … and the chance to introduce to new customers services they had not previously been offered … We see the US as an important growth market and we are also strengthening the position there of NatWest Markets and Coutts.

Troubles in Europe

A less dramatic series of setbacks took place in Europe, where NatWest had opened several branches. Its losses there and in the US were similar to those of Barclays and a likely result of their common strategy of pushing for geographic representation without assessing adequately enough the risks.

By 1993, after many years of European expansion, NatWest, like Barclays, was reporting big losses in France and Spain and was scaling down and/or exiting as a result. Rather than continue with retail banking in Europe, NatWest announced its intention to concentrate on investment and private banking there. Wanless was quoted as saying that 'NatWest believed retail banking was a "national game" and there was "no such thing" as a pan-European retail banking business.'[48]

Responses: better management, more focus, more streamlined organization

The jolts referred to above did not go unattended – nor could they, given their high visibility and their potential impact on NatWest's reputation and share price. In fact, they provided the impetus for wide-ranging changes within NatWest, aimed at improving its performance and future prospects. The issue now is whether the response was adequate enough.

By far the most damaging of the jolts was the Blue Arrow episode. One of the things that NatWest had most prided itself on was its long-standing reputation for integrity and professionalism in dealings with key stakeholders. The fraud charges related to the Blue Arrow flotation were devastating from that perspective, and NatWest responded with alacrity, using the episode as an opportunity to make significant reforms. These included:

(1) major personnel changes at the top: a new Chair, CEO, board members, and many senior managers, thereby speeding up the normal succession process;

(2) more rigorous strategic planning that had the potential at least to provide more focus and to limit the likelihood of such débâcles in the future; and

(3) a new organization to make the bank more responsive to customers and to eliminate much of its slow moving, dysfunctional bureaucracy by trimming the headquarters staff and transferring many of its past functions to the divisions.

Devolution thus became a significant NatWest policy, as did the search for synergies within and across its main divisions.

A new board

Blue Arrow was clearly a major catalyst for change, and a dramatic moment in NatWest's history was when its board Chairman, Lord Boardman, publicly announced his resignation in 1989, at the peak of the Blue Arrow case. Though NatWest had done well in the eighties under his stewardship, Boardman was not regarded within the industry as a dynamic leader, and his exit was hastened by that episode. A long-time banking reporter summarized his impressions of Boardman's term:

> Boardman had business and some government experience and was a very nice person, but he was not up to the job. In 1989, he announced his resignation on, of all places, the steps of his bank.

By contrast, Boardman's replacement, Lord Alexander, was a distinguished lawyer who had spent two years as part-time Chairman of the UK's Panel on Takeovers and Mergers. Although he had no background in banking or in management, he had an excellent reputation for integrity, for his negotiating skills, and for his ability to absorb new ideas and practices quickly. The appointment of Lord Alexander was thus an important one, providing NatWest with just the kind of leadership it was seen as lacking in the events leading up to Blue Arrow. In fact, NatWest's board saw Alexander's appointment as so important that he started as Deputy Chair in May 1989 and became Chair that October, several months earlier than originally planned.[49]

Alexander, acting as a crisis manager, immediately worked to get the bank's house in order. He soon reduced its board from 31 to 19 members, replacing some of the landed squires of the past with CEOs and other senior managers from major corporations.[50] When Alexander arrived in October 1989, 34.6 per cent of the board members had served for more than ten years; by 1994, none had.[51] A top NatWest staff person reported: 'These new people on the board include heavyweight corporate players in the UK, like the CEO of Unilever, the Vice-Chair of Hansen, the Chair of Tesco. And board meetings then included challenging and probing questions of our senior management that had never been asked before. So we became a much more businesslike organization.'

A new generation of senior managers

To concentrate on his defence in the Blue Arrow investigation, Frost retired from the post of NatWest's CEO in 1992, a year earlier than would otherwise have been the case. Lord Alexander and his board selected as Frost's successor 44-year-old Derek Wanless, at that time the youngest CEO ever at any British bank.[52] Wanless had been at the bank for some twenty years, but he was different from all previous NatWest CEOs – not only in age but in formal education and intellect. A graduate of Cambridge in mathematics, Wanless was highly regarded as a sophisticated technician and strategic thinker, just the kind of person Alexander and his colleagues felt could push NatWest back into the ranks as a leading UK and international bank.

Two others on the short-list who were passed over were John Tugwell, then 52, and John Melbourne, 56. Both had spent most of their working lives at NatWest and had served in various senior management positions. Tugwell in particular was the preferred choice of many knowledgeable outside observers: he had been head of the international division and then of NatWest Bancorp in the US, having done an excellent job in turning the latter around. Melbourne was also seen as a seasoned and shrewd banker, not likely to be captured by the latest fads and with thoughtful judgements about what businesses to pursue.

Instead, Lord Alexander and his board chose a younger man with a more formal educational background, with a deep understanding of the new technology coming into banking, and with strong analytical skills. Wanless had other things going for him as well: he was not tainted with any connection with Blue Arrow; and he had made his reputation in managing NatWest's UK retail banking, the very area that was the bank's greatest strength.[53] Wanless's appointment was heralded at the time as leapfrogging two generations. While somewhat exaggerated, this perception did call attention to Wanless's youth and new set of skills as strong considerations.

Other senior management appointments were made of new, young staff, many of them outsiders, around the time of Wanless's becoming CEO. Though he did not make any immediately dramatic appointments, within a year Wanless himself had begun to bring in enough such people to catch the notice of the financial press. Thus, by June 1993, some 15 months after Wanless's arrival as CEO, mention was being made of a 'new generation' of NatWest managers who might give it the critical mass and impetus it clearly needed to recover from its many recent knocks and financial losses.[54] These people included: Richard Goeltz, 49, as Chief Financial Officer, and formerly Executive Vice President at Seagram in the US; Stuart Chandler, 48, in charge of strategic development, and formerly with the Bank of England; Christopher Wathen, 48, Director of Human Resources, and former head of retail banking at Midland; John

Howland-Jackson, 45, Deputy Chair, NatWest Markets; Martin Gray, 46, CEO of UK retail; Martin Owen, 45, CEO of NatWest Markets; and Bernard Horn, 49, CEO of Group Operations. Gray, Owen and Horn were all old-time Natwest staff, totalling some eighty years collectively at the bank. But they had been promoted to senior positions at an unprecedentedly young age, and now there were many more outsiders than before.

This new group of senior managers, a mix of insiders and outsiders, represented a significant departure from the past. One of their big missions – as part of a drive to transform NatWest into a more focused, efficient, and adaptive organization – was to phase down much of the bank's dysfunctional bureaucracy. As one newcomer remarked: 'When I first came, I had not seen so many layers of bureaucracy since I read Milton's *Paradise Lost*. There were archangels and angels, and seraphim and cherubim everywhere I looked.'[55] Interviews with Barclays' managers indicated that the same conditions prevailed there as well.

A new organizational structure: devolution and synergy

Wanless, on becoming CEO, soon embarked on several initiatives to revamp NatWest's structure and fine-tune its strategy. None of these changes was done in a flashy or attention-grabbing fashion, that being neither his nor the bank's style. But they appeared on close examination to have the potential to improve markedly NatWest's adaptiveness and performance.

One of the most significant of the changes was to restructure relations between headquarters and the divisions to give the latter much more flexibility. This involved redefining the Office of the CEO and the role of headquarters as setting broad policy directions and making major strategy decisions but otherwise providing support and monitoring for the divisions, rather than making all their decisions. This policy was implemented, reducing the size of the corporate headquarters or head office staff from roughly 400 to 170.[56] A previously unwieldy central structure that had slowed down and obstructed the main business groups was to be replaced by a much more streamlined one, with many staff functions decentralized down to the businesses.

Human resource management decisions such as, for example, performance appraisals, salary recommendations, and training were transferred to the divisions. As a central staff person in that speciality noted:

We devolved human resource management to the business groupings and made the line managers there responsible for people management. At the same time, we only have twelve HR staff remaining at central, and we installed HR departments in all the business groups. They all have HR specialists, and we have been engaged in a massive re-engineering effort to get the line managers to have HR skills.

The same policy of decentralization or devolution took place with regard to strategic planning. 'We had a wide-ranging debate on the role of headquarters and the divisions, and we are very much committed to the divisions developing their own strategies,' explained a senior staff member at headquarters.

We do a lot of review and supportive probing, but now the separate businesses are expected to do far more of their strategic analysis for themselves. We network like mad among the planners in each of the businesses. But we need the divisions and the individual businesses to know more and more about change. So you can say that our management style has been to cascade authority from headquarters to the divisions to individual businesses.

These changes moved NatWest as an institution from a centralized bureaucracy to a more loosely coupled set of businesses with an enhanced capability to respond more quickly and more sensitively to customer demand. There remained, however, a small senior management group, part of the Office of the CEO, that met regularly to decide on strategy for the bank as a whole. That group was composed of Wanless, his Chief Financial Officer, the head of human resources for the bank, and a few other senior managers. Tugwell and Melbourne, for example, were part of that group in the mid-1990s, with Tugwell commuting regularly to London from his New Jersey office to attend those meetings. In addition, the CEOs from the investment bank (NatWest Markets), the UK retail bank, and headquarters services, as well as some top headquarters staff, would also attend some of the planning meetings.

Although devolution and divisional and business autonomy were stressed, there was more to this new organization than just a loose coupling. Much emphasis was placed as well on collaboration within and across the various businesses and divisions in an effort to find synergies among them, mirroring changes Taylor was making at Barclays – at least that was what the NatWest headquarters staff and senior managers kept reporting. One noted:

We have a lot of synergies between our retail businesses in the UK and US, including Ulster and Coutts, where we export best practice and have used the US as a test site for the UK. We bring ATMs, small business loan marketing, and private-placement services from Britain to our US retail branches. So, we have synergies retail-to-retail and wholesale-to-retail. And the common threads are management skills, technology, marketing. That would not happen if we were a specialized bank. The strategic-planning staff group at headquarters focus a lot on these key synergy issues.

Another headquarters staff member reported:

Maximizing synergies is important for us and we work hard on it. We want to make sure that our concerns for internal organization should not get in the way of finding solutions to customer problems. There must be synergies across divisions. If we do that well, we get another five to ten per cent profit. We are working on improving our skills in the retail bank – for example, at cross-selling – and the big challenge is there. We must do more.

Yet, other highly placed headquarters staff had a different perspective, arguing that it was not only difficult to get collaboration across product groups and divisions but also that far too little took place. One such staff person reported: 'Our portfolio is designed to have as few synergies between the SBUs [Strategic Business Units] as possible, focusing strongly instead on how they do it for themselves.' He went on to note that most collaborations took place within particular divisions and that, even there, it was difficult to do: 'Cross-divisional synergies are very difficult to find or implement, and most of the collaborations are within SBUs,' he explained. 'For example, right now, NatWest UK has been restructured to create linkages. Its whole logic is to build more integrated approaches to customers. But getting those people to work together to serve customers is hard, and there is the opportunity cost of the time required. Each one wants to run its business really well and not work on synergies. In the retail bank, they have a tendency to develop separate product silos and be very product-focused; but it tries to cross-sell as much as possible and all involving the six or seven product groups in that division.'

A consultant hoping to push NatWest toward more collaboration across product groups and divisions but not given much support in his efforts was deeply pessimistic about NatWest's prospects in this regard:

NatWest's weakness is in team building and integration. They need an integrated company, team development, and a long-term vision to rally people around. But I didn't see that as happening; in fact, they have gone backwards. In NatWest UK, for example, the degree of integration is very low. They need co-operation across their six separate businesses to service the customer, but instead they have increased the autonomy of each business. Integration is not in their culture, and they don't have the skills to pull it off.

This consultant had tried to work with Wanless, but he saw himself as unsuccessful in getting Wanless to take initiatives in integration. 'Wanless is a mathematician, and his head is not on integration and the behavioural side, no matter what he says. He can have a report with a load of numbers and he can condense it down quickly and well, but on getting people and businesses to collaborate – you can forget it with him. I know they talk a lot about synergy, but they don't do anything about it, as far as I can see. Wanless's style is one of avoidance and compromise, and there is less integration at the top in NatWest now [late 1995] than ever before.'

These reports suggest that while there is much *talk* about co-operation and synergies, *implementation* has proved difficult. The implementation that exists is more likely at the divisional level – as, for example, across product groups within NatWest UK retail or NatWest Markets. But, even there, it has been uneven. As we discussed above, the 'family of cultures' that Martin Owen talked about developing in NatWest Markets did not emerge there. Moreover, while it might have been easier to get such co-operation in the retail bank, it seems to have been slow there in coming as well.

NatWest had engaged in restructuring its organization since the early 1990s for what was reportedly the first time in its history. The concepts for that restructuring had considerable merit; their implementation, however, seems to have left much to be desired, and it is not all that clear that a new, more streamlined, flexible and responsive organization has emerged in the nineties. If it had emerged, it would have been unlikely that the serious problems at both NatWest UK and NatWest Markets, which contributed in the late 1990s to the bank's losses and high costs, would have arisen.

A new era of strategic planning

Just as NatWest undertook serious organizational-change initiatives after Blue Arrow, under Wanless as its new CEO, so too did it seemingly change its entire strategic planning process. NatWest senior managers reported enthusiastically about how the bank since the early nineties had replaced its less reflective drift of the past with a coherent, analytical approach to strategic planning. They attributed the change to Wanless's disciplined, systematic approach.

That approach bore much resemblance to strategic analysis models developed by academics.[57] It involved what NatWest strategy staff referred to as 'positioning the portfolio' by rating every business that NatWest was in on two dimensions: first, their attractiveness, which related to historic trends in their profitability; and, second, NatWest's market share within them. On the latter, NatWest staff made judgements about what they called the 'strategic stretch' needed to have the bank become a top performer.

Based on such an analysis, NatWest's senior management rated every business on a scale from one to five. A rating of one would indicate that NatWest's product was a first choice of customers and that it should therefore stay and expand. By contrast, a business rated four would be one that it would most likely want to downsize, and a rating of five would indicate a business from which the bank should exit. This sophisticated planning process generated much enthusiasm and pride within the bank, accompanied by an equally strong conviction that it could only help the bank develop more focus and perform better. 'This provided the discipline we never had before,' explained a planning staff member 'and it has been driven by Wanless's analytic approach. His vision is quite cerebral, as it follows this rigorous analytic process as opposed to the vision statements of other banks that may have more excitement value when presented to the public but are not nearly as well founded.'

NatWest senior managers and staff claim that this strategic management approach contributed to many exit and acquisition decisions. Some mentioned the sale of the US retail bank and the investment banking acquisitions as examples. Despite the new analytic process, bank analysts, consultants and financial reporters have not embraced it wth the same enthusiasm as have NatWest staff. Many such outside observers share the view that NatWest in fact had a quite diffuse and ambiguous strategy. For some, it was a matter of Wanless and his colleagues not articulating any clear vision or direction. Bank analysts and financial reporters not only shared this view but also suggested that it probably affected NatWest's reputation and share price. 'The analysts think NatWest's strategy is too fuzzy and expansionist without being thought through,' said one prominent banking reporter. A CEO at an investment bank observed: 'I don't know what NatWest's strategy is. I think Derek Wanless is smart and a very nice guy, but there is no strategy.' A veteran banking reporter mused: 'I find NatWest's direction unclear and hard to get one's hands around. It is a kind of amorphous jelly.'

Even some senior managers within NatWest acknowledged that the bank had not been effective in projecting a clear vision and strategy to the outside world. One very senior person conceded this point, comparing NatWest in this regard with Barclays: 'Taylor, Barclays' CEO, is a darling of the press,' he explained. 'He knows just what to say, and I know it is worth at least 50 basis points in Barclays' stock price. He presents himself very well, and we do less well in that regard. We are sensitive to how we project ourselves, and we are told that we do not project a clear strategy. We are seen as managing our businesses very well but not managing our reputation and image as well.'

Ultimately, one must look at the bank's financial performance to judge which side is right – the NatWest bankers applauding Wanless's new analytic planning approach, or the outside observers bemoaning the bank's lack of vision, clarity or coherent direction. One banking observer noted that 'measurement is not management', referring to the fact that Wanless's technical and mathematical skills as related to strategic analysis were not a substitute for articulating a clear vision and implementing it.

While it is reasonable to conclude that both could be right, with the bank's problem being one of failing to communicate externally in an attractive way the strengths of its strategic process, NatWest's lagging performance of the middle and late 1990s has suggested larger systemic problems that prevented the process from being effectively implemented. As George Vojta, Vice Chair of Bankers Trust has stated: 'Having a vision is important, but skill in execution is a big part of the task of becoming a high performer.' Skill in execution or implementation relates, in turn, to matters of managing the culture, organization and people, and to institutional style, all of which relate to NatWest's recent difficulties.

Notes and references

1. Bloomberg, *Financial Markets* (online).
2. *Annual Report and Accounts, 1997*, NatWest Group, pp. 5–7.
3. *Ibid.*
4. *Annual Abstract of Banking Statistics*, Vol. 14, 1997, British Bankers' Association, pp. 64 and 66.

5. *Annual Report and Accounts, 1997*, NatWest Group, p. 27.
6. *Financial Times*, 16 July 1997.
7. Lehman Brothers, *UK Clearing Banks, 1998 Annual Review*, pp. 76, 126.
8. Richard Reed, *National Westminster Bank, A Short History*, 1989, p. 3. National Westminster Bank plc, archived.
9. *Financial Times*, 19 April 1991.
10. Bloomberg, *Financial Markets* (online).
11. *Financial Times*, 5 August 1997.
12. Lehman Brothers, *UK Clearing Banks, 1997 Annual Review*, p. 123 and Bloomberg, *Financial markets* (online).
13. Stephen P. Robbins, *Organizational Behavior*, 6th edn, Prentice Hall, Englewood Cliffs NJ, 1993, pp. 139–40.
14. *Independent*, 26 February 1998.
15. *Financial Times*, 5 August 1998.
16. Lehman Brothers, *UK Clearing Banks, 1997 Annual Review*, p. 95, 131. See also its 1998 Annual Review.
17. Lehman Brothers, *UK Clearing Banks, 1997 Annual Review*. p. 122.
18. *Financial Times*, 20 December 1995.
19. *The Economist*, 22 March 1997, p. 94.
20. *Ibid.*, p. 78.
21. *Wall Street Journal*, 14 March 1997.
22. *The Economist*, 28 June 1997, p. 77.
23. *Ibid.*
24. *Wall Street Journal*, 14 March 1997.
25. Lehman Brothers, *UK Clearing Banks, 1997 Annual Review*, p. 128.
26. Lehman Brothers, *UK Clearing Banks, Annual Review, 1998*, p. 120.
27. Richard Reed, *op. cit.*, Part 1.
28. *Ibid.*, p. 43.
29. *Ibid.*, p. 43.
30. The discussion to follow draws heavily on Reed *op. cit.*
31. *Ibid.*, p. 49.
32. A good summary of the Blue Arrow experience appears in Roy C. Smith, *Comeback*, Harvard Business School Press, Boston MA, 1993, pp. 212–14.
33. *Financial Times*, 15 October 1991.
34. *The Economist* had a series of articles covering Blue Arrow from January 1988 through to 1992. See, in particular, its 28 January 1989 piece.
35. See *County NatWest Limited, County NatWest Securities Limited: Investigations under Section 432(2) of the Companies Act 1985, Report by Michael Crystal QC and David Lane Spence CA, Department of Trade and Industry*, 1989
36. *The Economist*, 6 March 1992.
37. *The Economist*, 23 January 1993.
38. From NatWest annual reports.
39. *The Economist*, 2 March 1991.
40. *Financial Times*, 31 January 1991.
41. *Ibid.*
42. *Financial Times*, 28 January 1992.
43. *Ibid.*

44. NatWest annual reports.
45. Interviews for this book.
46. *Financial Times*, 20 December 1995.
47. *Financial Times*, 23 December 1995.
48. *Financial Times*, 14 May 1993.
49. *Institutional Investor*, August 1980, pp. 80–4.
50. *Financial Times*, 16 January 1990.
51. NatWest annual reports.
52. *Financial Times*, 31 March 1992.
53. *Ibid.*
54. *Financial Times*, 8 June 1993.
55. *Ibid.*
56. *Financial Times*, 14 May 1993.
57. See, for example, Arnoldo C. Hax and Nicolas S. Majluf, 'The Use of The Industry Attractiveness–Business Strength Matrix in Strategic Planning', cited in William D. Guth (ed), *Business Strategy and Policy: Readings and Cases*, Copley Custom Publishing Group, Acton MA, 1993, pp. 323–38.

CHAPTER

8 *Can a Sleeping Giant Awake?*

AT THE beginning of the last chapter, I made the comparison of Barclays and NatWest with Citicorp and Chase. My profiles of those US banks in *The Future of American Banking* (1993) suggest some striking similarities between Barclays and Citicorp as one pair, pursuing entrepreneurial, first-mover strategies, and between NatWest and Chase as another, having a more risk-averse style.

A NatWest staff member thought likewise:

> You had a section in your book on the American banks where you described how Chase institutionalized and absorbed innovations in a way that they ended up not being innovative, and it sounded just like us. We were actually ready to merge with them, which would have been a big coup. And we are very much like what they were throughout their history.

This observation matches what many analysts, financial writers, regulators and other outside observers have noted over the years, in addition to NatWest managers themselves. Their view of NatWest as a reactive, slow-moving, bureaucratic institution throughout much of its history bears directly on the analysis to follow.[1]

A collegial but stodgy culture

Despite the frequent characterization of Barclays and NatWest as being similar in strategy and organization, they are also quite different in some respects. Those differences, particularly in culture and leadership – which may account in part for Barclays' having recovered more substantially in the late nineties than NatWest – are the focus of this chapter.

This is not to say that the NatWest franchise is without significant strengths and is not capable of returning to its former leadership position; its strong performance in 1998 suggests that that may well be the case. It is rather to argue that the overall NatWest style seems to have hampered its adaptation to increasing competitive threats, much as Chase's had in the seventies, eighties and early nineties in the US. Just as Chase has become stronger as a newly merged entity than it was before, so may NatWest have a similar experience in the near future.

The traditional NatWest culture includes several themes:

(1) reliability, integrity, steadiness and predictability in its dealings with key stakeholders;

(2) a strong emphasis on procedures and on consensus decision making, resulting in NatWest being more a follower and reactor to market changes than a first mover and paradigm breaker;

(3) much in-breeding, resulting from the promotion of high-street, retail bankers to senior management positions;

(4) an institutional modesty and lack of flashiness and charisma in representing the bank in public, reflecting again the dominance of traditional retail bankers;

(5) a clubby style, associated with strong ties of loyalty to one another and to the institution and its traditions and considerable homogeneity in backgrounds of senior managers; and

(6) a deep commitment to corporate social responsibility and community development.

Each of the above cultural characteristics could be interpreted in a positive as well as negative light. Thus, several observers emphasized the upside of the NatWest culture, characterizing its people and practices as humane, decent, reliable and professional. That would certainly be the case for NatWest's traditions of social responsibility that give it a record perhaps unsurpassed in either the UK or Europe. My argument is that, taken together and pursued with some intensity, the first four traits listed above represent a configuration that may have at times *hampered* NatWest's modernization and adaptation to a fast-changing, increasingly competitive market environment.

Risk-aversion was the cultural trait that outside observers and NatWest bankers cited perhaps most frequently as at the core of its culture. A positive interpretation was that this reflected a prudence and reliability in NatWest practices that inspired confidence among customers and regulators and limited NatWest's embarking on rash deals. By contrast, the negative interpretation emphasized how NatWest was consistently lagging behind its competition in adapting to market changes. This slowness, in turn, may be attributed to many factors: the continued influence of the retail bankers and a high-street mentality within NatWest, even after a newer generation had come in, particularly in the investment bank; and an historical legacy from the merger that brought together Westminster, National Provincial, and District as relative equals, leading to a style of consensus decision making that slowed NatWest's reaction time.

The NatWest culture and institutionalized style become particularly clear when contrasted with Barclays. Even though the two banks were similar in so many respects, including the school-leaver backgrounds of their retail bankers, NatWest and Barclays differed markedly in other ways, and bankers within each institution as well as outsiders continually noted those differences when describing the cultures of each.

NatWest was much more bureaucratic and slow-moving than Barclays. This reflected, in turn, differences in backgrounds of the banks' most senior managers and circumstances of their founding. While both banks were similar in the school-leaver backgrounds of their retail branch employees, the senior managers of Barclays – resulting largely from its history of the families – were a much more university-educated, cultured, and upper-middle-class group; and they were more entrepreneurial as a result. Senior managers at NatWest, by contrast, remained until the 1990s a predominantly school-leaver, high-street group, with more limited horizons.

These class differences then got played out in predictable ways. Some NatWest managers regarded those at Barclays as 'stuffy snobs', while the latter saw NatWest as 'plodding, grey, unimaginative bureaucrats'. The perceptions reflected, in turn, differences in the behavioural styles of the banks as institutions.

One former Barclays staff member noted, in summarizing many of these points:

> The Barclays senior people had much more flair than those at NatWest. Maybe some of that was because they came from old families, were posher, more upper-class, and didn't worry as much about being 'proper' and about status. The NatWest people were more branch dullards coming to the top. The Barclays senior people were just flakier. Barclays was a bank with more action people and was always entrepreneurial. NatWest was more like the Politburo. Even the new people like Wanless were that way.

Several observers made the point that these institutional differences were personified in the present CEOs of the two banks. One economist and analyst of the industry pointed out: 'Wanless is not prepared to rethink things. While Taylor has Barclays poised for action and major change, NatWest does not have that orientation. It has not asked the big questions and is not in ferment.' A former senior manager at NatWest recalled: 'NatWest was always very earnest. But its merger of equals led it to be slow in decision making. The issue was often about which way to go – Westminster, District or National Provincial. They spent too much time thinking about this and were late in acting. Also, Barclays was more entrepreneurial. It had an officer class, and they acted quicker and more decisively, though sometimes more disast-rously.' He went on to note: 'A big problem for this industry in Britain, which NatWest personifies, is that it has been dominated by branch banking, and those people are so absorbed by their culture that they cannot see paradigm shifts.'

Institutional styles are often reflected in a variety of symbolic ways – for example, in logos as well as in the public appearances of CEOs. One financial journalist, an astute analyst of the British banks' cultures, captured both in his comparisons of NatWest and Barclays: 'The corporate logo of NatWest is grey, while that of Barclays is peacock blue, and that really epitomizes the difference between them. Even their new CEOs reflect this. Taylor is more expressive and electric. Wanless is more restrained.'

Several NatWest senior managers agreed with these perceptions of its culture. One reported: 'Our culture is conservative, steady, and stable, with high ethical standards. We do not see ourselves as big innovators in products.' Another acknowledged: 'We are solid, dependable, a little slow and reactive, but now showing signs of being faster and changing more readily. And, right now, we are working hard to get rid of the dross and bureaucracy.' Finally, a senior staff person at headquarters explained:

> We tend to undersell ourselves, and we are quite modest and introverted. We don't present ourselves as well as we might. I take this to be a NatWest cultural characteristic. The positive at Barclays about its family people at the top was that because they were family they were not the grey bureaucrats who had to toe the line for their future. And they could take more risks and have a more free-wheeling, entrepreneurial spirit. We at NatWest are much less flamboyant and much more modest. Also, we have too much of a consensual decision-making style.

NatWest has pursued a practice of in-breeding throughout much of its history. All of the clearing banks followed this pattern, but it was particularly pronounced at NatWest. A common career line was to enter a branch as a clerk in one's middle or late teens, move on at some point in one's thirties or forties to an international branch assignment, and end up in one's fifties at headquarters. 'We have a homogeneous senior management team, who have followed that pattern,' explained an old-line staff member.

One of the features of that career line, in addition to its perpetuation of a homogeneous, insider, non-university group as senior managers, was the fact that it actually gave little management responsibility along the way. A former senior manager from NatWest explained: 'The problem was that the people coming in at seventeen were given no responsibility until quite late. By the time they were fifty and allowed to be in the running for top jobs, their minds had atrophied because they never had the responsibility.'

NatWest did make significant efforts to recruit university-educated and technically trained outsiders, even before the jolts described above forced them to speed up that process. The impact on the bank was minimal, however, as the old culture and established coalition of high-street bankers often rejected many of the newcomers. The latter were referred to as the 'officer class', and traditional NatWesters resented their presence. A human resources staff member from NatWest recalled:

> NatWest had programmes to bring in university graduates, and the turnover among those graduates was over ninety per cent until recently [late 1995]. There was little respect for academics within the bank, and the senior people did not want them in. Beyond that, NatWest had an archaic system of recognizing high-potential insiders, and the bank became more and more incestuous. For the last five years, however, university grads have increased their proportion of those who stay, whereas before that was not the case.

A former senior manager at NatWest further explained: 'There are more and more university graduates now. I remember, when I was there, one of the senior managers telling a group of us: "We will never have an officer class here," and that spoke of his narrowness of experience and imagination.'

Two consequences of this culture were, first, more limited innovation and slower adaptation to market changes than at Lloyds and Barclays; and, second, periodic lurches to compensate for the slow pace of change, whereby NatWest engaged in catch-up efforts that were not matched by a supportive infrastructure. Examples of both were the Blue Arrow episode and the experience in US retail banking, as presented in the previous chapter.

Blue Arrow could thus be seen as a catch-up attempt following NatWest's 'too timid start-up' relative to Barclays in investment banking in the mid-1980s. And it ended up such a disaster largely because NatWest did not have the expertise to implement the underwriting effectively.

The losses in US and European retail banking were similarly the result of trying to play catch-up in international banking, again without having either the strategy or the infrastructure to carry it off. Both Lloyds and Barclays were ahead of NatWest in attempts to develop strategic focus and concentrate on core businesses, and both sold off their US retail businesses as a result, several years before NatWest did. This was still a further example of where NatWest was behind its competitors by virtue of its starting later to develop new strategies and infrastructures to match the changing competitive environment.

A long-term senior staff member at NatWest summarized its history as having two main stages. The first was from its founding in 1970 to 1989, a time he characterized as one of very limited change. The bank started – and remained during that period – highly centralized, bureaucratic, with significant in-breeding of a homogeneous senior management team, being dominated by a branch manager coalition, very clubby, and following a strategy of universal banking. The latter included global and product expansion, but without a clear sense of what NatWest's core competences were and without a supportive enough infrastructure.

The second stage, brought about both by the increasingly competitive environment and by the impact of Blue Arrow and other failures, was from 1989 to the present day.[2] Its inception coincided with a recognition within NatWest that major changes were required for its survival, and many such changes were then introduced: a new appointment to the chair; a new board; a new CEO; new, younger senior managers recruited more from outside; a new, more sophisticated strategic planning process; a new, more decentralized, devolved organization; new technology; and efforts at culture change.

A basic question in this chapter relates to how successfully NatWest has implemented all of these changes, particularly in view of how antithetical they were to its old culture. Judging from its 1996 and

1997 results, indicating that it had fallen behind the other three clearers in ROE and in cost control in the all-important UK retail banking business, it appears that the implementation has not been adequate enough.

Yet, the improvement in all businesses for 1998 suggests a possible turnaround in which NatWest may be finally liberating itself from some of the most bureaucratic constraints of its past while concentrating more on areas of its past strengths, particularly UK retail and business banking.

NatWest's leadership

One means for overcoming such cultural obstacles to change is managerial leadership. Since such leadership is so essential in helping financial services institutions make the changes required to compete effectively, I turn now to an assessment of it at NatWest. The years of most relevance for this analysis are from the late 1980s to the present day.

The board Chair from 1983 to l989 was Lord Boardman. While he presided over NatWest in its years of steady expansion, his reputation in the British banking industry was as a decent person of limited distinction. One bank reporter was particularly outspoken on this: 'Lord Boardman was a man of low intellect and not confidence-inspiring,' he said. Boardman became one of the victims of Blue Arrow and resigned in 1989 to allow new leadership to take over that was untainted by any association with the case.

His successor, Lord Alexander, a well-known London trial lawyer, had many skills directly related to dealing with Blue Arrow. He had been chair of a highly visible commission on mergers and takeovers and had restored that body to a respectability it had lost before. The fact that he had this visibility and was in addition a skilled negotiator and analyst and was seen as a person of impeccable integrity was particularly beneficial to NatWest at this time.

From the outset, Lord Alexander was engaged in a crisis-management effort to restore NatWest's reputation. That involved orchestrating its defence in the Blue Arrow case and taking initiatives on the larger issue of speeding up NatWest's modernization. Although he was the board Chair and not NatWest's CEO, Alexander took charge much more forcefully than would have been the case had the bank not been facing such a public attack on its integrity. At the same time, he was sensitive to not encroach too much on the running of the bank and requested that his senior management and board warn him if he overstepped his own bounds.

On Blue Arrow, Alexander was most effective getting the charges disposed of as quickly as possible so that NatWest could move ahead expeditiously in its modernization efforts. One of his most aggressive initiatives was to request, in March 1992, an immediate, new inquiry in the case to clear CEO Tom Frost and the bank of charges of cover-up, over a year after the Department of Trade and Industry's main report had been completed.[3]

Lord Alexander took other major initiatives as well, including reducing the board from 31 to 19 members almost immediately on his arrival[4] and two years later appointing Derek Wanless as Tom Frost's successor as CEO. Lord Alexander's restructuring of the NatWest board helped make it less cumbersome and unfocused; and it encouraged the retirement of non-business oriented members, some of whom one senior NatWest manager referred to as 'Boardman's cronies'. Their replacement by senior managers of major corporations made a big improvement both in the board's functioning and in its reputation.

Most importantly, this board change became a platform for Lord Alexander's continued public pronouncements that banks had to be managed less like social institutions and clubs and more like business organizations with meritocracies. He was one of the main spokespeople for this point of view and his advocacy of it guided his and NatWest's later decisions.[5]

One of the most significant of those decisions was the selection of Wanless, in March 1992, as CEO. Wanless's predecessor, Tom Frost, had faced a stressful time as CEO since the Blue Arrow case went on during much of his term. Frost was praised in the industry for his long experience in branch and international banking, his persistence in NatWest's expansionist efforts, his interpersonal charm, and his strong commitment to community development efforts. But Frost was a traditional NatWester, having moved up in the conventional career sequence. Judgements about his leadership were mixed, with some observers seeing him as a strong and thoughtful leader and others seeing him as limited both in conceptual grasp of the industry's evolution and also as weak in managing the bank. Those negative judgements must be understood, however, in the context of the cloud that Blue Arrow cast over his time as CEO of NatWest.

The selection of Wanless was greeted with much praise and support at the time, although with some concern as well, given the magnitude of the task confronting him. Wanless came into the position with significant strengths. As a mathematical wizard, graduating with high honours from Cambridge, he had strong technical and analytical skills, enabling him to make well-informed strategic decisions. For a board chairman intent on making NatWest more businesslike, Lord Alexander had made an ideal choice in this regard. The fact that Wanless was not associated with Blue Arrow, that he had at different times been the head both of NatWest's UK retail bank and its investment bank, and that he had not been a senior manager long enough to be overly committed to any grandiose expansionist ideas held by some at that level were additional strengths. The fact that he was young and was sophisticated in the application of new technology was still another argument in his favour.[6]

The questions that some sceptics raised about Wanless, both at the time of his appointment and later, related to his breadth as a leader. 'Measurement is not management,' was the way one banking reporter and observer–critic phrased it. Some saw Wanless as similar in many respects to John Reed of Citicorp – in his interest in technology and quantitative approaches to managing the business, and in the fact that both were very young CEOs. Wanless was thus seen as a strong strategic thinker, but concern was expressed that, unlike John Reed, he did not seem to have any clear vision about how the bank should position itself and of how the industry was evolving.

Over time, there were increasing questions about Wanless's limited capacity to articulate his point of view to a wide public audience. He was, in a word, seen as not inspiring or charismatic, in the way that Pitman and Taylor were, with those being important aspects of managerial leadership. One bank analyst explained: 'Wanless is extremely bright, but he has no big vision, other than getting costs down in commodity businesses and getting good returns in non-commodity businesses. And it is clear that image now counts for a lot in this market.'

Other concerns have also been expressed. They relate to the judgement that despite his intelligence, youth and analytical skills, Wanless is not that much of an outsider or frame breaker. Having spent much of his working life at NatWest, he was criticized for consequently managing too much by consensus. Specifically, he was seen as too delegative with his senior managers, who were older than he, and thereby seen as failing to impose the controls that the bank needed.[7]

Based on this argument, he would not be expected, then, to move

NatWest ahead in more than small, incremental steps. 'Wanless is not prepared to rethink things,' said one analyst of the industry, 'while Taylor does have Barclays poised for action and major change. NatWest does not have that orientation. It has not asked the big questions and is not in ferment.' A banking reporter stated: 'Wanless says all the right things, but he is still more a product of the old NatWest, not the new.' A senior manager at an investment bank stated: 'Wanless is very smart but cautious, not leading-edge.'

Taken together, all the concerns raised by the critics indicate a scepticism regarding Wanless's skills at managing implementation. That was the issue raised in the previous chapter, in which I argued that despite Wanless's bringing in new people at the top, restructuring the bank's headquarters and instituting a sophisticated strategic-planning process, there did not appear to be that much improvement in NatWest's performance.

A critical issue on which NatWest foundered was the management of its investment bank. Blue Arrow was an example, as were the problems in 1997 with rogue trading. One long-time banking reporter explained:

> The culture of NatWest did not fit with investment banking. And nobody in NatWest knew about the business. That led to Blue Arrow and the complete clean-out, where they brought in a new totally different group at the top. And now it has happened again. Lord Boardman and Tom Frost were not confidence-inspiring then; nor were all of NatWest's past senior managers, who were cautious and completely at sea in the new investment banking. And Wanless has the same problems now.

The question then remains regarding future leadership at NatWest. Lord Alexander indicated in 1998 that he would retire at the end of that year; Wanless's fate is not as clear. Over the prior year, NatWest had been in discussions with Prudential and Abbey National about a possible merger; and in each case, one of the reasons the negotiations did not move ahead related to what role Wanless might play in the newly merged institution. He was reportedly unwilling to step down as CEO.

Wanless's future may depend in part on the strategic directions that NatWest's new board would like to see it follow. As at the time of writing, however, Wanless seems to have solidified his position within the bank, as indicated in more detail below.

A battle for the soul of NatWest

Many of these issues had at least begun to get played out in the 1990s as NatWest moved into and out of investment banking and as it increased the pace of modernizing its domestic retail bank. These two segments of NatWest have represented radically different subcultures, staff capabilities and interests within the bank, and the ways in which their relationships develop may well determine and then reflect the bank's immediate future. In order to understand what some of those dynamics are likely to be, it is useful to analyse how these groups differed and how they interacted.

Historically, as we know, the retail banking group prevailed. Its culture, its people, and its approaches to strategy and organization were the ones that the bank at large followed. And one of the biggest obstacles to modernization and adaptation to change that all of the Big Four clearers faced was having such a dominant coalition of traditional, retail branch bankers. This group had perpetuated itself over the years, was quite homogeneous, and set the culture and strategy of the bank. The problem was that the group was considerably out of synch with the accelerating changes that the industry was facing.

NatWest was certainly a prototype of that condition, as indicated in the earlier discussion of its risk-averse culture. Then, when it developed a large investment bank in the 1990s, it brought in a diametrically opposite culture. And much of the internal dynamic at NatWest over the past several years has been a playing-out of the conflict between the two, to see which would prevail.

On one side was the NatWest UK bank that reflected, in the words of one senior staff member, 'the remains of our old structure'. It was dominated by the non-university group who perpetuated the branch banking paradigm: hierarchical, highly structured, mass-producing, delivering of standard products, providing incremental salary increases and promotions, and maintaining a high cost/income ratio, with what one regulator referred to as 'antiquated customs and practices.' This group had dominated the larger NatWest culture throughout most of its history, having supplied disproportionate numbers of its senior managers.

On the other side were the new investment bankers, functioning in a much flatter, more loosely structured business, with shorter product life-cycles, much more innovation, fewer clients, and a faster pace of change. In the words of one of its senior managers, this group was 'constantly reinventing itself and the bank'. Its staff bore no resemblance to those in the retail bank: 'Ninety per cent of our staff here have university degrees,' explained a senior manager in the investment bank, 'and fifty per cent of our back office do. And we have a hundred Ph Ds among the six thousand employees in the division and five hundred masters degree people. Twenty years ago, there were no university grads in the entire bank. We are now drawing them in. but even now, under ten per cent of the retail banking staff are grads, so you can see the big cultural divide.'

This split between the two subcultures led to much mutual hostility and only limited co-operation. A top investment banker reported:

> Our people tell me they really don't want to go to meetings at headquarters, because they are seen as a complete waste of time. They have no interest in the issues, and the people are so slow-moving, nothing much happens. "It is not worth my time" is what they say. My people speak their mind and so do I. In our meetings, when I speak, they interrupt me, and we have a lot of combustion. At Derek Wanless's meetings, they are all too polite.

Moreover, the investment bankers had little respect for the competence of the senior management team directly under Wanless, and that, too, reflected their different backgrounds, cultures and styles of operation, as well as contributing to limited co-operation that was evident. 'I told the CFO recently that he couldn't make it in our shop as CFO. I also feel that, below Wanless, those group chiefs are almost worthless. We have fifty to sixty people who are better-quality than those people. One of my top managers – who feels even more strongly about these things than I do – is convinced that we have nothing to gain by being associated with the headquarters group.'

A senior manager in the NatWest retail bank acknowledged that this hostility existed: 'I remember during the late 1980s, I used to read the gossip column of the investment banking trade paper. It reflected the cultural divide. The terms used to describe the commercial bankers were very negative. We were referred to as "the nylon suited nine-to-five people". When Martin Owen, whose background was in commercial banking, was put in charge of them, the investment bankers saw him as the enemy.'

Not surprisingly, the retail bankers at NatWest had similarly negative stereotypes of the investment bankers. A senior manager in the retail bank said that he and his colleagues were very resentful of having to finance the big losses of the investment bank in the late eighties and early nineties, referring to that situation as 'lining the pockets of fancy-living, overpaid prima donnas.'

There were several ways in which this conflict affected the distribution of power and key strategic decisions at NatWest. One was for the senior people at headquarters to vacillate between not giving in to the investment bankers' demands, thereby excluding them from decision making, and being at times almost overcompliant with their demands. A banking reporter close to NatWest described the relationship: 'Every year they had a big lunch party for the international rugby matches held in London. And I would be sitting with a dozen or so top NatWest people. They were all buddies and were a closed club. And they used to talk about the merchant bankers they hated as 'stuck up' and as 'pains in the ass'. NatWest was back and forth between tight control and risk-smothering of the investment bankers versus letting them have their head. And the bank kept swinging from one to the other.'

Over time, however, aspects of the investment bank culture and paradigm were incorporated into the bank at large and were having an increasing impact on the retail bank's style and operations. The reasons for that were fairly obvious: the increasing pace of change in technology and products, new technical skill requirements, and increased competition – all characteristic of investment banking, were now pervasive in all types of financial services, including – retail banking. As a result, the retail bank and corporate wholesale banking began taking on more aspects of the investment banking model. A senior manager in retail banking explained the changes:

> The commercial bankers here changed toward the investment banking model. We no longer followed our old command-and-control model. Up to then, employment terms had been the same for everybody. The investment bank has a strong performance culture that was later in coming to the retail bank. People here had a nine-to-five, thirty-five-hour week. Also, the freedom to operate that the investment bank had was very healthy. They needed autonomy in that part of the business to respond to market changes. What happened was that it spread, and I now have more authority to run my operation here in retail banking. So headquarters created more autonomous business units, rather than one model.

There have been times, however, when the investment bankers felt so constrained by the commercial-banking culture represented at NatWest headquarters that they conducted big transactions on their own and took short cuts, without regard to the risks that that might incur for the bank. *Wall Street Journal* reporters interviewing NatWest staff regarding the options mispricings found this to be too commonplace:[8]

> One British banker said that many NatWest Markets traders criticize the parent bank's decision making for being too slow and too bureaucratic, forcing investment bank employees to cut corners to get things done. He described the relationship as a 'culture clash between the commercial bank, with its emphasis on safety and systems, and the merchant bank, where guys say, "I want to do it today; and if I can't do it today, there's no use doing it, because someone else will."'

Many aspects of the investment banking culture thus got incorporated into the bank at large: recruiting more university-educated people; hiring more technically trained people in sales, marketing and information technology; paying and promoting people on the basis of performance, rather than in a ratchet fashion; flattening the hierarchy and making it less procedure-driven and more responsive to customer needs. All these changes, incorporated from investment banking, were necessary for survival but traditionally alien to the dominant culture of the bank of the past.

As important as these changes have been, they still don't deal with the most important issue of all, namely, that of vision and strategy. The issue is what kind of financial services institution NatWest wants to be and what kind it *can* be in the increasingly competitive market environment that it faces. Notwithstanding the greater technical sophistication of NatWest's strategic planning process relative to what it had before Blue Arrow and other jolts had forced such changes, the bank has to develop a larger vision in order to survive. Whether and how it does this will determine its future, and the foregoing points are likely to be answered soon.

A common view among analysts, financial writers, regulators, and other outside observers is that NatWest will have to merge and most likely be acquired to survive: 'It won't make it as an independent corporation,' explained a bank analyst, 'and we all see an eventual merger partner where NatWest will not be dominant in the new firm. It seems to have destroyed its capacity to survive as a strong entity on its own or as the stronger one in a merger.'

In brief, the option whereby NatWest is the dominant player in a major acquisition may have been feasible in the past but appears less so now, as financial services in the UK and worldwide have become much more competitive and as NatWest's systemic weaknesses have continued to linger on. Thus, it may be too late for NatWest to survive on its own, just as it was for Chase, while that is clearly not the case for Lloyds and perhaps not so for Barclays either.

What is clear is that the universal banking model that NatWest increasingly followed since 1986's Big Bang is no longer appropriate. The need to develop a new model – and quickly – should be apparent from Chapters 7 and 8. NatWest, like Barclays, must reinvent itself quickly, if it is to have a future.

Retail banking: NatWest reinventing itself

The start of such reinvention at NatWest may well be in its domestic retail bank. NatWest is engaged in a series of reforms there that are a preview of its future.[9] Because of the substantial revenue generated from retail banking, it is not surprising that NatWest, along with the other clearers, has focused such efforts there.

Competition in retail banking has increased tremendously as many new players have entered the market. The UK's building societies are one such group. By the end of 1997, five of the ten largest societies had become shareholder-owned banks. They are more efficient than the commercial banks, their prices are lower, and polls indicate that consumers see them as friendlier than the banks. As *The Economist* observed: 'The three big societies converting this year [1997] – Halifax, Woolwich, and Alliance & Leicester – all have branches nationwide and plan to expand aggressively in fields such as pensions, insurance and consumer lending, where building societies are restricted.'[10]

Other new players include grocery chains, life insurers, department stores, Virgin Airways, and telecommunications firms such as British Telecom. These new competitors also have lower cost/income ratios than the banks, and they are driving down the margins on retail banking products: on credit cards, car loans, insurance, home mortgages, consumer lending, business loans, and pensions.

NatWest refers to its initiative as the Retail Transformation Programme (RTP), adding that it is the bank's biggest such effort in recent history. Since NatWest has a level of profitability below that produced by its peers (25 per cent ROE compared with over 30 per cent for Barclays in 1996), such an initiative is critical for its future.[11]

These innovative efforts, begun in 1996 and expected to be completed by 2000, include improving processing efficiency through regional 'factories' located around the UK, and developing multiple products distributed through multiple-delivery channels, thereby increasing market share. The strategy thus involves newly configured branches, new cash machines, and new delivery channels.

The new branches are referred to as 'stores', and NatWest has two, advanced, full-service, such stores in heavily populated suburban areas. One is in Basingstoke, some 40 miles west of London, and the other in Lakeside, 15 miles east of London. They are located in large shopping centres that have an estimated half-million customers coming through weekly.[12]

NatWest's new retail banking strategy, exemplified by its two new stores, is a complete antithesis to the traditional branch. One model that NatWest incorporated in them is from the Nordstrom department stores in the US: 'We got many of our design ideas from retailing in the States,' explained one of the 'store' managers, 'particularly Nordstrom and how it compensated and rewarded its sales staff.'

The essence of the Nordstrom model is to have an open, informal setting to facilitate customer service, building long-term relationships with customers and the wider community, and motivating and rewarding sales staff accordingly.[13] The branch facility of these stores has been completely transformed with that in mind. First, on entering the facility, there is a big waiting room with sofas, soft chairs, a large TV, and toilet facilities. Another room has a dispensing stamp machine, a change machine, and a machine to print business cards. There are also several conference rooms where customers can talk in private with a staff member, called a 'consultant', about their financial services needs. There is even a small TV in each conference room for children to watch while the adults' discussion takes place.

The ambience is thus open, bright and welcoming. The resulting traffic is unprecedented, particularly on weekends, when vast numbers of people come to conduct financial services transactions and to avail themselves of the many conveniences. 'Last weekend, people were here in big numbers to watch soccer on our TV,' a manager recalled. 'Who could ever imagine that you could watch international soccer matches on TV from a bank?'

The primary strategy is to create a climate that will make people want to conduct many of their financial transactions with the store. 'In the past, we had been transactionally led,' a store manager explained. 'People would come in and buy one product. Now we are pushing relationship banking, where the primary strategy is service. We encourage people to meet with our consultants and operate on the assumption that one-stop shopping still prevails among many British customers. Service is the key principle.'

In order for this service strategy to work, NatWest has incorporated many of Nordstrom's human resources policies. It follows a rigorous process during recruiting in order to ascertain applicants' sales skills. 'We feel that customer-service orientation and sales skills are much more important than technical banking knowledge and skills that can be taught easily,' explained a manager.

The branch gives performance bonuses at the end of each year, consultant-of-the-month and annual awards, all designed to build a sales-and-service culture. 'We recognize our staff for customer heroics,' said a manager. Examples of such customer-service heroics abound, and they resemble similar ones at Nordstrom. 'We didn't have a particular currency for one customer who was going to be travelling to another country on a Monday, and this was Saturday. Our salesperson went to a travel agent and delivered on Sunday morning the currency that the customer needed. It was a forty-mile round-trip. We had another case of a woman whose husband had just died, and her flat became flooded, and our salesperson went to her flooded flat and negotiated with plumbers and insurance agents to take care of her problem. Those heroics won service awards.'

Meanwhile, the branch managers play a very different role from the past. Their main job is recruiting, training and rewarding the salespeople, and otherwise watching over the operation of the store. The new stores are thus radically different from the traditional branch. They develop their own staff and sales programmes, rather than wait for commands and rely on managers above them. They focus primarily on servicing the customer and on developing a long-term relationship, by providing a wide variety of conveniences and services. Each salesperson is multi-functional and sells all the main products. And while the performance bonuses and awards have the potential to develop competition and conflict among the salespeople, as happens at Nordstrom's, that seems not to have happened at these Natwest stores. Instead, the store managers train the salespeople in team building, facilitating good bonding among them.

As part of a larger tiering strategy, these two full-service, demonstration stores are being evaluated to see if they may be replicated elsewhere. A second tier of large stores is being planned, with much the same full-service approach but not in such prime locations. A third tier of some 750–1000 outlets is planned for still smaller locations, and a bottom tier of more traditional outlets will continue to exist.[14]

A common theme in the strategy is to reconfigure the branches from their traditional process-oriented, service operation and inwardly focused culture to a more customer-oriented, sales-driven one. Paper processing and record keeping have largely been outsourced and automated. In brief, the bank teller function of staff has been replaced by machines, with the staff engaged primarily in selling various financial services products to customers.

In addition to these new-type stores, NatWest has new cash machines that include not only video screens of ATMs, but also advertising about NatWest's new products and promotional vouchers. The bank is also developing new delivery channels such as phone banking and financial services provided through machines in kiosks.

Physical branches as such will not disappear. Rather, there will be fewer of them and they will be reconfigured along the lines suggested in the demonstration projects, with electronic delivery systems via phone banking and ATMs gaining much wider usage. A big reason for maintaining many branches is that NatWest's 1.5 million small-business customers expect to visit a branch at least once a week. They also expect a branch to be within three or four miles of their place of business. 'The fact that we have so many branches has contributed a lot to our leading position in servicing small-business customers,' a senior manager in NatWest UK explained, adding:

> So I have a dilemma. Marks & Spencer and The Gap in the US have much higher foot flow than our bank branches. But what about the small businessman whose relative worth to us is ten times that of the average personal customer? He doesn't want to have to park in a mall and carry his money in crowded city streets. How to shake up the branch in the future to serve those two constituencies is a complex problem.

An issue in all such demonstration programmes is their replicability. The programme in these two stores obviously requires highly motivated and skilled salespeople as well as inspiring managers. There is an exchange programme with other branches, where the salespeople from these two stores go out and train their counterparts elsewhere. 'Our people go out to other branches. They feel like apostles in trying quietly to convert them to our concept,' explained a manager. 'The way we do things here is a new concept in British banking and certainly in NatWest.'

Much of what NatWest is doing in modernizing the delivery of services in its retail bank is similar to what the other clearers are doing. Reconfiguring the branches by outsourcing and automating the paper-processing functions, making the branches more customer-responsive and open, and developing new delivery systems through phone banking, pc banking, and the Internet are becoming standard practice. NatWest was also an innovator in developing its Mondex 'smart card' that enables the consumer to conduct multiple financial-services transactions through one source, and that may have a big return.

The basic story of NatWest with regard to this retail banking initiative is that it is driven in part from the bank's less competitive position in that area and from limited reforms in the past. Since the retail bank had always been a cash cow before, there was no sense of urgency about fixing it. Also, inadequate management and information technology skills further negated the limited attempts made in that direction. At present, NatWest is focused and working hard on this area of core competence. As one bank reporter noted:

> NatWest took its eye off the ball after Big Bang and now it is back on track. It is right for them to concentrate on what they are best at. Whether this will be enough to enable NatWest to survive as an independent firm remains to be seen.

The future

Despite these retail banking reforms, NatWest's future remains in doubt, just as Barclays' does. Having exited from many aspects of investment banking in 1997 and 1998, again as Barclays did, NatWest is searching for an identity. Specialized, retail niche banking in the UK, paralleling the Lloyds strategy, may be one option. While that segment of the industry has been a big revenue producer for all the clearers in the past, increasing competition from the other clearers, from the building societies, from non-banks in Britain, and from foreign non-banks and banks makes that alone an unlikely strategy for survival.

It might become more viable if NatWest merged with one of the other clearers. Martin Taylor had announced such an intention – for Barclays to merge with NatWest – in 1998, but nothing more came of it.[15] Concerns on both sides regarding who would be in control, as well as those of the Monopolies and Mergers Commission, appear to have combined to prevent further action on this proposal. Nevertheless, a merger like this would make NatWest and its new partner a powerhouse in UK retail banking, likely ensuring its survival as a big player for many years to come.

At the time that Taylor approached Wanless with the merger proposal (1997), Barclays' reputation and performance were higher than those of NatWest. Ironically, the reputations and performance of Barclays and NatWest have reversed somewhat since then: Barclays has had a series of setbacks, followed by Taylor's resignation, while NatWest has made a comeback with Wanless's position looking stronger than before.

Making a comeback?

After several dismal years, particularly 1997, when NatWest experienced big losses and fraud in its investment bank and serious doubts about its strategic direction and leadership, it had a temporary upswing in 1998. Defying the forecasters, it experienced a 49 per cent improvement in the first half of 1998. As the *Financial Times* reported, its post-tax ROE increased to 18.1 per cent, ahead of its long-term target of 17.5 per cent.[16]

Much of the improvement was in the core UK retail banking business, where the results of the transformation programme for NatWest's branch network were ahead of schedule. There were still remaining problems with the parts of NatWest's investment banking that it had not by then sold off, namely Greenwich NatWest, its debt-focused investment banking operations, and Gartmore, its fund management arm, along with Lombard, its long-time finance house. But the reversal of fortunes was marked. 'We finally achieved more focus,' explained one senior NatWest banker, 'as we moved out of investment banking businesses we were not skilled in and worked harder to improve on UK retail banking and corporate businesses, where we had always done well.'

Accompanying this short-term recovery has been a change in CEO Derek Wanless's management style. Earlier in the year, he had issued a stark warning to the bank's top 200 managers on the need for radical changes in its culture and organization. Indicating the crisis that NatWest faced, he told them: 'There will be no second chance. If we cling to our hierarchical, process-driven structure, we will not survive.'[17] He went on: 'We have two choices. We can continue to produce poor results and continue the inexorable slide downwards, or we can score some goals. The changes I am looking for are not optional, not negotiable, not nice to have; they are absolutely vital to the future of the group.'

Since then, all reports indicate that Wanless has in fact changed his management style in the direction of being more demanding and exerting stronger management controls than ever before. The bank is no longer run in the same delegative, consensus-management fashion of the past. 'Derek is a changed man. He's a much tougher manager now,' said one senior NatWest manager.[18]

Students of organizational behaviour suggest that institutions and their senior managers are most likely to change when they face major crises in the marketplace and when they recognize the severity of such crises. That may well have happened to NatWest and Derek Wanless. The year 1997 represented perhaps the low point of NatWest's decline in recent years. Articles in the financial press were even suggesting the prospect of a fraud inquiry into NatWest Markets' disappearing derivatives, as well as pointing to rumours of boardroom battles, failed merger talks with rivals, and then the ultimate humiliation of being offered a 'rescue' merger with Barclays, NatWest's arch-rival.[19] There were even hints that unless Wanless got NatWest on a better track, his future as CEO would be in doubt.

NatWest has not solved many of its strategic and culture-change problems, but Wanless's reputation and that of the bank have improved to a degree that his future is more secure than at the end of 1997. More importantly, the bank seems embarked on a series of more productive changes that may well reverse its decline of recent years. The main ones, toward a much more streamlined and customer-oriented UK retail bank, together with the exit from many parts of investment banking, seem to be having positive impacts.

It is unlikely that NatWest will give up wholesale and investment banking entirely. The question then becomes one of what kind of strategy it will pursue in this segment of financial services. Here again, significant merger activity will be required. Given the market power of the big US investment banks, and to a lesser extent of the European universal banks, NatWest, like Barclays, will have to narrow its choice to a market niche where it has a realistic chance of success. The most obvious choice might be a large European bank that already has a presence in European wholesale banking.

In the event that such a merger were to take place, NatWest might be seen as bringing less to the table than the European partner, making the combination more a merger of unequals than of equals. Much would depend on the extent of NatWest's recovery in 1998. That recovery might involve NatWest building up some segment of its wholesale banking over the next few years, as a pre-merger strategy, if it has that much time, preparatory to such a European bank merger. Regardless of what NatWest does in the coming years, commercial and investment banking are evolving globally in a fashion that requires major changes on its part just to survive. As was the case with Chase, the US bank with which it had much in common, NatWest's future requires much introspection, consolidation with a strong partner in retail and/or wholesale banking, and acceptance of the fact that it may not play a dominant role in the newly merged firm.

This may represent yet one more case of a major British bank being taken over by a foreign institution, and it could happen to Barclays as well as to NatWest. Even the US banks, however, are beginning to experience this, with Bankers Trust having been taken over by DeutscheBank and JP Morgan likely to merge during 1999 or 2000. Rather than just bemoan this development, if it happens to NatWest, the bank may be able to structure the merger so that its interests, however defined, are well represented.

Again, the comparison with Chase is relevant. While Chase's merger in 1995 with Chemical was defined at the time as a 'merger of equals', Chemical's Chair and CEO, Walter Shipley, took on those positions in the newly merged Chase. Tom Labrecque, former Chase CEO, became President but was thought to have a limited time there. 'I thought Labrecque would be gone in six months,' banking consultant Charles Wendel said, echoing a widely held view. 'That's the way these deals happen; the guy who is not the winner departs.'[20] Instead, Labrecque has both survived and thrived (until his announced retirement in June 1999).

Given the rapid pace of change in this industry, a merger of NatWest on both the wholesale and retail sides may well happen in 1999 or soon thereafter. One of its main tasks now is to ascertain which such mergers make the most sense – and then pursue them expeditiously.

Again, how it proceeds depends on the leadership that its board and Wanless provide. Since there are many new board members, prospects for change may be good. Lord Alexander, the Chair, left at the end of 1998, with two more members taking mandatory retirement (at age 70) in April 1999. New members of the board since then include: Sir David Rowland, President of Templeton College, Oxford University Business School and a former Chair of Lloyd's of London; Lord Blyth of Rowington, CEO of Boots the pharmaceuticals retailer; and Sir Richard Evans, Chair of British Aerospace. Rowland will take over as NatWest Chair in early 1999 and comes in with a long record of achievements within financial services. He is to spend just half the week as NatWest's Chair, suggesting his and the board's likely confidence in Wanless continuing to run the bank.[21]

Such a newly constituted board and rejuvenated CEO now face the task of reconfiguring NatWest to become once more a major player in British and international banking. They will not have much time, but their first order of business is to determine how they intend to strengthen NatWest's wholesale and retail banking and, in particular, what mergers they will pursue. Their arena is likely to be the UK and continental Europe. The develoment of the euro currency, even without Britain's direct participation at this time, makes the development of such a strategy by this new NatWest leadership an immediate priority.

Notes and references

1. Much of the analysis to follow comes from interviews with senior managers at NatWest and Barclays.
2. Richard Reed, *National Westminster Bank, A Short History*, National Westminster Bank plc (archives), 1989, p. 52.
3. *Financial Times*, 10 March 1992.
4. *Financial Times*, 16 January 1990.
5. *Financial Times*, 19 April 1991.
6. *Financial Times*, 31 March 1992.
7. *Guardian*, 8 August 1998.
8. *Wall Street Journal*, 14 March 1997.
9. Morgan Stanley Dean Whitter, *NatWest: Getting it Right in Retail Banking*, 25 November 1997.
10. *The Economist*, 7 June 1997.
11. Morgan Stanley Dean Whitter, *op. cit.*
12. The following discussion comes from a field trip to NatWest's Basingstoke store and from interviews with staff in NatWest's UK Retail Bank.
13. Richard Freedman and Jill Vohr, *Nordstrom*, Stern, NYU, 1991.
14. Interviews for this book.
15. *Financial Times*, 18 November 1997.
16. *Financial Times*, 5 August 1998.
17. *Financial Times*, 22 April 1998.
18. *Financial Times*, 5 August 1998. For a perceptive commentary on Wanless's changed management style and on culture change at NatWest, see Christopher Fildes article in the *Daily Telegraph*, 27 April 1998.
19. *Financial Times*, 30 June 1997.
20. *Wall Street Journal*, 25 November 1998, p. 1.
21. *Financial Times*, 1 September 1998.

9 Midland: Turnaround After a Near-fatal Decline

Dean Acheson once said that after Britain lost its empire, it failed to re-define its role in the world. Well, Midland was a very good example of that. It was a leading correspondent bank, but Barclays, Lloyds and NatWest left it far behind in international banking. And it had two CEOs at that time, in the seventies and early eighties, who rarely even talked to each other let alone agreed on anything.

Former Midland staff member

After the 1950s, Midland fell almost without a trace. It was very disorganized at the top. Graham, one of its co-CEOs, in charge of domestic banking, had to ask Crocker, a bank Midland bought, for its balance sheet, since he couldn't get it from Wilcox, the other co-CEO.

Former senior manager, Midland

In the seventies and eighties, they were by far the worst-performing of the Big Four. Now [1998] they are doing very well. They are the fastest-growing of the four, their costs are down, and they have a lot of market share in retail and corporate. After Hongkong and Shanghai Banking Corporation bought them, it shook up Midland dramatically. It took out lots of costs, including layers of middle management, and got away with it.

Bank Analyst

JUST AS Lloyds had been the best performer of the Big Four since the mid-1980s, so had Midland been the worst, until the past few years when it has made a remarkable recovery. From 1988 until 1993, for example, its average ROE after taxes was 4.8 per cent, compared with Lloyds at 19.7 per cent over the same period, NatWest at 6.8 per cent and Barclays at 5.8 per cent. By contrast, from 1994 to 1997,

Midland's average ROE after taxes was up to 22.9 per cent, comparing favourably with NatWest at 12.8 per cent, Barclays at 19.8 per cent, and Lloyds at 31.2 per cent.[1]

Midland was formed in 1836 in Birmingham, Britain's industrial heartland 120 miles north of London, as an amalgamation of Midland and Birmingham banks. By the 1920s it had emerged as Britain's, and the world's, largest bank.[2] It then went through a long period of stagnation and decline, from the late 1940s until the early 1990s. It only survived through two interventions: one by the Bank of England, which brought in two new CEOs, and the other by Hongkong and Shanghai Banking Corporation's purchase of it in 1992.

The account of Midland's evolution since 1836 shows extremes of both effective and ineffective management. Historically, Midland had some of Britain's most renowned bankers, including Sir Edward Holden, who initiated a series of mergers that moved it from relative obscurity in the early 1890s to being the largest bank in the world by the 1920s.[3] But the bank's mismanagement, which contributed to its decline from the 1940s onwards, was at least as dramatic.

Concentrating mainly on Midland's experience since the 1970s, this chapter analyses the elements of that decline, indicating as well how and why it has been turned around in recent years. After that, the chapter compares Midland with the other clearers in terms of what lessons may be learned about the mix of leadership, strategy, culture, organization and staff capabilities that may be necessary for success.

Midland in the late 1990s

The Midland of 1997 was the smallest of the Big Four, yet with total assets of £102 billion, a staff of over 48 000, and profits before taxes of £1.625 billion. The next largest clearer, Lloyds, had assets of over £158 billion, over 82 000 employees, and pre-tax profits of £3.16 billion.[4]

By 1997, Midland had made a significant recovery from its decline of previous decades. In addition to its 1997 post-tax ROE of 26.0 per cent, its cost/income ratio, a critical indicator of efficiency, was 57.5 per cent, comparing favourably with Barclays' 68.5 per cent and NatWest's 69.0 per cent, although the ratio for 1997 was not as strong as Lloyds' 51.9 per cent.[5] Moreover, most analysts note that the trend for Midland on these and other performance indicators is likely to improve in the coming years.

Midland, along with Barclays and NatWest, has pursued a strategy of universal banking, and it has continued to do so even while Barclays and NatWest have increasingly withdrawn from many global investment banking businesses and concentrated much more on their domestic retail franchise. Thus, Midland has a significant presence in both UK retail and wholesale corporate banking. Its UK retail banking encompassed some 1702 branches in 1996,[6] providing a standard portfolio of products and services: personal deposits and loans; home mortgages; credit cards; insurance services, including personal pension management; and loan and deposit services for small and medium-sized businesses.

Midland also maintains the UK's leading 24-hour telephone bank, First Direct, that it started in 1989. This subsidiary now has over 800 000 customers, whose satisfaction with it remains high, as measured by Midland's many surveys and by the fact that it continues to attract an average of over 10 000 new customers each month.[7]

In addition, Midland has a large, wholesale, corporate banking business, concentrated heavily in the UK and Europe. This includes securities-related corporate finance and trading services as well as more traditional foreign exchange, trust and custodial, trade finance, asset finance and leasing, and loan services that commercial banks have always provided.

Unlike the other three clearers, Midland is part of a larger holding company, HSBC Holdings plc (HSBC). HSBC does not provide disaggregated data on the contributions of various products and services related to Midland's total revenue, but from data presented in Lehman Brothers' annual review of 1997 we know that Midland's UK retail bank accounts for roughly two-thirds of Midland's total revenue – as it does in approximate terms for the other clearers.[8]

The Midland of the present is, by and large, a success story. The elements that turned it from nearly 50 years of stagnation and decline and set the stage for its being bought in 1992 by HSBC and its subsequent improvement are the subject of the rest of the chapter.

From country bank to the world's largest

Midland's history mirrors that of the wider British commercial banking industry, of which it has been such an important part. It started in 1836 as a small, joint-stock bank and grew tremendously through the nineteenth and early twentieth centuries by buying other joint-stock banks. Until the 1890s, Midland, despite its growth, remained a relatively obscure provincial bank; but by 1918, it was Britain's largest commercial bank.[9]

The growth took place by amalgamations with country banks in areas of the UK where its prior representation was thin, and with some big London banks in the late 1890s when it moved its headquarters there.[10] Midland thus became known as a London-and-country bank, but its deep roots throughout its history remained in the rural regions north and west of London. Even after it opened its London headquarters in 1898, Midland still emphasized the importance of provincial banking. Until the mid-1980s, it was referred to as 'historically the most parochial of the British clearers'. Until 1974, for example, it had no branches at all overseas, and its senior managers were 'men who have worked their way up from local Yorkshire branches.'[11]

The last big acquisition period for Midland was just after World War I. It bought Belfast Bank in 1917, Clydesdale in 1918, and North of Scotland Bank in 1924, giving it at the time the most and biggest affiliations in Scotland and Ireland of any British clearer. Then, in the period 1919–29, it almost doubled the number of its branches in England, Scotland, Ireland and Wales.[12]

Institutional weaknesses

As Midland grew at that time to become the world's biggest bank, it took on several characteristics that contributed to its later decline. They included the growth of a huge, centralized bureaucracy to standardize operations in its branches; a continuing attachment to its provincial roots and to the heavy industries in the Manchester and Birmingham areas; the development of a correspondent and consortium approach to international banking, reflecting that provincialism and limiting Midland's competitiveness; a predominance in senior management positions of retail bankers who had worked their way up from local branches; and a pronounced fragmentation of authority at the top, which made it difficult to develop any strategic coherence and focus.[13]

The development of a large bureaucracy was already under way by the 1860s when Midland built new, palatial headquarters in Birmingham.[14] The headquarters, accommodating Midland's accelerating growth, was accompanied by 'a growth of rules and regulations for the conduct of the bank's activities'.[15] Historians of Midland refer to these developments as 'signs of greater formality and institutional practice'.

Over time, the growth of bureaucracy continued as the bank's senior management standardized operations in its new branches. There was a constant emphasis within the bank that growth required uniform regulations and procedures and, in particular, a rule-driven and mechanistic approach to lending so as to minimize risk. This had been an approach common to commercial banks worldwide until the 1980s and 1990s, when the industry became more loosely regulated and also diversified into investment banking. Midland, like NatWest, was a prototype of that organizational form. Uniformity of procedures, ensuring tight controls over all its branches, was a hallmark of Midland's management.

Such a potentially ponderous, bureaucratic style had not, however, hampered the progress of Midland's many amalgamations. Instead, the entrepreneurial and negotiating heroics of a few individual senior managers, particularly Sir Edward Holden, contributed to the expansion. Known as 'a kind of superman in the banking world', Holden was the person largely responsible for Midland's growth from the early 1890s to 1919. He was seen as 'probably responsible for the greatest changes in the structure of banking between 1891 and 1914'.[16]

Holden's style was one of aggressiveness and dynamism as he converted Midland into a major London bank, in addition to its being one of the largest provincial banks. He reportedly terrorized competitors by threatening to open a new branch in towns where negotiations for an acquisition broke down. Within Midland, he established a pattern of 'one-man rule', with a management style characterized as personal and autocratic.[17]

Despite Holden's entrepreneurial proclivities for expansion, the accretion of bureaucratic rules, procedures and controls proceeded apace. After Holden died in 1919, his protégé, the distinguished Sir Reginald McKenna, former Chancellor of the Exchequer, succeeded him. All the while, Midland continued with its bureaucratization, adding layers of command and tighter accounting controls.[18]

By the end of the 1930s, a new and more cautious style pervaded the bank. For the first time in 50 years, Midland had lost its expansionary impetus. The depression and then World War II undoubtedly contributed; the bank's committee-ized decision-making style probably did as well.

Also, as part of Midland's provincial roots, it had a serious commitment to traditional heavy industries, such as coal, steel and ship-building, along with textiles in the north and north-west of England. When these industries declined, so too did Midland.[19] Despite Holden's many expansionary initiatives, Midland had remained underrepresented in the more rapidly growing areas of England to the South and East. Moreover, just when Midland needed to be revived by lending to new and growing companies, it became more deeply entrenched than ever, not just in centralized bureaucracy but in baronial in-fighting as well.[20]

By the 1930s and thereafter, Midland had replaced the expansionist, action-oriented, authoritarian approach of Holden with a much more consensus-oriented decision-making style that it carried forward right up to the 1980s. Midland's vast increase in size had led, then, both to an increase in bureaucracy and to a new, cautious, group-driven style of decision making. Taken together, these qualities contributed to a stagnation that Holden undoubtedly would have bemoaned, leading to Midland's lost leadership position as the biggest clearer.[21]

Late and slow in global banking

Other, related developments also contributed to Midland's decline. Its strong attachments to its provincial roots made Midland particularly cautious in its international business. The main international strategy was to develop a network of overseas correspondent banks and later to become involved in various consortium arrangements, rather than to open branches around the world as Barclays and Lloyds had done.[22]

Lloyds', Barclays' and NatWest's many international losses indicated that opening branches around the world was not in and of itself a guarantee of success. Midland's correspondent and consortium banking, however, was a strategy that its senior managers of the 1970s and 1980s felt was no longer appropriate. Midland's more cautious strategy had been a result of its positive alliances in Scotland and Ireland, the bad experience of other clearers in their overseas branches, and Midland's travails in Russia in 1917 at the time of the Revolution.[23]

Midland's decline was made worse in 1967 when Britain devalued sterling. A staff member from that era recalled: 'Harold Wilson, the Prime Minister, had constantly assured the banks that the UK would not devalue and none of them believed him, and correctly so. Midland did believe him. It was long in sterling and took a bath. It had not anticipated that devaluation.'

By the early 1970s, Midland continued to stagnate, as its core, heavy-industry customers in Britain became increasingly moribund. Its earlier CEO (1962–8), Howard Thackstone, had commissioned a study that concluded that it had to go beyond correspondent banking. He and some of his colleagues were increasingly concerned that, since the late forties and early fifties, Midland had been left behind as a result of its cautious, inward-looking and less flexible style in an increasingly competitive environment, where those qualities were hurting its market position.[24]

One prevailing interpretation of Midland's limited initiatives in international banking was that they reflected its provincial roots. Despite Midland having opened a headquarters in London in 1898 and various mergers with big London banks, its continued strong ties to its traditional banking businesses outside London indicated a discomfort with the newer world of international banking that its clearing bank competitors so eagerly sought out.

Who's in charge?

Perhaps Midland's most crippling weakness, a legacy from its past, related to its governance. It emerged from World War II very weak structurally at the top.[25] There were ambiguous relations between its board and its executives as to who was in charge. Even more devastating, there emerged a divided CEO structure. In the early 1970s Midland's board established two CEOs, one for domestic banking and one for international. Moreover, as many as five or six senior managers had unchecked power to run their own businesses. They showed little interest in collaborating to develop a coherent strategy for the bank as a whole.

A senior manager from Midland in the 1980s recalled: 'The bank had four sectors when I arrived: UK retail, corporate, international, and investment banking. None could run the bank and this group of four never talked to each other. They ran what were really four different banks. They had nothing in common: not the same technologies, systems, accounting practices or anything.' Another senior manager concurred: 'Within Midland in the 1980s, there was a big split between the international and domestic people. Malcolm Wilcox was the international person and Stuart Graham was the domestic man. They were the equivalent of co-CEOs, and they wouldn't speak to each other. They wouldn't even be photographed together in the same room.'

This fragmentation appeared as an extension of the decision-making-by-committee style that had emerged earlier. Whatever the cause, it was not working. In fact, it was contributing further to Midland's decline. Once more, a senior manager recalled: 'There was enormous bureaucracy at all levels in the eighties. In fact, with this split between international and domestic banking, there were two big bureaucracies.'

Disaster in the 1980s and early 1990s

Midland's decades of stagnation culminated in the 1980s and early 1990s in one of the most problem-ridden periods that any of the four clearers has ever gone through. Referred to in the financial press in the early 1990s as 'accident-prone', having 'an undiminished capacity to find trouble', as well as 'the weakest of the Big Four', in which 'management has never been its strong suit', and with the 'guts of income generation having been knocked out', Midland experienced close to 12 years of big losses, starting in 1980.[26] During that time, it became so depleted of capital that it only survived as a viable institution when HSBC bought it in 1992.[27]

Though the serious decline had been building for at least a decade before, it accelerated with Midland's acquisition of Crocker Bank of California in 1980, followed by its sale of Crocker in 1986 to Wells Fargo at an estimated loss of $1 billion. Other disasters included: an accumulation of third-world loans, both from Crocker and its own actions; a badly mismatched treasury book, resulting in losses of £250 million in 1990 alone; high costs in its UK retail bank; and HSBC's decision in late 1990 not to buy it, after much of Midland's planning had been based on the merger as its most viable survival strategy. It was only after HSBC changed its mind and bought Midland in mid-1992, following a similar Lloyds' bid, that significant improvements became a possibility.

The Crocker fiasco

Throughout the 1970s, some of Midland's senior management and board members grew increasingly concerned that it was falling far behind its clearing bank competitors in international banking. Its then director of international banking, Malcolm Wilcox, determined that Midland should overturn its traditional international banking strategy of correspondent and consortium banking. He was convinced that it should emulate Citicorp by establishing an international presence with branches around the world. His board vetoed the acquisition of a big factoring company in Chicago to establish its presence in the US. Concerned about the bank's continued slow pace of international expansion, the board then hastily endorsed a proposal to buy Crocker.[28] 'There was a late dash by Malcolm Wilcox to compensate for the fact that the bank had not done much international banking before,' recalled a former Midland staffer of that time.

In retrospect, the Crocker acquisition was extraordinarily ill-conceived. A bank reporter recalled: 'Midland's decision to buy Crocker was the most serious mistake any bank ever made, and Midland may never recover.' Midland's poor decision was seen as driven by its desperate attempt to catch up with competitors. 'This was an old industrial bank that got way behind the others in many areas and then blew it through the acquisition of Crocker,' remarked a veteran bank analyst.

The Crocker deal was consummated by two Wilcoxes (no relation): Malcolm, the head of international banking at Midland, and Thomas, the CEO at Crocker. Thomas Wilcox had been passed over as CEO at Citicorp in the late 1960s, in favour of Walter Wriston. The ambitious and fiery Wilcox then became CEO at Crocker, determined to make it the Citicorp of the West, and thereby showing Citicorp's board how wrong it had been in not choosing him. By the time Midland arrived, bent on making a jump-start in expanding its international banking franchise, Crocker had accumulated a bundle of problem loans, mainly to third-world nations and commercial real-estate projects. Tom Wilcox, having joined Crocker in 1974, had thus been pursuing his growth-at-any-price loan policy for some time before Midland's acquisition. He had even hired many Citicorp recruits to assist him in implementing that strategy, which was to come close to bringing down their former bank in 1990 and 1991, as it had Crocker in 1980.

Tom Wilcox not only pushed Crocker into this accelerating downward spiral before Midland's arrival but he was apparently so effective at disguising it through creative accounting techniques that Midland bankers had no idea just how bad Crocker's loan book was. Moreover, he was effective in keeping Crocker autonomous after the acquisition, referring to the relationship with Midland as 'an alliance' rather than a merger, and yet draining Midland of close to $800 million of its capital. As an indication of how far this autonomy went, it should be noted that Wilcox refused to allow a Midland nominee on his management team, would not find an office for Midland in San

Francisco or share offices elsewhere, and would not give Midland more information than any other shareholder.[29]

A bank analyst and former Midlander recalled: 'Tom Wilcox saw how desperate Midland was to get into international banking, and he knew he had them over a barrel. Midland's strategic error was to let Crocker control things while Midland just poured in capital. Crocker then vastly increased its lending capacity by 1982. It ran off like there was no tomorrow to Latin America, and the whole bank fell apart.'

Midland not only funded Crocker's questionable loans, but the conditions of its relationship with Crocker made it even more vulnerable to future losses. It had initially acquired less than 50 per cent ownership of Crocker's shares, and Crocker refused to give Midland oversight powers over its transactions. In addition, Crocker ignored queries from Midland regarding its loan practices. Yet, Midland kept providing capital. 'There was serious question about why Midland even bought Crocker,' a bank analyst explained, 'and why it then gave Crocker so much freedom seems, in hindsight, to have made no sense at all. Tom Wilcox sold Midland a bill of goods about how good a bank Crocker was, and they bought it.'

A Midland senior manager summed things up thus:

> In the eighties, the vogue was to go into international banking, and Midland had stood aloof from that while its competitors rushed in. Then it panicked and went international in a big way by buying Crocker. It was done out of desperation, with no judgement, and allowing the local Crocker guys to run rings around it. It was a disaster. Both Midland and Crocker had huge Latin American loans and to put them together was to compound the problem.

A senior banker from one of the clearers recalled his and his board chairman's astonishment at how the Crocker people proceeded in such a cavalier fashion in their loan policies: 'I'll never forget being in a taxi with our chairman and a couple of Crocker bankers,' he said, 'and they were crowing about how they were going to have all this money from Midland. When I asked them what they would do with it, they talked about all these commercial real-estate projects they wanted to fund. I looked at my chairman and we both concluded that these guys didn't know what they were doing.'

Realizing the extent of its increasing losses, Midland sold Crocker to Wells Fargo in 1986, but even then it remained burdened with an estimated $3.7 billion of Crocker's bad loans.[30] 'They took all the bad loans of Crocker and put them into a holding company called

Braxton,' explained a Midland manager, 'which was Midland's balance sheet. And the good ones went to Wells Fargo.' It was several years before Midland recovered from losses on those loans.

Actually, Midland had not completely sat still while Crocker drained its capital. By 1983, it had increased its ownership from under 50 per cent to 57 per cent, and in 1985 it bought the 43 per cent of shares it did not already own.[31] It had also installed new management by 1984, to protect its interests and monitor Crocker more closely than before. Judged by the losses that Midland ultimately experienced, these changes were too little too late, since much of the damage had already been done in the conditions of the initial agreement.

In addition, at least one key person that Midland put in did not necessarily represent its interests at all. 'They put in Frank Cahouet, for example,' recalled a former Midland staff member from that time, 'and he did not care about Midland's interests, but only about making Crocker the most powerful west-coast bank, as he saw it.' Russell Taylor, from interviews with key participants, characterized Cahouet as similar to Tom Wilcox in his high-loan-growth strategy and his refusal to accept Midland authority and oversight.[32]

An indication of how damaging the Crocker episode was to Midland was reflected in its board chairman, Sir Donald Barron's attempts to cancel publication of the company history that the bank had commissioned: the details of Crocker were not to be divulged.[33] After much internal discussion, a compromise was reached in which the bank allowed the book's publication and stopped the chronology at 1976.

European expansion

Crocker was not the only international initiative Midland had taken in the early 1980s. In February 1984, it hired Herve de Carmoy, a French aristocrat and Chase banker, as CEO of its international division.[34] De Carmoy and Midland then hired several other ex-Chase and ex-Citicorp bankers, forty or fifty of whom were lured from Chase alone. Many of these new people had had successful careers in European banking at Chase and Citicorp, and were lured away with an understanding that Midland was committed to major expansion. Some from Chase had chafed under its rigid culture and were concerned that, with David Rockefeller leaving, Chase would have less commitment to international banking. One of these 'international high fliers', Ernst Brutsch, who had had a successful career at Citicorp in foreign exchange, went on to become Midland's Group Treasurer.

The conflicts between Midland's traditional senior managers and this new group were understandably quite intense. The old-line Midland people had been retail bankers in areas far removed from London, both geographically and culturally. They had no experience of working abroad, and many of them felt there was little logic to the overseas initiatives.

Nevertheless, this new international group led a major European expansion. Midland bought the second-largest private bank in France and the largest investment bank in the then West Germany. As important as these acquisitions were, Crocker was by far the most significant. The losses there made the European acquisitions pale in importance.

Enter Sir Kit McMahon

By 1986, Midland's losses – and especially its depletion of capital resulting from Crocker and non-performing loans – were of such a magnitude that the Bank of England prevailed on Sir Kit McMahon, then its Deputy Governor, to restore Midland to health. The timing was good for McMahon. Although he had been reappointed as Deputy Governor of the Bank of England, he was ready to move on. McMahon, an Australian academic and economist and former Oxford don, was then appointed both Chair and CEO at Midland.

At the time of his appointment, there was much optimism about McMahon's capacity to turn Midland around, even though he had been a regulator rather than a banker and had little managerial experience. He had, however, a deserved reputation as a keen analyst of the banking industry, he was well networked within the financial services industry, and he was a well trained economist. 'If any one man can achieve this ambitious plan [to reverse Midland's fortunes], it will be Sir Kit McMahon,' said a staff writer for *The Economist* at the time.[35]

McMahon worked assiduously to reverse Midland's decline.[36] He immediately appointed several outsiders who had an expertise that Midland sorely needed. They moved into senior management positions in international and investment banking, retail banking, technology, and sales and marketing. Among the most prominent of these people were Gene Lockhart, an American information technology specialist and former consultant, and George Loudon, a Dutch international and investment banker. There were others as well, in human resource management and finance.

Much to the dismay of the traditional Midland bankers, these appointees soon constituted with McMahon a new 'counterculture' senior management team. 'When I arrived at Midland in the early eighties,' explained a former staffer, 'there was only one person of the twenty-odd in senior management on that floor who had not been at Midland all his working life. Five years later when I left, it was the reverse. There was only one person out of twenty who had worked there all his life. That shows how much change took place and how fast.'

It is necessary to understand the traditional Midland culture to realize the threat that these new managers posed. 'It was an extremely arrogant and inward-directed culture,' explained a senior manager. 'These were unclever people, and the culture was one of making no mistakes, obeying orders, and getting things right – and if you did not, your career was in jeopardy. The new people we brought in were very different: they were quite clever and totally un-Midland in culture.'

McMahon did many other things. He worked to combine Midland's two bureaucracies (wholesale and retail). As both CEO and Chair, he eliminated the split between the board and senior management. He encouraged the retirement of many traditional senior managers whose positions were no longer relevant in a more integrated structure. He gave Midland more focus. This included the sale of its brokerage, Samuel Montagu, along with that of Clydesdale Bank and an Irish bank. Meanwhile, McMahon worked to make Midland's investment bank, Midland Montagu, a one-stop business. And he introduced more of a sales-and-marketing culture in the UK retail bank. He was not alone amongst the clearers in this effort, but Midland was a leader in initiating such reforms, and he and his colleagues deserve credit for that.

McMahon's options had been limited throughout his time at Midland. 'He came in when huge damage had already been done,' explained a Midland member of staff, going on:

> He realized Midland could not be an investment bank. But then he got caught in the middle, where it was neither a strong specialized retail bank nor a strong diversified bank. To downsize and get more focus as a UK retail bank was not an option at that time. He ended up with a bank that was not strong in international, not strong in retail, not strong in corporate. It had no areas of competitive strength, and McMahon did not build one.

Lockhart: *enfant terrible*

McMahon facilitated yet other innovations. Several were related to the work of Gene Lockhart, the American computer specialist, who was recruited to Midland in late 1986. Lockhart's big early contribution was to develop and knit together a technological framework, first for the retail bank and then for the entire bank.

When Lockhart began his work there, Midland was both primitive and byzantine in its technologies; and so he worked quickly to modernize them. A senior manager who was there at the time explained:

> When Lockhart came, Midland's IT (information technology) was insane. We did many things by hand and were hopelessly behind. Lockhart cancelled parts of the retail banking system that made no sense at all and that had all kinds of bizarre networks – we had the largest ATM network in the UK but had no idea whether the machines worked or what worked. This was the first time any manager had ever sent to the Midland board the recommendation for a cancelled programme.

Lockhart went on to head all operations and strategic planning. He had several senior management positions, including one as head of the UK retail bank and another as Chair of Thomas Cook, Midland's subsidiary in travel-related services. And he was mentioned increasingly as a strong candidate eventually to succeed McMahon.[37]

Although he worked well with McMahon, Lockhart's style, his technical skills, and the innovations he developed and implemented alienated many of the traditional Midland managers. Variously referred to as 'crisp', 'abrasive', and having a 'prickly personality', Lockhard typified for the old-guard Midland clearers what was wrong with McMahon's strategy of bringing in a new countercultural managerial cadre. The Midland managers saw him as an outsider, not a banker; as a technocrat not familiar enough with substantive banking issues or with the legal framework of British banking, and as too arrogant about the value of his computerized approches to credit-related matters to appreciate the importance of the branch bankers' direct experience. Few doubted his brilliance and energy as an agent of change but, not surprisingly, many were not ready for the changes he introduced. One assessment by a Midland manager of the time was:

> Nobody inside understood what Lockhard was doing. He over-engineered in money-transmission capacity. He built a Rolls-Royce

instead of a Ford. He did rebuild the retail bank, but he overengineered that as well.

Some observers compared Lockhart with Citicorp's John Reed, another *enfant terrible*, who had many qualities similar to his: young, technically sophisticated, non-traditional in his computerized solutions to banking problems, and not always sensitive to the behavioural and political aspects of managing change. Reed at least had a strongly supportive coalition in CEO Walter Wriston and the senior people around Wriston, and he ended up becoming Citicorp's CEO. Lockhart, while he had McMahon's strong support, did not have that of many senior and middle managers. The fact that McMahon's later exit was not entirely voluntary and was associated with his inability to turn Midland around probably did not help Lockhart, since McMahon had brought him in and they had worked so well together. Lockhart left not long after McMahon.

Lockhart's innovations are important to note, since some survived long after his exit and helped constitute part of the infrastructure that contributed to Midland's later recovery. He was involved in the precursors to First Direct, the first telephone banking service among the clearers, which has continued to grow and flourish. He centralized cheque clearing, securities processing, money-market deposits, and mortgage origination. Also, he supervised Midland's branch-closure programme and staff reduction so as to bring down costs.

Given an eventual HSBC take-over of Midland, Lockhart would probably have had to leave anyway. His ambition likely speeded up that process. A Midland staff member reported: 'He had a huge need for power and wanted to control as much as he could. That was obvious in his becoming the CEO of the retail bank and Chair of Thomas Cook. The accrual of power was a big goal of his, and in the end, that hurt him. It also probably hurt McMahon, who was a big fan of his.' Another Midland person commented: 'Lockhart was more involved in empire building than doing what Midland could afford, and it was overkill.'

The HSBC connection

One of McMahon's most significant actions was to develop a relationship with HSBC. In 1987, HSBC bought a 14.9 per cent interest in Midland, with the long-term plan of having the two banks merge as a way to ensure Midland's survival.[38] The two banks collaborated well for the next three years, seemingly intending to deepen the relationship, and in 1990 the acquisition of Midland by HSBC nearly took place.

Both William Purves, HSBC's Chair and CEO, and McMahon stated publicly in early 1990 that they favoured a merger of the two organizations. The banks had already moved since 1987 toward greater integration and had much complementarity. Midland's strength was in the UK and Europe, while HSBC's was in the Far East and North America. Midland had a strong retail franchise, while HSBC's was largely in wholesale banking. And HSBC was strongly capitalized, a resource Midland sorely needed.[39] One potential obstacle was the requirement that HSBC move its headquarters to England, but it appeared that HSBC would comply with that.

Unfortunately for Midland, deteriorating economic conditions in Britain and worldwide in 1990 made the merger increasingly unattractive to HSBC. In December 1990, when its ownership agreement of the preceding three years expired, HSBC announced that it was not ready to consummate the merger, although it was willing to continue with the past relationship. Each bank had accumulated more bad debts that year in the form of non-performing loans. The fall in the share price of each organization made their respective valuations unclear, thereby increasing the uncertainty surrounding the structure of such a deal. And even if that uncertainty were minimized, the merged group's financial structure would still have been complex.[40]

Furthermore, Midland's poor performance appeared to give HSBC considerable pause for thought. Notwithstanding McMahon's heroic efforts to turn Midland around, its 1990 financial results were unsatisfactory. It had accumulated the worst third-world debt exposure of the Big Four. It had the highest costs in domestic retail banking. It had major losses in its investment banking, with its Treasury group having made a bad bet on interest rates in 1989 as a result of which the bank lost over £200 million.[41]

When HSBC pulled out of the possible merger, McMahon had in many respects played his last trump card. He had taken on the job as Chair and CEO just after the Crocker sale. He was therefore immediately burdened with that big loss, estimated at roughly $1 billion. Despite the appropriateness of many of his actions, once the recession set in, it was going to be extraordinarily difficult for him to be a successful change manager. That would have required a big overhaul, giving the bank much more focus, making bigger dents in its high cost structure, changing the corporate culture, integrating the organization, and effectively incorporating new managers at several levels to help ensure that these changes actually took place.

Instead, McMahon was forced by circumstance to engage in much crisis management. He was overwhelmed both by the difficulties he inherited and by the recession. In that sense, his timing could not have been worse. A senior manager there at the time explained:

> We very nearly did the acquisition in 1990, but the recession was so great we had to fire-fight on that most of the time. We were so damaged after Crocker that we were no longer strong enough on our own to survive. And once HSBC pulled out, Midland was hurting more than ever, and McMahon was up a gum tree.

Another judgment, however, was that McMahon's demise, after five years at Midland, was partly of his own doing. He was ultimately seen as a very good Chair but not a strong CEO. His past experience as a central banker, his training as an economist, his astuteness as an analyst of financial services, and his wide networks of relationships within the industry all served him well in chair-relevant tasks, particularly developing strategy for the bank. That was different, however, from managing the bank on a day-to-day basis. A Midland staffer explained:

> McMahon had never run anything before, having been a central banker. He was extremely bright, but he made many mistakes. He brought in some impressive but volatile new people, of whom Lockhart was only one. Also, he has participated in the risky bet on interest rates coming down that brought those big losses in 1990. If he had just been the Chairman, with somebody like Pearse as his CEO, it might well have gone much better. We all liked and respected McMahon, so it was one of the tragedies of this industry that it didn't work out for him at the end.

One more Bank of England rescue attempt: Brian Pearse

In early March of 1991, in order to try to bail out Midland, the Bank of England intervened a second time. It prevailed upon Sir John Quinton of Barclays to give up his CFO, Brian Pearse, to succeed McMahon, who by this time had served for five years. It also invited Peter Walters, former Chair of British Telecom and member of NatWest's board, to become Chair of Midland.[42]

Pearse was in many respects an excellent choice. He was highly regarded at Barclays and in wider British banking circles. He came from the same roots as Midland, in the Birmingham and Manchester areas, and provided a good fit with the Midland culture that had resisted fiercely McMahon's efforts to bring in a new one. He could in that sense help restore morale within an institution whose staff at all levels was understandably downcast at their bank's poor performance and at being 'invaded' by McMahon's new managers, who they did not think were always qualified. Pearse was known particularly for his skill as a manager in motivating people.[43]

The only other senior managers mentioned publicly at the time as possible successors were Brian Goldthorpe, a 40-year Midland wholesale banker who was characterized as 'too pedestrian', and Gene Lockhart, seen for reasons mentioned above as 'too exciting'.[44]

In retrospect, McMahon had probably moved too quickly in trying to change Midland, although at the time its problems were so great that he had to do dramatic things. Maintaining an appropriate balance between pushing ahead quickly with needed innovations and new staff while not alienating the old guard is very difficult. A senior manager there explained: 'McMahon was trying to introduce a lot of change, and maybe he tried to do it too fast. Maybe he overlooked the culture. But he had to do something. And we did have the highest cost/income ratio of all the clearers. He may have made a mistake in trying to get rid of so many old timers and bringing so many younger ones in.'

Pearse and restoring tradition

Pearse took over as Midland's CEO in early 1991. His background, loyalties and likely strategic preferences were almost immediately made known to the traditional Midland managers, who thus welcomed him with great relief. 'Brian Pearse looks like one of us,' a staff member was quoted as saying at the time, having shared with his colleagues a distrust of the new senior managers whom McMahon had hired.[45] In that sense, Pearse was seen as, in the words of one former Midlander, 'a safe pair of hands for Midland, at a troubled time'.

Pearse accepted the challenge offered to him with enthusiasm, although he reportedly had some initial discomfort about leaving Barclays to work for a competitor. He thus chose to retire formally from Barclays first, before moving on to Midland. Reflecting the traditional British commerical banking culture, he still valued the banks' no-poaching tradition, even in the 1990s, and his depth of loyalty to his original bank went back several decades. One banker observed: 'Brian Pearse started with Martins Bank in the North [of England] and became a Barclays person only when it bought Martins in 1968. When you talked with him years later about what bank he was from, he always identified himself as a Martins man. That was how strongly he felt about those ties.'

Managing symbols is a critical aspect of an executive's job, and one of the first symbolic things Pearse was reported to have done was to instil much more informality, *esprit* and cohesion among Midland's senior managers than had existed before. He did it by keeping his door open as much as possible, contrary to established practice at Midland. One of his former colleagues at Barclays reported: 'The first day he was there, he told me that he looked down the hall on his floor where the senior managers sat, and he noticed that all the doors were closed. He couldn't understand it because at Barclays all our doors were open. So he asked his driver to make a little wooden wedge and put it under his door, to keep it open. And within a week, lo and behold, all the senior managers had little wooden wedges under their door.'

In addition to this symbolism, Pearse embarked on a significant reversal of the McMahon–Lockhart strategy of computerization and centralization. He announced a few months after taking office that he believed the way to the future for Midland was to get back to basics. He meant by that giving a bigger role to the traditional branch managers – delegating more authority to them to exercise their own judgements regarding the creditworthiness of customers, to deliver more products directly through the branch network, and to become pillars once again in their local communities. The trend among all four clearers had been to substitute automated, computerized programmes for branch manager initiatives and to remove from the latter and their immediate field supervisors many of the functions that they had engaged in before.

In brief, Pearse was sceptical about using technology to replace the human judgements of the branch managers, and he wanted to re-establish the branches as the point of contact for personal and corporate customers. In a well publicized speech in 1994 as President of the Institute of Bankers, Pearse took issue strongly with Martin Taylor just after Taylor, with much fanfare, had become Barclays' CEO. Taylor took the position that new technology was a much more efficient tool than relying on the branch manager's judgements and that it was making the the branch manager obsolete.[46] Without taking an extreme Luddite position, Pearse was arguing that retail banking had become too clever and overengineered. He maintained that there wasn't much more to do in cutting costs in the branch network, although he saw considerable room for reducing them at head office.[47] Most importantly, he believed that the big banks had been hurt in the 1980s in their ability to control risk and meet customer needs by centralization of decision making, and that huge loan losses were the result.[48]

Pearse's solution, then, was to devolve power to the regions and branches. He started by identifying some 200 of the best-performing branch managers and giving them more authority, with the eventual plan to extend it to others. Robert Peston, the *FT*'s banking writer at the time, referred to this as 'giving pride to the people in grey suits'.[49] Needless to say, Pearse's devolution strategy went over well with many Midland bankers. After five years at the hands of outsider technocrats and change managers, they were more than receptive to Pearse's traditional approach. They regarded him as restoring the clearing bank culture to Midland.

A different point of view, however, held by some sophisticated observers of British banking, was that Pearse's was a regressive move. It was seen as more of a 'feel good' approach in an era when the winners in financial services would have to harness advancing technology more effectively. 'It was a return to a more gracious age, after the troubles of the eighties,' explained a former Midland manager. 'Midland, like other banks, had major problems of internal integration and, given its history, maybe it had more of them. All Pearse did was to push those organization-design problems down to the regions and local branches. He didn't deal with them head-on and, if anything, he only made the bank more difficult to manage. Cutting back on the head office was not going to solve the organization-design problems.'

HSBC revisited

In late February of 1992, after Pearse had been CEO for just under a year, HSBC announced fresh plans to take over Midland. The announcement came a couple of months after Lloyds had indicated a similar desire to merge with Midland. Represented by Brian Pearse and Sir Peter Walters, Midland rejected Lloyds' bid, partly on legal advice that the Monopoly and Mergers Commission would oppose such a merger. In addition, Pearse expressed concern that a merger with Lloyds would set back his new devolution programme in Midland's UK retail bank. He had every reason to be concerned, since Sir Brian Pitman, Lloyds CEO, intended to close branches of the newly merged banks, to shed up to 20 000 staff, and thereby to cut costs.[50] For Pearse, that was unacceptable, and he threatened to resign if such a merger went through.[51]

Pearse's threat did not end Lloyds' efforts, however, and over the next several months there was much jockeying back and forth among Lloyds, HSBC and Midland over which offer might prevail. One result of the competition between Lloyds and HSBC was that the latter's purchase offer went up. HSBC's initial offer was £3.1 billion in shares and bonds, compared with the Lloyds offer of closer to £4 billion. By April, HSBC offered £3.3 billion and the final price was £3.9 billion.[52]

While expressing sadness that Midland would give up some of its independence in the event of an HSBC acquisition, Pearse also acknowledged that such a deal would give Midland sorely needed capital.[53] The deal was actually completed in June 1992, with Pearse staying on as CEO but with the top management group otherwise undergoing considerable change.

Pearse had been an aggressive, action-oriented CEO before the HSBC takeover, and he continued to be so immediately after it was consummated. Less than two months later, for example, he stated that the task of rebuilding Midland was still only half done and that he did not know when he would retire and would be around until 'the job is complete'.[54]

HSBC's autocratic culture – and Pearse's exit

Pearse's continuation in the CEO role was not to be so, however, because William Purves, CEO and chair of HSBC, was to exercise increasing control over Midland to a degree that made Pearse's freedom to pursue his strategies increasingly untenable. HSBC had an essentially cost-cutting, controlling, autocratic, quasi-military culture. Long known as a tightly-managed colonial bank, HSBC had in Purves a Chair and CEO who ran the bank in a seemingly imperious fashion.

Purves's and HSBC's controls over Midland seemed to many observers inevitable, especially after the Bank of England insisted that HSBC move its headquarters from Hong Kong to London as part of the deal. The financial press was full of commentaries to the effect that Purves would be intimidating when he arrived in London, that this would involve unscheduled visits to branches, and that Pearse had better get used to having Purves down the street, constantly looking over his shoulder. One Midland manager announced when quitting: 'Messages would arrive from Hong Kong. The role became less that of an advisor, and more one of carrying out instructions in the military.'[55]

Midland managers thus saw Purves as autocratic, dominating, impatient, and intolerant of any independent spirit. Over time, HSBC's control of Midland gradually increased. A month after the take-over, HSBC named Keith Whitson as Midland's Deputy CEO. He had been former CEO at subsidiary Marine Midland, where he had been an active, hands-on manager and had implemented cost-cutting and re-structuring measures.[56] That was followed by the announcement of the departures of Gene Lockhart, then CEO of UK banking, and George Loudon, CEO of Midland Montagu.

Purves then announced that he was changing the management style at Midland, stating as well that he thought Pearse, who he rated highly, agreed with his views. He noted that 'there were many more committees and many more committee decisions were being made in Midland than HSBC had. But I think they are welcoming the change. I think Mr Pearse himself is not a great committee man.'[57]

By early 1993, Pearse was quoted as saying: 'I have found my masters very receptive. I'd be very surprised if they went against anything I thought was right.'[58] At the same time, HSBC's new CEO, John Bond, who had just arrived in London in January 1993, indicated that if Pearse did not produce results in the form of transformed profits, HBSC's patience would otherwise wear uncomfortably thin.[59]

While Pearse worked tirelessly to develop more revenues from Midland's UK retail bank, he kept trying to convince HSBC that there was little scope for cost reductions at the branch level. That point of view was reportedly unacceptable to Purves, Whitson and HSBC, and it became increasingly clear that HSBC, as the parent organization, would in the end get its way.

Sir Peter Walters, Midland's Chair at the time, was due to leave at the end of 1993 to become Chair of SmithKline Beecham, and while Midland managers had expected that Pearse would succeed Walters as its Chair, Purves decided that he would take the position himself. By November 1993, Pearse had resigned. At the time, he acknowledged that Purves's becoming Chair might have helped to integrate the HSBC and Midland cultures even more. Perhaps on a more plaintive note, he added: 'I don't feel sixty.'[60]

Comments from knowledgeable bank analysts, reporters, consultants and academics all indicate a combination of respect for

Purves for continuing to move Midland on an upward trajectory and criticism for the way in which he exerted more control on Pearse, whom they also regarded highly. One analyst, sympathetic with Pearse, noted: 'Pearse is a wonderful person – very smart, intelligent, and tried to do new things. He tried to innovate and was risk-oriented. The HSBC people were not risk takers. They were middle-market, meat-and-potatoes people, and that was it for Pearse. Willie Purves is very tough, but not a risk taker. He's focused on grinding down costs and counting the paper clips, and that is unfortunate. Pearse was very competent. When he was at Midland, people went there because it was exciting. No more.' A bank analyst with less emphasis on the personalities explained: 'HSBC is still sorting out Midland. After the 1992 merger, it made Midland much more of a focused, lean, and low-cost operation.'

An academic with strong ties to the clearing banks gave his version of the merger: 'As a bank, Midland had always been a weak, problem-riddled place from the seventies. But then, when HSBC took over, Purves was a martinet, and he was always intervening with Pearse and never leaving him alone. He was trying to demonstrate that he had his man in there.'

The basic issues, then, were conflicts between Pearse and Purves over control and over Midland's appropriate strategy. Pearse's view was that cost cutting at the branch level was not the critical step to take and that his devolution strategy would increase revenues substantially if given a chance. He kept trying to convince Purves and other HSBC managers of that. Purves, by contrast, wanted more immediate results, since cost cutting and efficiency were central to his strategy. He seemed unwilling to wait around for the results of Pearse's strategy. And he certainly wanted more control over Midland than he had with Pearse as its CEO, since Midland accounted for so much of HSBC's costs and revenue.

Pearse was thus too much of an independent spirit – not the kind of person Purves wanted to be running Midland. For Purves, he ensured his control by becoming Chair of Midland and also keeping the similar position at HSBC.

In that regard, the story of Midland since Pearse left has been one of HSBC putting more and more of its own people into top management positions. At times, this has meant pushing out other highly capable people in order to ensure even more HSBC control. One example (other than Pearse) was Midland's managing director of branch banking, who had ironically pressed so hard to facilitate the HSBC merger. Purves unceremoniously removed this well regarded person for an HSBC executive, leading a *Financial Times* writer to comment that such personnel changes 'will also put an end to any suggestion that Midland "merged" with HSBC. It was taken over by an autocratic outfit which is out to prove that it can run a UK clearing bank better than anybody else. We shall see.'[61]

One test of Pearse's impact on Midland was the fate of his devolution strategy. In early 1995, HSBC committed itself to giving three years to making Pearse's 'gamble' on increasing the responsibilities of the branch managers pay off.

Ultimately, the HSBC takeover of Midland will be judged on the latter's financial performance. The record since 1992 has been positive enough to suggest that HSBC is doing well in that task. Midland had in 1997 the second-highest ROE of the clearers, behind Lloyds, and its cost/income ratio has been coming down, from 71.3 per cent in 1992 to 57.5 per cent in 1997.[62] This has to be attributable in large part to HSBC initiatives, in cutting costs, divesting Midland of losing businesses, and putting in many HSBC managers to manage those changes. The larger question of what Midland's future strategy will be remains to be addressed.

Reversing a failed culture and configuration

A central theme of these case studies is that the particular mixes of strategy, culture, organization, people and leadership that institutions evolve all directly affect their performance. Midland was an extreme example of a dysfunctional mix throughout much of the last five decades. That mix included an ill-conceived, poorly formulated strategy that bore little relationship to emerging opportunities and threats in financial services, and an infrastructure that perpetuated that condition. The infrastructure included a risk-averse and inward-oriented culture; a bloated, in-bred, bureaucratic organization; a homogeneous dominant coalition of retail bankers; and a condition of divided authority and organizational fragmentation.

Midland had this configuration to a greater degree than any of the other clearing banks in the seventies and eighties. Lloyds broke out of the mould much earlier and in a more comprehensive way, followed by Barclays and then NatWest. Indeed, if one were to array the four clearers on a continuum, NatWest seems to come closest to Midland in having more of this cluster of characteristics than any of the others, although it never had them to anywhere near the same degree.

One of the things that was so striking in interviews with senior managers at Midland in this regard was the tendency of several to speak spontaneously about how similar it was in many respects to NatWest. One Midland senior manager made that observation from direct experience. He recalled:

> NatWest is the bank most like Midland. It always took them much longer to change, given their enormous hierarchy. I knew about this first-hand, because we at Midland were involved in financing Eurotunnel, and so was NatWest. The NatWest banker was very professional, but he had to operate through a series of committees and they were extremely bureaucratic, like us. NatWest got some very good marketing people from Midland; but it is a high-cost, slow-moving bank, and still with big management suites for the top people, and with an inflated cost structure.

Another senior Midland manager made a similar point. 'Midland was run by tough clearing bankers who did not understand change. It was closest to NatWest, and the many problems NatWest is now going through – not having focus and not having adequate systems – are problems that we went through from 1986 on. I respect both Wanless [NatWest's CEO] and Lord Alexander [its board Chair] as professionals, but they are going through these problems.'

Midland's future

Although HSBC has improved Midland's infrastructure considerably, and that has included helping Midland focus more on core business competences, there still remains the problem of how HSBC defines Midland's strategy for the future. Given the constant changes in the industry, that institutional definition obviously cannot be a static one. Nevertheless, Midland needs what Lloyds was able to do and what NatWest and (to a lesser extent) Barclays must do.

HSBC has not been known as a bank with that capability for vision. Yet, it must now provide it, if Midland is to take the next step of becoming more of a leading bank in the future. Given the considerable improvements made since 1992, taking that next step may be possible. Otherwise, Midland may sink back into mediocrity. It would not likely be as mismanaged and poorly performing as in the nearly five decades immediately preceding HSBC's take-over, but it would still not be capable of competing effectively in the fast-changing world of financial services.

Notes and references

1. Big Four annual reports.
2. The following accounts draws heavily from the company history by A.R. Holmes and Edwin Green, *Midland*, Battsford, 1986.
3. *Ibid.*, Chs 3–6.
4. Lehman Brothers, *UK Clearing Banks, 1998 Annual Review*, pp. 113 and 114 on Lloyds; and Midland Bank plc, *Annual Report and Accounts, 1997*, pp. 1 and 10.
5. Midland data come from its 1997 annual report, p. 1; data on Barclays, NatWest, and Lloyds are from Lehman Brothers, *UK Clearing Banks, 1998 Annual Review*, 23 July 1998.
6. *Annual Abstract of Banking Statistics*, Vol. 14, 1997, p. 66.
7. Midland Bank plc, *Annual Report and Accounts, 1997*, p. 7.
8. Lehman Brothers, *UK Clearing Banks, 1997 Annual Review*, pp. 91–107.
9. Michael Collins, *Money and Banking in the UK: a History*, Croom Helm, London, 1988, p. 207 and Holmes and Green, *op. cit.*, p. 150.
10. Holmes and Green, *op. cit.*, Ch. 4.
11. *Euromoney*, 'Midland's Foreign Adventures', July 1984, p. 68.
12. Holmes and Green, *op. cit.*, Ch. 6.
13. This summary is from interviews with senior staff at Midland.
14. Holmes and Green, *op. cit.*, pp. 53–6.
15. *Ibid.*, p. 53.
16. *Ibid.*, p. 122.
17. *Ibid.*, Ch. 4.
18. *Ibid.*, Ch. 7.
19. Russell Taylor, *Going for Broke*, Simon & Schuster, New York, 1993, pp. 87–8.
20. *Ibid.*, pp. 232–5.
21. Holmes and Green, *op. cit.*, Ch. 9
22. *Euromoney*, July 1984.
23. Holmes and Green, *op. cit.*, p. 140.
24. *Ibid.*, p. 250ff.
25. *Ibid.*, p. 213.
26. These phrases are taken from various articles in the *Financial Times*.
27. *Financial Times*, 3 June 1992.
28. A summary of the Crocker acquisition appears in Taylor, *op. cit.*, Ch. 15.
29. *Ibid.*, p. 224.
30. *Ibid.*, p. 235.
31. *Financial Times*, 16 January 1985.
32. Taylor, *op. cit.*, p. 232.
33. *Ibid.*, pp. 214–5.
34. See *Euromoney*, July 1984, pp. 68-73, for a further discussion.
35. *The Economist*, 1 October 1988.
36. This review of Sir Kit McMahon's experiences as CEO of Midland relies heavily on interviews with Midland senior management and staff who were there at the time.
37. *Financial Times*, 10 May 1990.

38. *Financial Times*, 7 February 1990.
39. *Financial Times*, 7 February 1990.
40. *Financial Times*, 18 December 1990.
41. *Financial Times*, 22 December 1990.
42. *Financial Times*, 6 March 1991.
43. *Ibid.*, p. 20.
44. *Financial Times*, 6 March 1991.
45. *Ibid.*
46. *Financial Times*, 23 March 1994.
47. *Financial Times*, 27 December 1991.
48. *Financial Times*, 31 July 1992.
49. *Financial Times*, 27 December 1991.
50. *Financial Times*, 19 March 1992.
51. *Financial Times*, 25 March 1992.
52. *Financial Times*, 16 July 1992.
53. *Financial Times*, 15 April 1992.
54. *Financial Times*, 31 July 1992.
55. *Financial Times*, 27 September 1993.
56. *Financial Times*, 16 July 1992.
57. *Financial Times*, 22 September 1992.
58. *Financial Times*, 16 March 1993.
59. *Ibid.*
60. *Financial Times*, 30 November 1993.
61. *Financial Times*, 6 April 1994.
62. Midland Bank plc, *Annual Report and Accounts, 1997*, p. 1.

10 Universal Banking: Benchmarks from Britain

> *Large universal banks are like battleships – powerful but not very manoeuvrable. In financial innovation, manoeuvrability and specialization are needed. Bureaucracy and institutional rigidity are counterproductive.*
>
> **Roy Smith, *Comeback*, Harvard Business School Press,**
> **Boston, MA, 1993, p. 184**

A CENTRAL issue of this book relates to how well universal banking succeeded in Britain, as one nation whose commercial banks pursued a version of that strategy. In the British variant, these banks diversified into a variety of financial services, particularly investment banking and insurance, grouping them in a loosely coupled fashion into one common holding company. In contrast to the German and Swiss versions of universal banking, the British version has not included significant holdings and voting power in big, non-banking corporations.[1]

Viewed in a broader context, commercial banks worldwide have pursued some form of universal banking for all the reasons discussed in Chapter 1: to retain their corporate and individual customers by providing them with securities products; to spread risk across many different businesses, levelling income streams; to achieve economies of scale and scope; and to attain synergies from product diversity and from cross-selling that would not have been possible in a more specialized bank.

This preferred strategy emerged in recent decades, as commercial banks worldwide have faced increasingly competitive threats from other commercial banks, investment or 'merchant' banks, savings-and-loan institutions, and non-banks. The increased competition, in turn, has reflected a blurring of market boundaries across various financial services. The forces that have driven it include deregulation, new technology, globalization, and the rise of capital markets.

This chapter draws together data on how universal banking was implemented in the four British clearing banks, in order to identify the benchmarks that these cases give us that US banks might use. The benchmarks deal with two issues. The first relates to the viability of the organizational forms that the British banks developed to manage the positioning of investment banking within the overall bank. The second deals with the banks' attempts at cross-selling, a critical promised benefit of following that strategy.

Even though 'financial supermarkets', a version of universal banking, were not working well in the US in the 1980s, the British banks tried them in 1986, after Big Bang. The case studies presented in this book, particularly those of Barclays and NatWest, indicate that the British banks were also ineffective in implementing this strategy.

At the present time, British banks are moving away from universal banking. That need not indicate, however, that some version of the strategy is no longer a viable choice for commercial banks. In fact, in the 1990s, support for the concept in the US and worldwide has increased, with massive bank consolidation and diversification taking place as a result. The initiatives have come from many segments of financial services, as firms from each segment have merged with those from the others. As background for examining the relevance of the British experience for US banks, a review of the US experience is in order.

The early US experience

In the US, commercial banks were not allowed to diversify domestically into investment banking and insurance, and in a previous study I indicated how constrained their senior management felt about the many regulations that prevented their doing just that – for example the Glass Steagall Act.[2] One of the more dramatic characterizations of those reactions is the description of Citicorp's CEO, Walter Wriston, who in the 1970s and early 1980s initiated a major lobbying effort in Washington to repeal such legislation. JP Morgan, Bankers Trust and other US banks engaged in similar lobbying. Wriston reportedly wanted Citicorp to be able to become a financial supermarket, just like American Express, Prudential, Sears, and Merrill Lynch. 'If those guys can do it,' he was reported to have said, 'why can't we?'

Notwithstanding Wriston's great vision on many financial-services-related issues, the concept of the financial supermarket, a manifestation of the universal bank, had been widely discredited from negative experiences in the 1980s – at least in the US. American Express is a classic example, along with Sears and Prudential. For a variety of reasons, these attempts at achieving synergies through so-called 'one-stop shopping' and cross-selling multiple products to the same customers were not successful.[3]

Problems associated with managing the complexity and scale that such financial supermarkets represented were overwhelming and frequently prevented the synergies from occuring. Instead, these newly diversified conglomerates often experienced a form of 'internal pollution' in the many seemingly unmanageable conflicts that got generated.[4] Culture clashes, territorial disputes, and consequent difficulties in team building and providing incentives for collaboration across product groups, along with a limited consumer interest in one-stop shopping, were among the main obstacles to effective implementation.

Despite these experiences, the financial-supermarket strategy re-appeared to such a degree that there has been a worldwide consolidation frenzy in the 1990s that shows no signs of letting up. It has spread to mergers not only within particular financial services segments but also across them – and across national boundaries as well. If anything, the merger movement is increasing, although pressures on banks to update their technologies for the year 2000 (in other words, the millennium bug) may temporarily slow it down.

The most notable example is Citigroup, the newly merged conglomerate of Citicorp and Travelers–Salomon, which went well beyond what was permissible under existing laws, on the assumption that its mere existence would speed up their repeal. After some 15 years of inaction on such regulatory reforms, it remains to be seen whether the US will enact them in the face of these mergers.

Ironically, one of the leaders in the US, Sanford Weill, who is co-CEO in the newly formed Citigroup, was a central figure in the failed American Express attempt to put together a financial supermarket in the 1980s.[5]

To the informed observer of American financial services, it seems anomalous that Weill would continue to pursue the supermarket strategy, after the American Express experience. Judging from his many merger initiatives since leaving American Express, however, culminating with the Citicorp one, he clearly remains strongly committed to the strategy. Other leaders in financial services worldwide are similarly committed, as indicated by the mergers of (amongst others) Deutsche with Morgan Grenfell and later with Bankers Trust, Swiss Bank with Dillon Read, Nation's Bank with Montgomery Securities, and BankAmerica with Robertson, Stephens.

The British experience as a benchmark for the US

By contrast with the US, British bankers have recently abandoned many aspects of universal banking, particularly those related to investment banking. It is important to understand why and what broader implications may flow from such actions for the viability of commercial banks taking on investment banking elsewhere.

In this regard, the book began with the specific intention of exploring how the British experience with universal banking might have relevance for the US. Largely because of the more restrictive regulatory system in the US, American commercial banks were at an earlier stage in diversifying into investment banking and insurance domestically in the early 1990s, although the pace in the US is quickening now, despite nominal regulatory constraints.

For many reasons, the universal banking strategy that combines commercial and investment banking businesses in one bank did not work particularly well among the four clearers in Britain. By far the highest performer was Lloyds, whose success seemed directly associated with its having abandoned universal banking since the 1980s, pursuing instead a strategy of focusing mainly on its strong UK retail banking franchise. It did diversify into new retail banking businesses such as insurance and home mortgages, but it exited from investment banking and many aspects of its wholesale international banking.

By contrast, Barclays and NatWest, clearers that followed the universal banking strategy most intensely, experienced big losses in their investment banks and major problems in understanding and controlling them – witness NatWest's Blue Arrow episode, which badly hurt its reputation. As a result, these two banks sold off much of their investment banking in 1997 and 1998, particularly the equities and corporate advisory parts. With ROEs from investment banking in single digits, and with enormous costs in technology and compensation trying to keep up with (foreign) competitors, their senior managers felt they could no longer justify to shareholders the pursuit of those businesses. In that sense, they adopted a strategy similar to Lloyds', only they did so ten years later.

The fourth clearer, Midland, had so many internal problems – those of leadership, culture, and organization – that it could not be seen as a test of any strategy. It survived only by HSBC's taking it over. While Midland's financial performance is much improved since then (1992), it is not clear what strategy Midland will pursue in the future. Interestingly, European banks such as Deutsche, Dredsner, and Commerzbank had similarly poor performances in investment banking, but they have persisted. Their boards and large, institutional shareholders have more tolerance for such failures.

Different organizational design solutions

Supporters of universal banking may well argue that just because it did not work in Britain doesn't necessarily mean that it will not work in the US. Indeed, there may be some idiosyncratic features of the British case that had an impact – for instance the early cartelized structure of the industry in Britain and the nature of its embeddedness in the wider society.

My argument is that, notwithstanding cultural differences between nations, the British experience with investment banking faced broad managerial–organizational issues that banks in every country, including the US, must encounter. The rest of the chapter examines two such issues: first, the organizational forms selected to structure the relationships between investment banking and the bank at large; and, second, the degree of success in cross-selling.

To analyse how well universal banking has worked, I have examined the many conflicts commonly reported between commercial and investment banking divisions within the clearing banks. It turns out that they pursued different approaches, none of them particularly productive, in maintaining both sets of businesses under the same corporate umbrella. In the end, however, all the clearers converged on a common approach. It involved giving the investment bank much autonomy and proved unsatisfactory enough to hasten the clearers' exit from investment banking.

NatWest was perhaps earliest in adopting what could be called an integrated model, having all wholesale businesses that had been part of its commercial bank, including Treasury and foreign exchange, incorporated into the investment bank. While the NatWest group, as the wider bank was called, was a somewhat loosely coupled aggregation of financial services businesses, some were nevertheless more tightly coupled than in the other clearers. NatWest had considerable integration of the investment bank into the wider one, for example, and moved in that direction earlier than the others.

There was good reason for NatWest's moving toward such early integration. It had been hurt badly in Blue Arrow and wasn't about to have that happen again. Integrating the investment bank into the wider bank, so that the latter might have more oversight than before, seemed a logical way to proceed.

Over time, however, NatWest's investment bankers exerted renewed pressures to become more independent, and they were largely successful. The investment bankers felt that collaboration with the larger group was irrelevant to their mission, and they claim to have participated minimally in bank-wide meetings on strategy and operations. Moreover, when they did attend such meetings, they came away with the view that the commercial bankers were incompetent and too slow-moving. 'My people tell me they really don't want to go to meetings of the NatWest group,' explained a senior manager of NatWest Markets, 'because they are seen as a complete waste of time. We have become the catalyst for continued culture change in the larger NatWest group. But some of my senior people are convinced that we have nothing to gain by being associated with it. I told the CFO recently that he couldn't make it in my shop as CFO. I have fifty to sixty people who are better quality than the clearing bankers.'

Reflecting such sentiments, the investment bankers moved to reverse the wider bank's integration strategy. That development had, however, some negative results. Having become independent once more, and proceeding with minimal oversight, NatWest's investment bank then stumbled into another débâcle, namely the 'mispriced derivatives' escapade. The subsequent £77 million loss and further damage to NatWest's reputation then hastened NatWest's decision to exit many aspects of investment banking as being no longer viable.

A lesson from the NatWest experience is that even when pressures for integration are strong, those for separateness are seemingly stronger. That then puts the bank as a whole at the mercy of the investment bank, making it vulnerable to the latter's mismanagement. It is little wonder, then, that a senior NatWest executive reported in late 1995 that he saw one of his tasks to be that of saving the rest of the bank from the investment bankers. As he put it: 'A critical issue for me is to protect the rest of the bank from the investment bankers – from NatWest Markets. The problem is that the investment bankers are brighter, more aggressive and regard the commercial bankers as drones.'

Barclays proceeded differently. It maintained much separateness and autonomy for its investment bank, BZW, only integrating it into the larger group in the mid-1990s, long after NatWest had done so. This coincided with CEO Martin Taylor's strong push for more collaboration and synergy across Barclays' various businesses. His view was that no business should exist as an island unto itself, and if it did not collaborate with the other businesses then it should not be allowed to continue.

Poised for action, in the event that any of the businesses did not measure up, Taylor then moved quickly to sell off much of BZW, as its costs kept rising after 1995, its ROE was under 10 per cent, and it was therefore pulling down the rest of the bank. Even though BZW did not experience the rogue-trader losses that NatWest's investment bank had, its overall performance was very low and no longer justifiable to shareholders. One might argue that Taylor having followed the more hands-on and integrative model enabled him to act quickly, once he decided that BZW could not compete, particularly in the equities and corporate advisory businesses.

NatWest also acted quickly, however, after its big losses in derivatives trading. Wanless, like Taylor, recognized the difficulties of remaining in a business that both experienced such low profitability and was careening out of control.

Midland's approach was different from that of NatWest and Barclays, reflecting its particular history of extreme internal conflict and fragmented authority. Given its past difficulties in bringing together the wholesale and retail bankers, its investment bank, Midland Montagu, remained quite separate from the rest of the bank. Midland's rationale for the separation was that the cultures of commercial and investment banking were too different. At present, it retains Midland Montagu as a separate subsidiary.

Where do the synergies take place?

Students of corporate strategy have written extensively about achieving synergies in diversified firms. Sociologist Rosabeth Kanter argues that there is no other justification for a multibusiness company except the achievement of synergies.[6] As Campbell and Sommers note, however:[7]

> While synergy has been a basic component in the thinking about diversification for at least three decades, it often seems to promise more than it delivers ... we discovered that it is much easier to find examples of failure than of success.

Senior managers and staff at all four clearers talked at great length about their strong commitment to cross-selling as a way of getting synergies across various businesses and product groups. It did not take much prompting to get such a conversation going, since cross-selling, along with one-stop shopping, had become a clarion call for the industry, both in Britain and worldwide. As reported, Martin Taylor had made cross-business collaboration a centrepiece of his strategy at Barclays; and NatWest had a similar emphasis, in its continued quest for synergies. Yet, the quest for synergies and the preoccupation with internal organizational design and conflict management that it requires may undermine a firm's flexibility to pursue external market options and increase opportunity costs.

There were three arenas within which the clearers attempted to get cross-business collaborations: within the retail bank, within the investment bank, and between them. The general consensus was that it was extraordinarily difficult to develop and then sustain such collaboration in all three.

The complexities of cross-selling

An extensive literature exists in economics and finance on the costs and benefits of one-stop shopping and cross-selling.[8] It is largely an abstract, non-empirical literature, containing little or no data on how these techniques work in particular financial services firms. There are no reported studies, for example, about how much cross-selling exists in individual banks, why it occurs, what implementation problems may arise, and what impacts occur on bank performance. The discussion to follow, based mainly on interviews at the four clearing banks and among knowledgeable outsiders, provides some preliminary data on how cross-selling is working in Britain.

Cross-selling seemed to have greater support among product groups within retail banking than it did within wholesale services. 'The management challenge in retail banking is not nearly as great as getting the various investment bankers together,' reported a senior banker in one of the clearers. 'Investment bankers are prima donnas. Cross selling and teams are easier to put together between retail bankers selling life and general insurance, home mortgages, credit cards, and long-term savings.' Another commented: 'The investment bankers are non-team-oriented. They are deal makers and do not band together naturally into large teams.'

Senior management among the clearers also stated that they were at a very early stage in promoting cross-selling and could do a lot more yet in that regard. One CEO noted:

> We are so inefficient at cross-selling, it is pathetic. Our success is so limited. We are hopelessly bad at converting credit-card or home mortgage customers, and we still make a fortune in retail banking. We could so easily increase our penetration rate through better products, better targeting, and more sales efforts. Even as we do it so poorly, our retail business makes a lot of money.

Moreover, there was widespread agreement that cross-selling was not only not being done as much as it might be, but that doing more of it would significantly improve the banks' profitability. 'Cross-selling is perhaps the biggest issue in our retail bank,' stated a senior manager. 'We must improve our skills at cross-selling, and the same is true at corporate. If we do it well, we get another five to ten per cent profit in the retail bank. We must use our many opportunities to multiple-sell. We sell two or three products to customers, and that is not high.'

Managers and staff at headquarters, as well as retail bankers discussed constantly the importance of selling multiple products to the same customer. Home mortgage customers were often mentioned as a good place to begin the cycle, as were credit-card customers. A consensus seemed to be that most banks averaged between 2.5 and 3 products per customer, but that there were unexploited opportunities to push for more.

TSB: a model

One of the highly acclaimed performers had been Trustee Savings Bank (TSB), which merged with Lloyds in 1995. Several British bankers singled it out for special attention and offered a series of explanations as to why it had been so successful. The explanations emphasized the businesses that TSB had been in, its client base, and the organization design it adopted. Specifically, its emphasis on retail banking, its lower-income customers, and its matrix organization were all seen as contributing. One banker explained:

> TSB is the British bank that has been the most active and successful on synergies. It was first in that field and was able to do that in part because it was never serious in the corporate market. It was a federation of banks

and had a strong focus on retail banking and bancassurance. And they developed a matrix to encourage co-operation across product groups.

A senior manager from TSB explained:

> We are far and away the insurance leader in Britain. We are the only bank that has integrated the bank and insurance operation. We have developed a matrix to encourage co-operation across product groups. One advantage we have is that our customers tend to be a lower socio-economic group. It is natural for that customer group to do business with us on many products.

After Lloyds merged with TSB, it took on that cross-selling expertise. Moreover, by virtue of its acquisitions of Abbey Life, Cheltenham & Gloucester, and TSB, Lloyds has now become a retail financial-services power, with a strong cross-selling capability.

Obstacles to cross-selling in retail banking: lack of collaboration and team building

Not surprisingly, while cross-selling makes much sense in theory as a way of getting economies of scope, and has many supporters, it has been very difficult to develop and sustain in practice (apart from at TSB and Lloyds). One consultant who worked with a clearer's retail bank defined it as an organizational design issue in which team building across the various product groups was one of his main tasks. He reported deep and continuing frustration at how those who worked in each product group would close ranks by limiting its collaboration with bankers from other groups, largely because of a fear of losing direct contact with the customers and of losing bonus compensation for the sale. He also expressed dismay at not getting more support for his team-building efforts from the bank's senior management at headquarters:

> For banks heavily into retailing, cross-selling is absolutely key. The long-term direction for the banks is to take a holistic view of the customer. The question is how to do that, how to organize such product specialities as life insurance, loans, mortgages, investment services like unit trusts, underneath marketing.

As this consultant saw it, few retail banks have carried out this process well. He identified two, however, that had done so: TSB in Britain and Wells Fargo in the US. The latter had long been recognized as one of the best-managed US banks until its difficulties in 1997 and 1998 in absorbing First InterState. 'Wells Fargo has been one of the best at such team building,' he explained. 'They meet weekly and five key product managers talk and figure out how they can work together better. TSB has done the best of all the banks in Britain in cross-selling and product integration. All the product people report to the same boss.'

An even better case in the US is Norwest, which has been more successful than perhaps any other US bank in selling multiple products to its retail banking customers. At the time of its recent merger with Wells Fargo, Norwest had a reported 3.8 products per customer, and had publicly committed itself to doubling that (although not indicating over what time period).[9]

A consultant who had worked with one of the larger clearers found it particularly frustrating that the clearer's normal operations kept thwarting his attempts at promoting team building. One obstacle was poor management within individual product groups. As he put it: 'The integration must be staged, after you have each of these product groups together.'

Still another obstacle was the fact that the career progression of effective product group managers and the consequent turnover in their positions prevented needed continuity in team-building efforts. 'Effective managers are often earmarked early and never stay in one job for more than twelve to eighteen months,' he explained. 'They move up quickly and don't stick around long enough to see through these programmes to their resolution. The bank singles them out for career success and this hurts our programmes.'

The consultant expressed much disappointment that the bank was not more committed to its cross-selling efforts. 'They develop these team-building programmes with some fanfare,' he bemoaned, 'and then underresource and undermanage them up front. Many good managers move constantly, and there is too much churn to get continuity and get things done.'

In brief, while bankers and consultants agree on the importance of securing much more collaboration and team building across product groups in retail banking than has traditionally existed, the gap between theory and practice remains enormous. A critical question for bankers and consultants committed to team building is to identify the conditions under which such collaboration and actual cross-selling are more and less likely to take place. Specifically, what types of organizational designs and team-building efforts are likely to be successful? How should they be pursued – in other words, with what types of incentives and leadership styles, and on what types of customer populations?

To some, the TSB success suggests that lower-income customers are the more receptive to cross-selling. The reasoning is that they may be a more compliant population, more accepting of the policies of financial services providers, less sophisticated about possible variations in prices and products among various providers, and more limited in where to go to learn about them. But the well educated, some financial services analysts say, lead busy professional lives and they seek to simplify the management of their financial affairs. Other analysts disagree and suggest that this population prefers shopping around among several providers, particularly since the Internet minimizes search costs.

The bottom line is that banks need to know much more than they do about what drives different customer groups or market segments to either concentrate their financial services purchases with one provider or spread them among several.

Team-building problems in investment banking

If providing integrated packages of financial services through collaborative teams of different product specialists is problematic in retail banking, British bankers and outside observers report that it may be even more so in wholesale banking. Eccles and Crain, in their now classic study, *Doing Deals*,[10] argue that the essence of managing effective investment banks is to customize packages of financial services to the particular needs of the customer. This involves getting the various product specialists together in collaborative teams, referred to by Eccles and Crain as an 'adhocracy', project-management approach. A variety of factors already discussed or suggested in the case studies, however, mitigate against that approach.

British investment bankers, like those elsewhere, have been strongly resistant to such collaboration and team building, reflecting their broader career orientations. Sociologists distinguish between white-collar professionals with more local interests and those with more cosmopolitan orientations; investment bankers are an extreme example of the latter. They often have minimal commitment to the firm where they are currently employed; they do not like to be managed, preferring instead as much autonomy as possible; and, as a corollary, they resist being melded into teams of collaborative financial services providers.

There have been investment banks where such teamwork and co-operation have existed, largely through supportive cultures. Goldman Sachs and Morgan Stanley are examples in the US, but they may well be the exceptions rather than the rule. Instead, investment bankers are highly mobile, measuring their success in large part by the extent to which their present employer is providing base salaries and bonuses that at least match – if not surpass – those of the highest-paying competitors. In an industry where firms are constantly bidding for the services of talented specialists, investment bankers have much leverage. They want the freedom to trade, do deals and provide financial advice with a minimum of interference, and they want to be compensated well, regardless of their performance in a given year. In the present seller's market, they often get their way.

Given such conditions in the labour market, it is not surprising that many investment bankers exist in their firms with power in the form of a series of independent baronies. When Martin Owen was unable to develop a 'family of cultures' among NatWest's investment bankers after pledging to do so, it appeared that he was constrained and defeated by the forces just discussed. While separatism also exists among retail bankers, it has nowhere near the same intensity as among investment bankers. Retail bankers seem not to be as mobile, they are not bid for with escalating compensation packages to nearly the same degree as are investment bankers, and they are therefore more amenable to incentives for team building.

Collaboration between wholesale and retail bankers

As for the prospects of getting investment bankers and retail bankers to collaborate, that seems to have been the most difficult task of all. Professor Roy Smith of New York University's Stern School of Business maintains that wholesale and retail financial services businesses have such different cultures and modes of operation as to be inherently incompatible within the same enterprise.

As discussed earlier, investment banking has a much more customized strategy, adapting its expertise to the idiosyncratic needs of clients. It exists, as Eccles and Crain describe, as a flat, decentralized, organic (anti-bureaucratic), self-designing organization.[11] By contrast, retail banking is much more of a top-down, bureaucratic business, providing standard products for individual customers in a fashion similar to a continuous-flow type of operation. Investment banking is thus structured much like an R&D firm, while retail banking operates more like a factory.

Despite such differences, there are potentials for synergies. The distribution system and customers of retail banking are important potential outlets for investment banking services – for example mutual funds, securitized loans, and asset management. Conversely, investment banking benefits from the capital and reputation of the commercial bank, and from its credit business expertise. In that sense – again, at least in theory – there are synergies in having both within the same firm. The British experience suggests, however, that such synergies are difficult to develop.

Instead, these two sets of financial services businesses (retail and wholesale) compete vigorously for the bank's resources. Their cultural differences and conflicting interests make it very difficult to get them to collaborate. The power of the investment bankers enables them to exist with minimal controls from the larger bank, whose senior managers too often are not as informed as they should be about what is happening in the investment bank. And the bank as a whole is then vulnerable to high costs and huge losses on the investment banking side, which drag it down and erode shareholder confidence and its larger reputation.

If some form of universal banking was not conducive to high performance among the clearers, it is important to establish what strategy *is* more productive. The four case studies provide some answers.

Throughout much of the last two decades, Lloyds has emerged as the highest performer of the clearers, and Midland the lowest, although it has now recovered after being acquired by HSBC. The culture and leadership of Barclays gave it an edge over NatWest until 1998, even though both banks suffered from being too committed until that time to size, growth and diversification. As I argued in the case studies described in earlier chapters, these were fuzzy, ill-thought-out strategies that were increasingly untenable in the late 1990s. As competition intensified in this most recent period, it was necessary to be much more selective than Barclays and NatWest had been. Barclays seems to have picked up on that earlier than NatWest.

One implication of this ranking is that focusing on one's core competence is critical to success. Lloyds moved in that direction much earlier than the other three, and it was reflected, for example, in its ROEs and cost/income ratios, which far surpassed those of its clearing bank rivals during the nineties. Starting in the early 1990s, Barclays also moved toward greater focus, resulting in its pulling ahead of NatWest, which seemed to take longer to divest itself of losing businesses.

The experience of the late 1990s, however, suggests that relying on a single formula, such as strategic focus, and concentrating on core competencies may be inadequate as a guide for future success. The pace of change has accelerated so much in recent years, with the movement toward consolidation and the continued impact of new technology, that future success will require more than following a particular strategy and organizational configuration. Rather, future winners will be financial services firms that have high levels of flexibility and a readiness to adapt to rapid and sudden changes in the industry's competitive environment. The capacity for organizational learning may thus be much more significant than positioning the firm in any particular way.

Contradictions in universal banking

Reviewing the failures of financial conglomerates in both the US and Britain, we can detect a basic organizational contradiction inherent in the concept of universal banking and in its implementation, and this may provide an explanation.[12] That contradiction relates to the need for simultaneously maintaining both high levels of diversity or differentiation and of integration. Universal banking cannot work unless it brings together a wide variety of different businesses and product groups: commercial and investment banking, asset management, and insurance. And yet, each of these businesses exists in a different competitive environment and requires a different set of skills.

In brief, each has its own differentiated culture and must maintain that to be effective. At the same time, universal banking can only work when there are synergies across these businesses. That can only take place, however, when the businesses are tightly coupled or linked. There is a need in that sense for the high-performing universal bank that reduces transactions costs for customers and provides much cross-selling to be a 'seamless organization'.

The problem is that no financial services institution to date has figured out how to make these two demands compatible. There is a need for the diversity of businesses and therefore of cultures. But that diversity is only a means to provide one-stop shopping opportunities for the consumer through extensive cross-selling. The managerial challenge is then one of managing such diverse cultures in an integrated way. With the exception of the limited successes in retail banking cited above – TSB, Norwest and Wells Fargo, for example – no financial services organization has been able to do that.

The conflicts across these businesses are so great that the firms end up keeping them apart. That just increases agency costs, however, with each pursuing its own goals, following its own compensation practices and maintaining its own culture. Seamless organizations that provide one-stop shopping do not develop from such separatism.

In brief, the centrifugal forces or those for differentiation are so strong that they prevent managers from fostering powerful enough centripetal or integrative ones to make universal banking work. The cultural integrity of each of the many financial services businesses must be maintained for it to be effective. Yet, maintaining those differences makes it hard to bring them together to provide one-stop shopping. Furthermore, the fact that each of these businesses itself exists in a highly changing, uncertain market environment makes the challenge of integration even more difficult, since they must keep adapting themselves to that changing environment to be effective.

Future options

New organizational forms have emerged in recent years that provide an array of choices for British banks and those of other nations. These forms may be particularly desirable where the banks see many benefits in offering retail and wholesale customers a wide range of products, but where the costs of containing them all within a single holding company are too great.

One such choice is to form strategic alliances with outside investment banks and work out arrangements where both parties jointly provide a range of financial services. Another is to outsource the delivery of some services. In each instance, there are problems of control. Several senior British bankers have indicated that they would find outsourcing for some financial services unacceptable for that specific reason. One stated:

> We do a lot of outsourcing now with things like administering wages and salaries, but we would never outsource core competences. It boils down to reputation, and our reputation would be affected if anything went wrong in an outsourced service that we didn't deliver directly.

It may well be, however, that this clearing banker had too broad a definition of core competences for his bank. Had he and his colleagues narrowed that to services where the bank clearly excelled, there might be investment banking services that it could deliver in partnership with outside investment banks.

Looking back at the experiences of the four clearers, commercial banking in Britain may well be at more of a crossroads now than at any time in the industry's long history. Even the Lloyds strategy of being primarily a diversified financial services company in domestic retail banking may only be a temporary solution; indeed, some observers of British banking predict that Lloyds will soon expand its retail bank by an aggressive acquisition foray in Europe. As for Barclays and NatWest, having exited from many aspects of investment banking, they too are pondering the future. Will it be mainly to build on their cash cow businesses in UK retail operations, through further computerization, developing new delivery systems, closing down branches and modernizing those that remain? Will they supplement this by building on their emerging private-banking franchise, and concentrating their wholesale banking in the UK? Or will they, like Lloyds, seek to become a significant European retail-banking and even wholesale-banking presence?

What does seem clear is that investment banking has largely been taken over by the US bulge-bracket firms. They are now so far ahead of the rest of the world in technology, staff and product capabilities, customer linkages, and distribution systems that it seems unlikely that commercial or investment banks from other nations, including Britain, can compete with them. Perhaps the only way that will be possible is for each of these British banks to specialize in one or a few areas of investment banking, where they have some significant core competence, and try to become global players in that niche. Given the emergence and development of the European Union, that seems the most promising arena for such expansion. In the meantime, this is a time for introspection and regrouping.

The importance of culture

In addition to universal banking, this book has also examined the slower modernization and lesser capacity for adaptiveness of the British commercial banks relative to those in the US. As the case studies have indicated, commercial banking in the UK has historically been an industry of the lower middle class, by contrast with investment banking, which has always been a much more prestigious calling, dealing as it does with the financing and development needs of sovereign nations and large corporations. While this class difference between investment and commercial bankers is mirrored in other industrial nations, it has seemed particularly pronounced in Britain in the years of interest to this study.

Even though many in the non-university, school-leaver group who became senior managers in the clearing banks had strong entrepreneurial and commercial banking skills, their capabilities as change managers were, by and large, not as strong as those of the university-educated investment bankers. The argument that many observers and analysts have put forward is that, given similarly sized cohorts or pools of non-university and university graduates, the latter are likely to include more people with the conceptual, analytical, and action skills so essential for becoming effective change managers.

There are always exceptions, and Sir Brian Pitman, CEO and (later) Chair of Lloyds, is one. But even in that case, Pitman had achieved a partial equivalent of a university education through his extensive early experiences as an international banker in Europe and the US. He had spent much time looking at well managed US corporations and meeting prominent US management consultants. In that sense, he had attained a sophistication in management as well as banking at an early age.

Even so, overall, the people that British commercial banking have attracted may have contributed to its struggles in the eighties and nineties to adapt to change. A second factor may have been that the industry had reached a high degree of economic concentration much earlier than it did in such nations as the US. After World War I, a Big Five – and later a Big Four – was to dominate British banking. They were protected from competition to such a degree and for so long that they had limited capability to adapt quickly to emerging market and technological changes during the 1970s and subsequently. Still a third factor was the close ties between the industry and its regulator, the Bank of England, which probably encouraged inertia.

A combination, then, of early cartelization and of having attracted bankers with more limited horizons than their counterparts in investment banking in Britain or in commercial banking in the US, appears to have produced an institutional mind-set and practices that made it difficult to adapt. The British clearers were slower-moving institutions than commercial banks in the US. And at least two of them, Barclays and NatWest, had become huge, encrusted organizations since the early 1970s, with Midland having already developed a similarly rigid bureaucracy in an earlier era.

In sum, British commercial banking in recent decades was less innovative and entrepreneurial than such banking in the US. This is not to say that American banks were that well managed either. They also had expanded and diversified with little thought given to the viability of their strategies. In his book, *Breaking up the Bank*, Lowell Bryan, one of McKinsey's leading bank consultants, has written at length about how little strategic analysis US banks had engaged in.[13] He attributed it largely to the failure to assess the strengths and weaknesses of their various product groups as separate businesses and to make larger strategic decisions (to expand, stay the same, contract or divest) in the context of such an assessment.

An indication of the US banks' mismanagement in recent years was their enormous losses in Latin American, commercial real estate, and leveraged buyout (LBO) loans. The US banks seemed driven more by a concern to expand their loan portfolio than by an examination of the loans' viability as measured by the creditworthiness of their clients. A herd-like mentality prevailed, in which banks vied with one another to see who could book the most loans the fastest. One of the US banks, Citicorp, led the pack, to such a degree that it came under extreme regulatory scrutiny and supervision in 1990 and 1991, when its losses multiplied.

Temporarily chastened by these mistakes, and helped considerably by an expanding national and global economy, Citicorp – and, in turn, many of its US competitors – has made a remarkable comeback since 1991. Several such banks are now leading financial services institutions of the world.

Overall, US commercial banks have been earlier and more advanced than the British banks in the development of new technology, in establishing a meritocracy, in aggressive sales and marketing policies, in strategic analysis, and in change management.

British culture

Wider cultural values within the nation at large may have also contributed to the slower pace of adaptation in Britain. A considerable academic literature now exists on the possible impact of British culture on the nation's supposed economic decline in the twentieth century.[14] Without taking a position in the debate as to whether there has in fact been a decline in Britain relative to other industrial nations, it is worthwhile to speculate on the possible impact of British cultural values on the slower pace of modernization in its commercial banking relative to the US.

Sociologist Sir Ralf Dahrendorf writes about the 'cultural environment' in Britain, in which 'there is very little attraction for people to move into that in-between area in which technological advance is translated into industrial production'.[15] He attributes Britain's limited support for entrepreneurship and business management to its class structure and social values. However impressionistic the historical data may be, he suggests that in the highly stratified society that still exists in Britain, there remains a set of dominant upper-class values 'which involve a view of life which is more geared to peer group understanding, to living nicely and pleasantly with others, to leisure and perhaps to sports, than to industrial values'.[16]

Others write of the continuing ideal of the leisured gentleman who devalued business, technology, entrepreneurship and material achievement. They also write of a culture of amateurism, and of gentlemanly sportsmanship in competition. Historian George Smith speculates that 'the British historically were very ambivalent about competition as a means to a better economy. Relative to Americans, they had a culture of not liking to compete, at least not too openly. Instead, they valued fair play and gentlemanly sportsmanship.'[17]

Broad speculation at this level, linking assumed societal values in Britain to the extent of modernization and competitive strength in its commercial banking system must obviously be made with caution. Some observers suggest, however, that it may have merit. One is historian Martin Wiener, who suggests that economic explanations of Britain's slow economic development by themselves explain little.[18] He ends by urging more tolerance by scholars of British economic history of the admittedly more difficult problems of evaluating cultural, social or ideological factors.

A parallel to this speculation is the common observation that the adoption of modern management skills in the banking industry was late in coming, compared with the US. There are varied explanations: being late to attach importance to MBA education; the protected, oligopolistic nature of banking; and the homogeneous backgrounds of British commercial bankers. Regardless of the explanations, a wide consensus exists on the lateness-in-modernization view.

In addition to these perceptual judgements, anecdotal data suggest a similar pattern. For example, when Citicorp expanded its corporate loan services in London in the late 1960s and early 1970s, it almost immediately took over 30–35 per cent of that market from the clearing banks.

As another example, a British consultant, a professor of strategic management at British and American universities, reported on his experiences in the 1970s, working for one of the clearers. He compared the work styles of US and British bankers: 'In commercial and investment banking, they [the US banks] were having their working breakfasts at the office at 7:30, while the Brits were sauntering in from the suburbs closer to 9:30 or 10:00. That alone suggested to me some of the source of the trouble. We were being out-hustled.'

If there is any validity to this cultural thesis, British banks face a formidable challenge in this increasingly competitive industry. They have certainly been responding in more aggressive ways since the 1970s. They will have to do so more intensively in the future.

British and continental European banks: who's ahead?

A final perspective on the state of British commercial banking may be provided by comparing it with banking in other industrialized nations, particular the US and continental Europe. I have already made comparisons throughout the book with US banks, indicating the many ways that US banks are ahead of their British competitors in technology, management and performance. Not surprisingly, since Lloyds, Barclays and NatWest have all dropped out of much of global wholesale and investment banking, the US banks are way ahead there. The US banks would have been ahead anyway.

In what Professor Roy Smith of NYU's Stern School of Business refers to as his 'Gorilla Tables', US banks constituted eight of the world's top ten in market share at the end of 1997, with Barclays Capital and NatWest Markets finishing 19th and 20th respectively.[19] Moreover, two US commercial banks appeared within that group: JP Morgan and Nations Bank. Citicorp just missed the top group, as number 11. After its merger in April 1998 with Salomon Smith Barney, however, it is likely to have moved into the top five by 1999.

On the retail banking side, the British clearers, as has been emphasized throughout, have been strong performers in their domestic UK market. Also, they are continuing to modernize those businesses, making bigger and more sophisticated investments in new technologies in order to improve efficiency in existing branches, to close down many branches, and to develop alternative delivery systems.

US commercial banks have also been aggressively pursuing these goals. In addition, with the repeal of restrictive legislation (such as the McCarran Act), which has limited the US banks' capacity to expand their interstate branching, there have been big consolidations there by the super-regional banks. Bank of America (with Nations Bank), Wells Fargo (with First Interstate and then Norwest), and First Union (with Core States) are among the largest of those consolidations, as a step in the emergence of perhaps five or six giant national retail banks. Such consolidation may yet take place in Britain – as, for example, between NatWest and Barclays.

Retail banking is much more of a domestic than a global business, but Citicorp (now Citigroup) has indicated that it has the capacity for being global as well. It remains to be seen whether the British banks – particularly Lloyds, the most successful in retail banking in the UK, embark on a new retail initiative in Europe.

Comparisons of British with European banks are more ambiguous. Two of the latter appeared in the world's top ten in market share at the end of 1997: Credit Suisse First Boston (CSFB) and Union Bank of Switzerland/Swiss Bank Corporation (UBS/SBC), as sixth and ninth respectively.[20] The overall financial performance of the main European universal banks, however, as indicated earlier, has been poor: they exist as second- and third-tier players, with little likelihood of much improvement over the short term. Even in a bull market, they have had ROEs in single digits and have faced rapidly rising costs for technology and compensation.

A comparison with Deutsche Bank

Deutsche Bank is one of the most dramatic examples. Despite its merger with Morgan Grenfell in 1989 and its stated goal of becoming a top global player in wholesale and investment banking, it only emerged at the end of 1997 as 15th in the world, with a modest 2.26 per cent of market share in global securities, M&A, arranged bank loans and lead-managed medium-term notes.[21] Moreover, Deutsche Morgan Grenfell had only a 6.4 per cent ROE in 1997.[22] The biggest and most significant capital markets that an aspiring player like Deutsche Bank would have to penetrate are in the US, and its efforts there at acquisition – JP Morgan, Merrill Lynch, and Goldman Sachs – ended in failure until its recent (November 1998) success in taking over Bankers Trust.

Even that acquisition, however, does not get positive early reviews. And even if it had taken place a year earlier, it would only have lifted Deutsche from 13th to 11th place in 1998 in M&A, the market where it is particularly weak. In brief, Deutsche might perhaps move from a third- to a second-tier global investment bank by this merger, and then only if the implementation goes well.

Predictions of that taking place are pessimistic, however, especially in view of Deutsche's past experiences and of the sharp contrasts of the two banks' cultures. Deutsche's record with Morgan Grenfell, before the Bankers Trust acquisition, was particularly dismal. It included many conflicts and subsequent staff defections; a fund-management fraud, leading to serious questions about internal controls; and constant reorganizations, in which Morgan Grenfell was first kept autonomous and later integrated, but with great confusion among the investment bankers. Also, since that acquisition, Deutsche did much poaching of teams of investment bankers from top competitors for enormous compensation packages, leading its board 'to worry that it was creating a monster of an investment bank, based on hugely expensive egos'.[23]

As for integrating Bankers Trust into Deutsche Bank, that will be a most problematic challenge. As *The Economist* concludes: 'Take a transatlantic combination of a lumbering, accident-prone universal bank with a prickly, free-wheeling investment bank, and only the foolhardy would bet on success.'[24]

Other comparisons

Deutsche is only one of many cases, however. Most other European universal banks have had similarly negative results in their efforts to build global investment banks. None has become a significant player in US capital markets. In a piece entitled 'Out of Their League?' *The Economist* reports Dredsner Kleinwort Benson as facing much internal strife and earnings of little more than Deutsche's, and Dutch-owned ING as having experienced defections on such a scale as to leave its securities division 'on its knees'. A later piece reports the German banks in a 'sorry state': Commerzbank, the nation's second-largest, as a take-over target and having no strategic direction; Dredsner as 'staid and bureaucratic'; and the German banking industry as generally having too few profits, too many branches, much inefficiency, and under possible threat of acquisition by foreign banks. Credit Suisse, ABN AMRO, and HSBC have all been said to be contemplating bids for a big German bank.[25]

Where does this leave the British banks? Taking such a comparative perspective, perhaps they are not as badly off as the detailed case studies would at first suggest. They still have tremendous strengths in domestic UK retail banking, and they would do well to work intensively on rationalizing that business in preparation for the increasingly likely competitive invasion of British and foreign competitors, banks and non-banks.

As for their exit from wholesale banking, what might seem to some observers as a narrowly inward-looking, risk-averse strategy of isolationism may make much sense in view of how European and British universal banking has fared. Indeed, it may be seen instead as a prudent or even a shrewd judgement that the bulge bracket of US global giants and their European would-be competitors will soon prove less manageable, once the Wall Street bull market fades away.

Such a withdrawal need not be permanent. Rather, it may – and should – be accompanied by a searching assessment of why the British and European universal banks have performed so poorly. That might, in turn, lead to a much more promising later re-entry into selected aspects of European wholesale and investment banking that does not distract from further developing their strong retail franchises and may lead to much more than the mediocre profits (at best) of the past.

One might argue that the competitive environment in Britain and the rest of the UK is more conducive to such improvements than that in many European nations. British banks in recent years have been under more critical purview by large institutional shareholders and boards than have their European competitors. They have also functioned for a longer time in an open-market environment rather than a state-driven competitive environment, with less rigid labour laws and less unsympathetic socialist states. The latter two conditions may well have made the European banks much more rigidly bureaucratic than the British banks.

The net result of these differences is that British banks, rather than being seen as having 'given up and gone home' to become second-rate global players, may be seen instead as having made prudent decisions in order to focus on their area of strength, namely UK retail banking, and to rethink their future wholesale banking strategy. Having assessed in some depth the many managerial and implementational problems associated with embarking on a major global wholesale and investment banking strategy, they may then return on a selected niche basis. Meanwhile, as the bull market declines, many of the US and European universal banks may well experience the kinds of losses that British banks may be in a position to temper in the future.

In brief, size, market share, broad geographic representation and product diversity may not be the 'holy grail' of financial services in the future. And the British banks may have been right in continuing to question that strategy. They may yet end up as important global players by re-examining critically where they have been and pursuing a more reasoned wholesale expansion strategy in the future.

Notes and references

1. See Roy Smith, *Comeback*, Harvard Business School Press, Boston MA, 1993, Ch. 5; Jordi Canals, *Universal Banking*, Clarendon Press, Oxford, 1997; and Anthony Saunders and Ingo Walter, *Universal Banking in The United States*, Oxford University Press, New York, 1994, Ch. 4.
2. David Rogers, *The Future of American Banking*, McGraw Hill, New York, 1993.
3. See Robert Grant, 'Diversification in the Financial Services Industries', in Andrew Campbell and Kathleen Sommers Luchs (eds), *Strategic Synergies*, Butterworth Heinemann, 1992, pp. 203–42, for one of the only empirical studies documenting the limits of the financial supermarket.
4. I am indebted to Andrew Campbell for this insight, based on his research and his executive development programmes with managers of multiproduct firms.
5. Jon Friedman, *House of Cards: Inside the Troubled Empire of American Express*, New York, Pitman, 1992; and Richard Freedman and Jill Vohr, *American Express*, Stern School of Business, NYU, 1991. Now, Sandy Weill, former CEO of Travelers Saloman, and John Reed, former CEO of Citicorp, have, as co-CEOs of the newly merged Citigroup, extended the 'supermarket' or universal banking model to include not just commercial and investment banking but retail brokerage and insurance as well. This is reported in *The New York Times*, 7 April 1998, pp. A1 and D10.
6. Andrew Campbell and Kathleen Sommers Luchs (eds), *op.cit.*, p. 3.
7. *Ibid.*, p. 4.
8. See Robert Grant, 'Diversification in the Financial Services Industry' in Andrew Campbell and Kathleen Sommers Luchs (eds), *Strategic Synergy*, Butterworth Heinemann, Oxford, 1992, pp. 210–11.
9. *American Banker*, 11 June 1998, p. 20.
10. Robert G.Eccles and Dwight B. Crane, *Doing Deals*, Harvard Business School Press, Boston MA, 1988.
11. *Ibid.*, Ch. 6.
12. I am indebted to Professor Richard Freedman of the Stern School of Business, New York University, for his insights regarding contradictions built into the universal banking strategy.
13. Lowell L. Bryan, *Breaking up the Bank*, Dow Jones-Irwin, Homewood IL, 1988.
14. *Explaining the Decline of the British Economy*, Harvard Business School, 9-391-254. See also W.D. Rubinstein, *Capitalism, Culture, and Decline in Britain*, Routledge, London, 1993; Martin J. Wiener, *English Culture and the Decline of the Industrial Spirit, 1850–1980*, Cambridge University Press, London, 1981; and Bruce Collins and Keith Robbins (eds), *British Culture and Economic Decline*, St Martins, New York, 1990.

15. *Explaining the Decline of the British Economy, op. cit.,* p. 14.
16. *Ibid.,* pp. 15–16.
17. Interview with George Smith.
18. J. Weiner, *op.cit.,* p. 167.
19. Professor Roy Smith, whose information comes from Securities Data Corporation. See Tables 5 and 6 in the Appendix for data on 1996 and 1998.
20. *Ibid.*
21. *Ibid.*
22. *The Economist,* 28 November 1998, p.73.
23. *Ibid.*
24. *Ibid.*
25. *The Economist,* 26 July 1997, p. 67.

Appendix

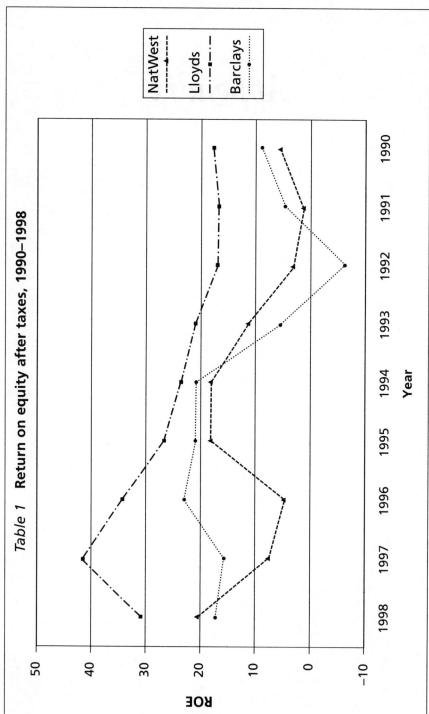

Table 1 **Return on equity after taxes, 1990–1998**

Source for Tables 1–4: Bloomberg, *Financial Markets* (on-line). Midland was not included, since HSBC acquired it in 1992 and Bloomberg does not publish data on subsidiary banks

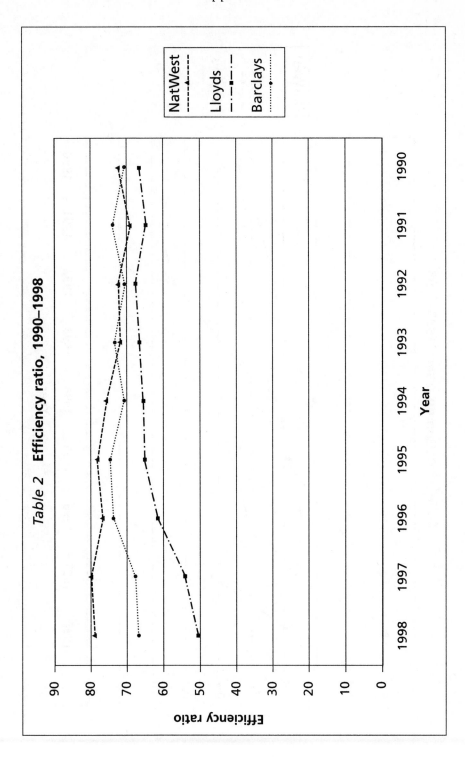

Table 2 **Efficiency ratio, 1990–1998**

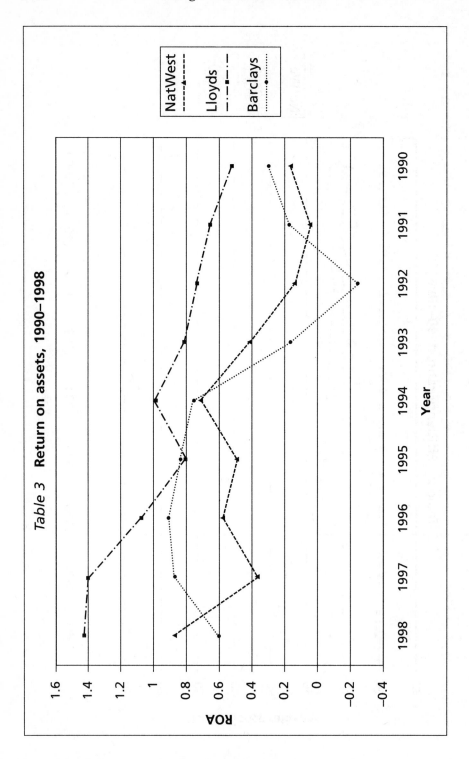

Table 3 **Return on assets, 1990–1998**

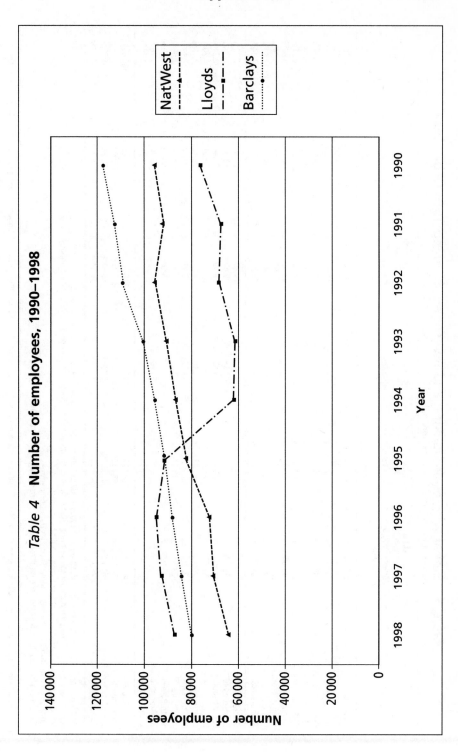

Table 4 **Number of employees, 1990–1998**

Table 5   Global wholesale banking and investment banking 1996 ($ billions)
Full credit to book running manager only

Firm	Global Debt & Equity Securities Underwriting & Placement (a)		Global M & A Advisory (b)		International Loans Arranged (c)		Medium-Term Notes Lead-Managed		Total (d)		% of Industry Total
Merrill Lynch	215.74	1	100.06	3	2.97	27	54.82	1	373.58	1	10.15%
Chase Manhattan Bank	31.53	15	17.37	18	249.12	1	2.99	24	301.00	2	8.18%
JP Morgan	104.34	7	77.95	4	90.43	2	19.77	6	292.49	3	7.95%
Goldman Sachs	146.71	2	116.50	2	2.70	28	24.02	4	289.92	4	7.88%
Morgan Stanley	125.47	4	116.72	1	–		28.52	3	270.72	5	7.36%
CS First Boston	107.33	6	60.88	5	39.44	6	17.06	7	224.71	6	6.11%
Salomon Brothers	119.06	5	47.94	7	–		41.46	2	208.46	7	5.67%
Lehman Brothers	125.61	3	47.41	8	–		19.89	5	192.91	8	5.24%
UBS	34.96	13	46.38	9	38.16	7	9.86	9	129.37	9	3.52%
Bear Stearns	57.75	8	18.58	17	–		13.39	8	89.73	10	2.44%
Citicorp	–		–		84.51	3	4.89	20	89.40	11	2.43%
Deutsche MG	36.87	11	13.15	22	27.85	10	7.40	13	85.64	12	2.33%
SBC Warburg	37.58	10	29.41	11	5.47	26	8.99	10	81.44	16	2.21%
DLJ	52.93	9	28.07	13	–		–		81.01	13	2.20%
NatWest	20.72	20	33.21	10	25.19	12	–		79.12	14	2.15%
Nations Bank	22.94	12	–		49.27	5	5.41	18	77.62	15	2.11%
ABN/Amro	23.64	16	13.11	23	30.90	8	7.63	12	75.28	17	2.05%
Smith Barney	36.02	12	28.36	12	–		5.20	19	69.58	18	1.89%
Bank of America	–		–		65.40	4	–		65.40	19	1.78%
Lazard Houses	–		51.95	6	–		–		51.95	20	1.14%
Total Top 25	1462.98		982.22		918.24		316.24		3679.68		100.00%
Total Industry	1769.86		684.62*		1093.71		371.73		3919.92		–
Top 10 as % of Total	61.73%		102.10%		64.33%		63.97%		55.89%		55.89%
Top 20 as % of Total	77.77%		134.31%		79.17%		80.48%		73.62%		73.62%

(a) Global rankings, top 25. Completed deals only. Includes all US private placements. Source: Securities Data Company.
(b) By market value of completed global transactions, full credit to both advisors, top 25 advisors. Source: Securities Data Company.
(c) Top arrangers of International Syndicated credits by volume.
(d) Global MTNs, top 25 managers. Source: Securities Data Company.
*As a result of 'double accounting', the total for the top 25 firms is higher than the industry total.

Source: Smith, Roy C. and Walter, Ingo, 'Global Capital Market Activity and Market Shares of Leading Competitors for 1996 and 1998'. New York University Salomon Center, Stern School of Business

Table 6 **Global wholesale banking and investment banking 1998 ($ millions)**
Full credit to book running manager only

Firm Rank 1998 (1997 in paren.)	Global Securities Underwriting and Private Placements	Global M&A Advisory (a)	International Bank Loans Arranged	Medium-Term Notes Lead-Managed (b)	Total	Percent of Top 25 (c)
Goldman Sachs & Co (2)	388,765.9	1,067,258.8	16,404.5	54,419.6	1,526,848.8	13.89%
Merrill Lynch & Co (1)	549,797.3	692,920.3	10,999.7	129,629.4	1,383,346.7	12.59%
Morgan Stanley Dean Witter (4)	404,497.5	635,623.9		32,680.2	1,072,801.6	9.76%
Salomon Smith Barney/Citigroup (7/11)	366,353.8	483,761.8	107,565.7	51,412.2	1,009,093.5	9.18%
Credit Suisse First Boston (6)	290,502.0	431,756.5	19,086.9	60,166.1	801,511.5	7.29%
JP Morgan & Co. Inc. (5)	250,064.7	324,207.0	115,665.7	27,502.8	717,440.2	6.53%
Chase Manhattan Corporation (3)	122,602.9	172,858.9	307,131.0	20,448.8	623,040.8	5.67%
Lehman Brothers (8)	264,339.6	225,415.6	26,311.8	48,982.5	565,049.5	5.14%
Deutsche Bank/BT (15/16)	158,681.0	147,874.4	53,780.3	84,419.0	444,754.7	4.05%
Warburg Dillon Read/UBS (9)	201,809.6	143,743.3	17,009.9	53,780.1	416,342.9	3.79%
Bank of America Corp. (14)	57,975.7	83,679.4	200,100.1	42,250.0	384,005.2	3.49%
Bear Stearns (12)	140,608.7	184,752.8		17,610.0	342,971.5	3.12%
Donaldson, Lufkin & Jenrette (13)	111,498.7	217,614.0	12,618.8		341,731.5	3.11%
ABN AMRO (17)	127,077.6	34,143.3	16,282.5	125,333.1	302,836.5	2.76%
Paribas/Société Générale (25/41)	153,649.0	54,472.3		11,398.0	219,519.3	2.00%
Lazard Houses (18)		160,775.5			160,775.5	1.46%
Barclays Capital (19)	81,236.9		14,457.3	6,370.2	102,064.4	0.93%
Dresdner Kleinwort Benson (30)	54,611.5	37,373.2		8,273.0	100,257.7	0.91%
Rothschild Group (28)		84,291.2			84,291.2	0.77%
Nomura Securities (34)	58,998.1			14,556.0	73,554.1	0.67%
Schroder Group (22)		69,179.4			69,179.4	0.63%
BankBoston (38)		49,903.0	19,124.8		69,027.8	0.63%
First Union Corp. (39)	24,972.3		21,591.7	20,000.0	66,564.0	0.61%
PaineWebber (23)	57,604.2				57,604.2	0.52%
HSBC (24)	57,260.5				57,260.5	0.52%
Top 25 firms	3,992,907.5	5,301,604.6	958,130.7	809,230.2	10,991,873.0	
Top 10 as % of top 25	76.41%	81.59%	70.34%	69.63%	77.88%	
Top 20 as % of top 25	96.44%	97.75%	95.75%	97.53%	97.09%	

(a) Completed deals only. Full credit to both advisors to targets and acquirers.
(b) Equal credit to both book runners if acting jointly.
(c) To avoid overestimation, the top 25 total ($10,991,873.0 million) was used instead of the industry total ($8,470,261.3 million)
Data: Securities Data Corporation

Source: Smith, Roy C. and Walter, Ingo, 'Global Capital Market Activity and Market Shares of Leading Competitors for 1996 and 1998'. New York University Salomon Center, Stern School of Business

Bibliography

1. Books

Auletta, K., *Greed and Glory on Wall Street*, New York: Warner, 1986.

Bordo, M. & Sylla, R. (eds), *Anglo-American Financial Systems*, Burr Ridge: Irvin, 1995.

Bryan, L., *Bankrupt*, New York: Harper, 1991.
        Breaking up The Bank, Homewood: Dow Jones-Irwin, 1988.

Campbell, A. and Luchs, K. (eds), *Strategic Synergy*, Oxford: Butterworth Heinemann, 1992.

Canals, J., *Universal Banking*, Oxford: Clarendon Press, 1997.

Channon, D., *British Banking Strategy*, London: Macmillan, 1977.

Cases in Bank Strategic Management and Marketing, New York, Wiley, 1986.

Cleveland, H., and Huertas, *Citibank*, Cambridge: Harvard University Press, 1985.

Collins B., and Robbins, K. (eds), *British Culture and Economic Decline*, New York: St Martins, 1990.

Collins, M., *Money and Banking in The UK: A History*, London: Croom Helm, 1988.

Davis, S., *Excellence in Banking*, London: Macmillan, 1985.
        Managing Change in Excellent Banks, London: Macmillan, 1989.
        Leadership in Financial Services, London: Macmillan Business, 1997.

Eccles, R. and Crane, D., *Doing Deals*, Boston: Harvard Business School Press, 1988.

Friedman, J., *House of Cards: Inside the Troubled Empire of American Express*, New York: Pitman, 1992.

Goold, M., Campbell, A. and Alexander, M., *Corporate-Level Strategy*, New York: Wiley, 1994.

Goold, M. and Luchs (eds), *Managing the Multibusiness Company*, London: Routledge, 1996.

Grant, R. *Contemporary Strategy Analysis*, Cambridge, MA: Blackwell, 1995.

Holmes, A.R. and Green, E., *Midland*, London: Battsford, 1986.

Hodge, B.J., Anthony, W.P., and Gales, L., *Organization Theory*, Upper Saddle River, NJ: Prentice Hall, 1996.

Lorenz, A., *BZW: The First Ten Years*, London: BZW house press: October, 1996.

Markides, C., *Diversification, Refocusing, and Economic Performance*, Cambridge, MA: MIT Press, 1995.

Miles, R. and Snow, C., *Organizational Strategy, Structure, and Process*, New York: McGraw-Hill, 1978.

Miller, D. and Friesen, P., *Organizations*, Englewood Cliffs: Prentice Hall, 1984.

Mintzberg, H., *The Structuring of Organizations*, Englewood Cliffs: Prentice Hall, 1979.

Pfeffer, J., *Managing with Power*, Boston: Harvard Business School Press, 1992.

Porter, M., *Competitive Analysis*, New York: The Free Press, 1985.

Ratner, S. Soltow, J., and Sylla, R., *The Evolution of The American Economy*, 2nd edn, New York: Macmillan, 1993.

Reed, R., *National Westminster Bank, A Short History*, NatWest Archives, 1989.

Rogers, D., *The Future of American Banking*, New York: McGraw-Hill, 1993.

Rubinstein, W., *Capitalism, Culture, and Decline in Britain*, London: Routledge, 1993.

Saunders, A. and Walter, I., *Universal Banking in The United States*, New York: Oxford, 1994.

Saunders, A. and Walter, I. (eds), *Universal Banking*, Chicago: Irwin, 1996.

Sayers, R., *Lloyds Bank in the History of English Banking*, Oxford: Oxford University Press, 1957.

Smith, R., *Comeback*, Boston: Harvard Business School Press, 1993.
            The Global Bankers, New York: Dutton, 1989.

Swary, I. and Topf, B., *Global Financial Deregulation*, Cambridge: Blackwell, 1992.

Taylor, R., *Going for Broke*, New York: Simon & Schuster, 1993.

Wiener, M., *British Culture and the Decline of the Industrial Spirit, 1850–1980*, London: Cambridge University Press, 1981.

Winston, J., *Lloyds Bank*, Oxford: Oxford University Press, 1982.

2. Monographs, reports, and conference proceedings

Center for The Study of Financial Innovation, *Banking Banana Skins*, June 1994.
                              Banking Banana Skins II,
    November, 1994.

Crystal, Q.C. and Spence, David Lane, *County NatWest Limited, County NatWest Securities Limited*, Department of Trade and Industry Investigation under Section 432(2) of the Companies Act 1985, 1989.

Goffee, Rob, *A Review of Professional and Managerial Skills*, City Research Project, London Business School and Corporation of London, September 1994.

Conference on Mergers of Financial Institutions, New York University Salomon Center in association with New York University Law School Center for the Study of Central Banks, 11 October 1996:
Boyd, John J., and Graham, Stanley L., 'Consolidation in US Banking: Implications for Efficiency, Competition, and Risk', Session III.
Macey Jonathan R. and Miller, Geoffrey P., 'Bank Mergers and American Bank Competitiveness', Session III.
Pilloff, Steven J. and Santomero, Anthony M., 'The Value Effects of Mergers and Acquisitions', Session I.
Smith, Roy C. and Walter, Ingo, 'Global Patterns of Mergers and Acquisition Activity in The Financial Services Industry', Session II.

Annual Reports
Barclays (1980–1998)
Lloyds   (1980–1998)
Midland   (1980–1998)
NatWest   (1980–1998)

3. Business and Financial Press

Banking World
The Economist
Euromoney
Financial Times
Guardian
Institutional Investor
The Wall Street Journal

4. Annual Reports

Barclays (1980–1998)
Lloyds   (1980–1998)
Midland   (1980–1998)
NatWest   (1980–1998)

5. Selected Bank Analyst Reports

Brown Brothers Harriman:
Banking Outlook, Global Investment Banking, 1 April 1996

Kleinwort Benson:
Reaching The Crossroads, 14 March 1996.

Lehman Brothers:
Global Investment Banking: Which New Players Will Make the Team?
    February 1994.
Global Banking Conference, 31 October–2 November 1995, December 1995.
UK Banks – Results Season Should Confirm Promising 1997 Outlook,
    22 January 1997.
UK Clearing Banks, Annual Review, 1996, 1997 and 1998.

Morgan Stanley:
Banking on Quality Improvement, 5 April 1995.
UK Banks: Achieving Peak Profitability, 25 July 1995.
Lloyds TSB: Superior Profitability, Superior Rating, 21 February 1997.
The Converting Building Societies: Wait for a Weighting, 17 April 1997.

UBS Global Research:
Building Societies Research: The Major Players, Rob Thomas, September
    1995.

7. Industry Abstracts

British Bankers Association:
Annual Abstract of Banking Statistics, 1995–1998.

Index